This book is due back on or before
the date stamped below.

BPP Business School Library, 2 St.
Mary Axe, London. EC3A 8BF.
Tel. 0207 025 0486

library@bpp.com

BPP

UNIVERSITY

Sustainability in Hospitality

HOW INNOVATIVE HOTELS ARE TRANSFORMING THE INDUSTRY

EDITED BY MIGUEL ANGEL GARDETTI
AND ANA LAURA TORRES

Greenleaf
PUBLISHING

© 2016 Greenleaf Publishing Limited

Published by Greenleaf Publishing Limited
Aizlewood's Mill
Nursery Street
Sheffield S3 8GG
UK
www.greenleaf-publishing.com

Cover by Sadie Gornall-Jones.
Printed and bound by Printondemand-worldwide.com, UK.

British Library Cataloguing in Publication Data:
  A catalogue record for this book is available from the British Library.

ISBN-13: 978-1-78353-199-8 [paperback]
ISBN-13: 978-1-78353-264-3 [hardback]
ISBN-13: 978-1-78353-197-4 [PDF ebook]
ISBN-13: 978-1-78353-198-1 [ePub ebook]

Contents

Introduction[1]

Miguel Angel Gardetti
Center for Studies on Sustainable Luxury, Argentina

Ana Laura Torres
Center for Study on Sustainable Hotels, Argentina

Sustainability in the hospitality industry

To better address this issue, it seems appropriate to explain what is understood by sustainable development and sustainability.

Sustainable development is a problematic expression, the meaning of which few people can agree on. We take the term and "reinvent" it to suit our own needs. It is a concept that continuously leads us to change objectives and priorities since it is an open process and, as such, it cannot be captured definitively. However, one of the most widely accepted definitions of sustainable development—though diffuse and non-operating—is the one proposed by the World Commission on Environment and Development (WCED) report, *Our Common Future*—also known as the Brundtland report—which defines sustainable development as the development model that allows us to meet present needs without compromising the ability of future generations to meet their own needs. The essential objective of this development model is to raise the quality of life by long-term maximization of the productive potential of ecosystems, through the appropriate technologies for this purpose (Gardetti, 2005).

While achieving sustainability is the goal of sustainable development (Doppelt, 2010), the word "sustainability" has several meanings nowadays, and is frequently reduced by associating it with "environment". Some authors—Frankel (1998) and Elkington (1998)—define sustainability as the balance between three elements:

---

1 Our special thanks go to the review panel for their outstanding work. This book would not have been possible without their dedication and commitment.

economy, environment and social equity. Though this definition is closely linked to *organizations*, it can also be applied at the *societal* level. But not everybody agrees with Frankel and Elkington: Paul Gilding (2000) argues that much of the "complexity" of sustainability is lost when considering only the three mentioned aspects. Sustainable development is not only a new concept, but also a new paradigm, and this requires looking at things differently. It is a notion of the world that is deeply different to the one that dominates our current thinking and it includes satisfying basic human needs like justice, freedom and dignity (Ehrenfeld, 1999).

The importance of promoting sustainability in the hospitality industry

For many countries the tourism industry represents one of the most important sources of income and employment generation. Hotels and all the various forms of accommodation comprise the largest sector of this industry and, being commercial buildings, have a great impact on the environment, economies, cultures and societies in general (Chen *et al.*, 2009).

There is strong recognition that uncontrolled growth in hospitality industry development aimed at short-term benefits often results in negative impacts, harming the environment and societies, and destroying the very basis on which hospitality is built (Chen *et al.*, 2009).

In a world characterized by natural resources scarcity, pollution, climate change, social inequity and vulnerable economic conditions, there is an increasing need for the lodging sector to demonstrate a commitment to reducing its environmental footprint and to addressing social concerns. Whatever their size, location and target market, hotel services are finding themselves held to account for their sustainability practices and policies.

In a report published by the consulting firm Deloitte, in which trends that are shaping the hotel industry are explored, sustainability is considered such an important issue that, if integrated in a business strategy, can define a company's success in the marketplace. There are several drivers that are making sustainability a top priority for organizations in the hospitality sector. Conscious consumers, increased government pressures, competitors' actions, rising costs and the need to improve operational efficiencies are contributing to the business imperative to adopt green technologies, processes and operating procedures (Deloitte, 2010).

Since awareness for environmental and social issues is growing, sustainability will increasingly become the norm and part of consumer expectations. Strategy and operations that are considered irresponsible will negatively impact stakeholder decision-making, from investors through to consumers (Deloitte, 2010).

Integrating sustainability in the hospitality industry

Rather than perceiving sustainability solely as regulatory compliance and risk management, businesses in the hospitality sector have to recognize its value-creating potential. Today's hospitality leaders promoting sustainability recognize the opportunities inherent in adapting their business to a more sustainable approach. A sustainable strategy not only brings cost savings through operational efficiency but also other economic benefits can be gained, including customer loyalty, employee retention, awards and recognition, and increased brand value. (Graci & Kuehnel, n.d.). Importantly, understanding of consumer values and expectations relative to sustainability should be one of the guiding principles for action (Deloitte, 2008).

With initiatives such as education programs, reforestation programs, eco-resorts, the implementation of energy-efficient practices, and the development of buildings that comply with government-defined standards, among others, hotel companies are increasingly encouraging environmentally friendly practices and embracing sustainability through both developmental and operational strategies (Ernst & Young, 2008).

Leading hospitality companies realize that truly sustainable business models are fundamentally different, have far-reaching implications and are not merely incremental to today's business operations. Companies that embed sustainability into their core business strategy and corporate culture are in a better position to gain competitive advantage and, ultimately, to be successful.

The book

This book intends to explore the different dimensions of sustainability within the hospitality industry. The call for papers for this book attracted 23 submissions, 19 of which were invited to the second round for full manuscript review. Finally, and with the help of the review panel throughout this process, 14 high-quality papers were selected which deal with essential aspects of sustainability in the hospitality sector. At this point we would like to make a clarification: at the end of the collection of papers we have added an article that, given the current importance of the topic it addresses, we considered should be included.

The book is divided into two parts: In the first one we have gathered the chapters referring to "The relevance of business sustainability in the hospitality sector". The second part of the book refers to the practice of sustainability within the sector, and thus bringing together several case studies developed in this field.

Part I begins with the chapter written by **Theresa Bauer**, titled "Human rights obligations of international hotel chains". Arguing that the issue of human rights in the hospitality industry has rarely been explicitly dealt with, the author examines the human rights obligations and responses of three international hotel chains.

In the following chapter, "The relevance of business sustainability in the hotel industry", by **Zabihollah Rezaee** and **Eun Kyong Choi**, the authors examine five dimensions of sustainability performance, namely EGSEE (economic, governance, social, ethical and environmental) and their relevance to the hotel industry.

Following this, **Susan Tinnish** presents "Strategic decision elements for hotel managers embarking on a sustainable supply chain management initiative". The author contends that this chapter will allow hotel managers to think more purposefully about the role of supply chains and the opportunity they represent for developing sustainable initiatives.

In turn, **Duane Windsor**, in his work "Exotic tourism to very fragile locations: Sustainable value creation in environmentally and socially fragile locations", examines the theory and practice of sustainable value creation for environmentally and socially fragile locations attracting increasing exotic tourism. The chapter explains how stakeholder management theory and TBL (triple bottom line) performance theory should be combined with environmental stewardship for sustainable exotic tourism.

Then, in the chapter titled "The role of leadership and organizational competencies in corporate social responsibility programs", written by **Susan Tinnish** and **Kevin D. Lynch**, the authors identify—through the use of a model—key competencies required to embed sustainability into a culture and create sustainable CSR programs for hotels.

Following this, and in order to gain an overview of extant definitions of sustainability and value, **Ruth Mattimoe**, author of the chapter "Effective delivery of the finance function and sustainable business in hotels in the British Isles", presents a deep review of the professional accountancy literature.

With the chapter "Evolving towards truly sustainable hotels through a 'well-being' lens: the S-WELL sustainability grid", **Gulen Z. Hashmi** and **Katrin Muff** aim to provide hotels, academia and students with an analytical tool for understanding and challenging hotel sustainability strategies and practices to benefit society at large.

In the eighth chapter titled "The Swiss ibex sustainability scheme: A comprehensive sustainability orientation for hotels", **Arthur Braunschweig** and **Domenico Saladino** present the "ibex fairstay", a label for hotels denoting the hotels' level of sustainability performance and management. Its structure and methodology, as well as some learnings from participating hotels and across all ibex certified houses, are described.

In the following chapter **John Hirst**, author of "Can hotels educate consumers about sustainability?", presents a very interesting project, delivered as an MBA at Durham University Business School, which seeks to link theory to practice in a way that can make a distinctive contribution to the quest for sustainability.

Part II begins with the work of **Alison Dempsey** titled "A resort for generations—Maintaining, protecting, renewing, improving". This case study is intended to exemplify how a small resort is making steps to increase and protect its environment, community and commitment to a sustainable future while recognizing the inherent limitations and challenges of scale and cost for a smaller enterprise.

In turn, **Benjamin H. Gill** and **Beverly K. Burden** present "Optimizing performance of a remote African hotel: Using the One Planet Living framework to maximize the sustainability performance of Singita Gruneti in Tanzania". Through the analysis of this case, the authors aim to demonstrate that it is possible to enjoy a high quality of life within the productive capacity of the planet.

The following contribution, "Business and sustainable tourism: Sextantio—a case study", written by **Salvatore Moccia**, presents the case of Sextantio, a company that focuses on the reclamation of abandoned areas to create hotels.

In order to better understand motivations towards an adopted practice in a competitive environment, **Marlon Delano Nangle**, in his chapter "Compliance or the deviant response: Implementation patterns of the TTTIC quality practice in Trinidad & Tobago", studies the implementation patterns of a quality practice that has been introduced to the tourist accommodation industry in the Caribbean republic. He examines which factors lead managers to interpret the practice as an opportunity for gain versus a threat of loss. Closing this selection of contributions, the chapter written by **Fran Hughes**, "Human trafficking: Why it's time for the hotel industry to act", provides facts, figures and practical information to help a hotel or hotel company understand the issue of human trafficking and its implications to the business. It also includes a selection of case studies highlighting best practice from the hotel sector.

In closing, these diverse contributions certainly offer a wide and representative compilation of writings on the subject. Note that this initiative has received a large international response. We hope this book represents a major step forward in expanding the knowledge base of the relationship between hospitality and sustainability and that it continues to stimulate further debate.

References

Chen, Joseph S., Sloan, Philip, & Legrand, Willy (2009). *Sustainability in the Hospitality Industry: Principles of Sustainable Operations.* Oxford, UK: Elsevier.

Deloitte Development LLC (2008). *The Staying Power of Sustainability—Balancing Opportunity and Risk in the Hospitality Industry.* London.

Deloitte (2010). *Hospitality 2015: Game Changers or Spectators.* London.

Doppelt, B. (2010). *Leading Change Toward Sustainability: A Change-Management Guide for Business, Government and Civil Society.* 2nd ed. Sheffield, UK: Greenleaf Publishing.

Ehrenfeld, J.R. (1999). Cultural Structure and the Challenge of Sustainability. In Ken Sexton, Alfred A. Marcus, K. Williams Easter & Timothy D. Burkhardt (eds). *Better Environmental Decisions—Strategies for Governments, Businesses, and Communities.* Washington: Island Press.

Elkington, J. (1998). *Cannibals with Forks.* Gabriola Island: New Society Publishers.

Ernst & Young (2008). Global Hospitality Insights-Hospitality going green.

Frankel, C. (1998). *In Earth´s Company.* Gabriola Island: New Society Publishers.

Gardetti, M.A. (2005). Sustainable Development, Sustainability and Corporate Sustainability. In M.A. Gardetti (ed.), *Texts in Corporate Sustainability—Integrating Social, Environmental and Economic Considerations with Short and Long Term*. Buenos Aires: LA-BELL.

Gilding, Paul (2000). Sustainability-Doing. In D. Dunphy, J. Benveniste, A. Griffiths, & P. Sutton (eds). *Sustainability—The Corporate Challenge of the 21st Century*. St Leonards: Allen & Unwin.

Graci, S. & Kuehnel, J. (n.d.). How to increase your bottom line by going green. Green Hotels and Responsible Tourism Initiative. Retrieved from http://green.hotelscombined.com, accessed 10 March 2014.

Part I
The relevance of business sustainability in the hospitality sector

1

Human rights obligations of international hotel chains

Theresa Bauer

SRH FernHochschule Riedlingen, Germany

The issue of human rights in the hospitality industry has rarely been explicitly dealt with. This chapter aims to fill this gap by examining the human rights obligations and responses of international hotel chains. The chapter introduces negative and positive responsibilities and describes distinctive challenges in different institutional environments, i.e. in democratic and in non-democratic countries. It investigates the actions of three large hotel chains: InterContinental Hotels, Hyatt and Shangri-La. These companies have explicitly recognized their human rights obligations and have implemented measures such as human rights policies, reporting on human rights issues, ethics training and signing up to the UN (United Nations) Global Compact. While the negative duty to "do no harm" has been recognized, there is a need for further appropriate responses for acting in an environment of unjust law.

Introduction

CSR (corporate social responsibility) has become an increasingly relevant topic. Various groups such as consumers, investors, governments and NGOs (non-governmental organizations) have demanded that companies meet their responsibilities towards society and ensure that operations are not only profitable, but also desirable in terms of the objectives and values of society. More recently, the corporate responsibility of respecting human rights has been recognized, both in CSR literature (Kobrin, 2009; Wettstein, 2012a, 2012b; Wettstein & Waddock, 2005; Arnold, 2010; Cragg, 2010, 2000) and in practice. The work by the UN's special representative John Ruggie, appointed in 2005, contributed to this development with the introduction of the UN "Protect, Respect and Remedy" framework (United Nations, 2008a, 2008b) and "Guiding Principles on Business and Human Rights" (United Nations, 2011).

At the same time, "sustainable tourism", respectively "responsible tourism", has become a trend and underlines the relevance of CSR for companies in the hospitality industry. Already in 1999, the UNWTO (UN World Tourism Organization) had devised and adopted a global code of ethics for tourism, designed to minimize the negative effects of tourism activity on destinations and local communities. Since then, a growing number of hotels have explicitly embraced CSR and sustainability and have developed clearly articulated and communicated CSR policies that are a result of planned decisions (see, e.g. Sloan, Legrand & Chen, 2013; Bohdanowicz & Zientara, 2008). Core CSR areas range from philanthropy and environmental concerns to the improvement of working conditions and the engagement in community development.

While CSR activities and sustainable management in the hospitality industry have received considerable attention, human rights obligations have been rarely explicitly dealt with. This chapter aims to fill this gap by examining human rights obligations in the sector conceptually and empirically. What are the human rights obligations of hotel chains and what measures are taken to fulfil them? These questions will be at the core of the chapter.

Some human rights challenges are relevant for large chains as well as smaller independent hotels, e.g. working conditions or the possible abuse of a hotel for the sexual exploitation of adults and children. Other human rights related issues only arise in the case of international chains, e.g. the decision whether to enter a non-democratic country where basic human rights are violated by the state. The empirical part of this chapter focuses on large international chains, because these have considerable power and potential to influence because of their size and resources.

The first section of this chapter explains the relation between business and human rights and briefly introduces relevant literature before negative and positive duties to "do no harm" and "do good" are elaborated on and applied to hotels. Next, the chapter provides ethical and economic/strategic justifications and analyses how human rights obligations relate to different institutional environments. The empirical part exemplifies how hotel chains approach their human rights obligations by examining the actions of three large chains: InterContinental Hotels, Hyatt and Shangri-La. This part is based on company internal and publicly available secondary sources.

Business and human rights

Human rights are "inalienable rights of all members of the human family" (UN General Assembly, 1948) whose modern conceptualization is influenced by the Enlightenment thinkers who propagated natural rights grounded on human nature (Donnelly, 1982). The protection, promotion and implementation of human rights has been accepted as one of the main responsibilities of countries and has become a core concern in international relations (Schmitz and Sikkink, 2002). Complementary obligations of companies have been identified more recently based on the insight that business conduct can significantly enhance or curb almost all kinds of human rights. International law does not directly relate to companies, and global agreements that formally require companies to respect human rights have not been reached. Yet some companies have started to integrate human rights into business practice and to cooperate in initiatives such as the BLIHR (Business Leaders Initiative on Human Rights) and its successor, the GBI (Global Business Initiative) on Human Rights. Several international institutions have designed non-binding guidelines and codes of conduct for businesses to improve the human rights situation, among the earliest being the Guidelines for Multinational Enterprises, which were originally adopted by the OECD in 1976, and the Tripartite Declaration of Principles Concerning Multinational Enterprises and Social Policy, introduced by the ILO (International Labour Organization) in 1977. The UN Global Compact, "the world's leading corporate responsibility initiative" (Rasche, 2012, p. 33), promotes human rights by obliging member companies to "support and respect the protection of internationally proclaimed human rights" and to "make sure that they are not complicit in human rights abuses" (UN Global Compact, 2012b). Moreover, the work by the UN Special Representative John Ruggie has contributed to clarifying the meaning of corporate human rights obligations. According to Ruggie, the state has the duty to protect against human rights abuses by regulating and adjudicating corporate activities, while companies must respect human rights by not infringing on the rights of others as the baseline expectation (United Nations, 2008b, p. 9). Ruggie claims that "companies cannot be held responsible for the human rights impacts of every entity over which they may have some influence" (United Nations, 2008a, p. 5), but still recognizes the risk of becoming complicit in violations committed by third parties. Thus, companies should "seek to prevent or mitigate adverse human rights impacts that are directly linked to their operations, products or services by their business relationships, even if they have not contributed to those impacts" (United Nations, 2011, p. 14). Ruggie has developed a number of concrete recommendations that have been widely accepted among governments, business and civil society, although some critical voices have noted lacking external monitoring mechanisms (e.g. Frankental, 2013).

Companies that are committed to uphold business ethics will not necessarily see human rights as constraining guidelines; instead they may view them as helpful ones. Operating in a large number of countries (with differing value systems) can be a challenge when it comes to taking morally appropriate decisions that comply with various guest country and home country expectations. Human rights provide an important point of reference across countries and regions; yet they need to be interpreted and implemented in a "culturally sensitive" way (Wettstein, 2009, p. 144).

Human rights issues have long been neglected by business ethics and CSR scholars (see Wettstein, 2009), but have increasingly attracted attention especially in the context of multinational corporations operating in developing countries (Kobrin, 2009; Wettstein, 2012a, 2012b; Wettstein & Waddock, 2005; Arnold, 2010; Cragg, 2010; Cragg, 2000). Controversies have arisen on the issue as to whether corporate human rights obligations extend to all human rights equally, or whether they are limited to specific rights. For example, Arnold (2010) argues that the obligations of companies differ depending on the sort of rights; he distinguishes basic human rights that are essential for a decent human life, namely liberty, physical security and subsistence, from aspirational rights such as unlimited access to high-quality education and healthcare.

Human rights obligations in the hospitality industry have been seldom investigated explicitly. Yet a number of studies have dealt with specific issues that clearly touch upon human rights. This holds especially in the context of human resources management, where key topics (among others) have been labour practices, gender and diversity management (e.g. Manoharan et al., 2014) and prevention of sexual harassment of employees (e.g. Oliveira & Ambrósio, 2013). Other central issues relating to human rights issues in the sector are children's rights (e.g. Sadar, 2011), i.e. prevention of child labour and child sex tourism, and human trafficking (e.g. Tepelus, 2008). The studies on these specific aspects lay an important basis for considering the human rights obligations of hotel chains in a more general way, as this chapter aims to show.

Negative and positive duties: "Do no harm" and "Do good"

When establishing human rights as guiding principles for hotel chains, two alternative approaches can be taken. The focus could be on the *negative* duty to "do no harm" or on the *positive* duty to "do good" (Wood, 2012, pp. 64–5). Negative duties are broadly accepted among scholars in the human rights field, i.e. there is wide agreement regarding the claim that business operations may not infringe on human rights. In the case of international hotel chains, the negative duty requires specific measures to forestall human rights violations through business activities.

The positive duty to "do good" is controversial and calls for further explanation. Positive duties could be established by following Hsieh (2004, 2009). He builds on the philosophy of John Rawls to identify a "duty of assistance" for companies owned by members of well-ordered societies to help burdened societies.[1] In his view, a company ought to help to achieve reasonably just or decent institutions, provided the government of a well-ordered society does not fulfil its duty of assistance and the company is to benefit from operating in countries that are not well ordered. A company may promote well-ordered institutions: indirectly through normal business activities by contributing to economic development; and/or directly, e.g. in the form of technical assistance and training. Wettstein (2012b) goes one step further and propagates a positive duty of large international companies when another party harms human rights, i.e. the company ought to come to the victims' help or assistance, speak out and put pressure on perpetrating host governments. Otherwise, moral approval of human rights violations is given. Not only academics but also practitioners argue for positive duties of that kind. The UN Global Compact recommends that companies should "privately and publicly condemn systematic and continuous human rights abuses" (UN Global Compact, 2012a). In the case of international hotel chains, the positive duty to "do good" could entail contributing to economic prosperity in developing countries through normal business operations; but it could also be interpreted as the duty to intervene with the local government, e.g. in case a critic of the regime has taken refuge in the hotel and is about to be arrested simply because he or she has claimed freedom of opinion.

However, there are concerns regarding positive duties among scholars and practitioners. One could object that the expectation to "do good" is too far-reaching. Besides, one might argue that businesses should not be involved in politics by intervening with governments in order to improve the human rights situation. Defenders of liberalism such as the influential US economist Milton Friedman argue that policymakers and managers each have responsibilities only for their specific realm (Friedman, 1970). Yet the notion of business, society and politics as entirely separate aspects is questionable—especially in today's globalized world where power is shared between governments, civil society and business and increasingly companies participate in efforts to establish global governance. Countries still do have the primary responsibility for providing sufficient laws and enforcing human rights; however, if they are not willing or able to provide appropriate protection and the international community fails to pressure for change, companies that have the potential to influence are required to act.

Overall, both negative and positive responsibilities are principally relevant for international hotel chains. Yet this does not entail limitless expectations; in some situations, meeting negative responsibilities is sufficient, while in others positive ones need to be fulfilled. Criteria to distinguish situations that call for doing good in the form of intervention are introduced later on.

---

1 Rawls defines burdened societies as societies that "lack the political and cultural traditions, the human capital and knowhow, and, often, the material and technological resources needed to be well-ordered" (Rawls, 1999, p. 106).

Ethical and economic/strategic justifications

This section explains the motivation of companies to meet human rights obligations. First, it is helpful to consider how CSR has been justified. The respective literature has generated "duty-aligned/ethical" and "economic/strategic" perspectives (Gond *et al.*, 2009, p. 66; Swanson, 1995). Both perspectives do not necessarily contradict each other. Taking impacts on broader society into account may not only be the "right thing to do", but can also serve the self-interest of companies, e.g. by providing competitive advantages and/or improving reputation. Regarding the economic/strategic perspective in the case of hotel chains, positive effects of CSR can be expected particularly in terms of the brand image and guest retention (see e.g. Othman & Hemdi, 2013; Kang *et al.*, 2010).

Similarly, human rights obligations can be justified by ethical and economic/strategic reasoning. The ethical perspective entails that companies have moral responsibilities and "moral reasoning ought to motivate management decisions" (Quinn & Jones, 1995, p. 22). Avoiding any harm to human rights must be considered as morally compulsory. When it comes to the additional positive duty to intervene in case others (particularly the state or business partners) violate human rights, defining what is morally required is not possible in a straightforward way. Combining the recommendations by Santoro (2010), Wood (2012) and Wettstein (2012b), the following criteria can help to determine whether it is morally obligatory for international companies to "do good":

- *Nature and degree of violation:* Corporate intervention becomes imperative when actual or potential violations of the most basic rights are "severe, systematic, and ongoing" (Wettstein, 2012b, p. 54)

- *Connection:* The closer the link between the company and the human rights violation, respectively between the company and "either the perpetrator of human rights abuse or the human rights-holder" (Wood, 2012, p. 64), the more pressure is placed on the company to act

- *Ability to influence:* Another factor is whether companies have the ability "to make a difference to the state of affairs" (Wood, 2012, p. 64). The ability to influence depends on the company's "power to significantly influence the perpetrator" and "a certain social or political status" that implies potential to influence the public perception (Wettstein, 2012b, p. 39)

- *Capacity to influence:* Companies with considerable resources are expected to act, i.e. when "the capacity to withstand economic retaliation or to absorb the costs of an action" (Santoro, 2010, p. 292) is great

The more criteria that are satisfied, the higher is the moral expectation for a company to act. These factors are not to be understood as exclusion criteria, but rather as moving up the scale from optional to compulsory action.

In addition to moral grounds, respecting and promoting human rights may be justified by economic/strategic considerations. Fulfilling the negative duty to "do no harm" to human rights is clearly in the self-interest of the company when national laws provide respective stipulations. Besides, avoiding criticism by external actors such as NGOs and thereby forestalling reputational damage provides a strong self-related motive to pay attention to human rights issues (Putten *et al.*, 2003). This holds not only for the imperative to "do no harm", but also to "do good". For example, if a globally active company (such as an international hotel chain) speaks out against a government infringement of human rights and thereby triggers improved human rights protection in an oppressive environment, the company might be able to forestall public criticism and consumer boycotts at home and gain a reputation as a responsible business.

The context matters: Democratic and non-democratic environments

Some countries provide a high degree of human rights protection, while others are characterized by gaps between internationally agreed human rights standards and national law and practice. Generally, companies have to take into account all internationally recognized human rights (cf. United Nations, 2011, p. 13), as expressed in the Universal Declaration of Human Rights, the ICCPR (International Covenant on Civil and Political Rights), the ICESCR (International Covenant on Economic, Social and Cultural Rights) and the ILO's Declaration on Fundamental Principles and Rights at Work. The exact human rights challenges of companies (including hotel chains) vary depending on the institutional environment. Hence, the following section considers obligations in two different institutional settings: stable countries with democratic institutions and procedures and a generally high level of human rights protection; and non-democratic environments with a weak rule of the law and low protection of human rights.

Democratic context

In a functioning democracy, the state provides effective legislation and enforcement measures to promote human rights. For companies, legal stipulations constitute the imperative to "do no harm" to human rights (in addition to moral obligations). However, business self-regulation is still important, especially in case regulatory loopholes occur, e.g. when complex processes of law-making do not keep pace with rapid economic and social change. The positive duty to "do good" is less relevant in this institutional context, as the country meets its responsibilities to a large extent.

Principally, two categories of rights need to be taken into account by businesses: CPR (Civil and Political Rights) and ESCR (Economic, Social and Cultural Rights).[2] Companies are seldom directly involved in the protection or abuse of CPR, like the right to life, right to liberty and security of person, freedom of expression. Yet there are exceptions. For example, the right to religious observance might affect hotel chains on account of the beliefs and religious practices of employees; respecting religious customs (such as prayer times, dietary needs) is required. Many ESCR have a clear link to business activities, particularly in the form of employees' rights that are touched upon directly through management decisions. Most industrialized countries have implemented regulation to guarantee rights such as freedom of association, equal opportunities in the workplace and fair wages. In addition, companies should commit to protecting employees' rights in these areas. Hotel chains often have a global workforce where individuals from all types of backgrounds, with different experiences and viewpoints, meet. Hence, inclusion and diversity management is a major field to show awareness of employees' rights, e.g. through leadership training programmes, mentoring opportunities and educational support. In many Western countries, efforts have been undertaken recently to achieve lesbian, gay, bisexual and transgender (LGBT)-friendly practices and policies; for example, in the US, hotel chains such as Choice Hotels and Wyndham Worldwide have been included and honoured in the HRC's (Human Rights Campaign) Corporate Equality Index. In other cases, hotel chains have been accused of failing to incorporate employees' rights sufficiently. One prominent example is the health-related case of Neil Francey and Sue Meeuwissen versus Hilton Hotels of Australia. The Australian Human Rights and Equal Opportunity Commission (1997) found the hotel's failure to provide access to a smoke-free environment an unlawful discrimination of a person with a disability due to asthmatic lungs. Another more recent example is the lawsuit by Ronald Tobin against his former employer, the Californian Fess Parker DoubleTree Hilton, for unsafe working conditions and alleged race discrimination (he is African-American). The list of accusations and litigations against hotels could be continued. Yet such examples not only point to a failure by the respective hotels to respect employees' rights sufficiently, but also underline that voluntary human rights commitments by companies are to be welcomed as a sign of goodwill, but they are less needed when means such as litigation exist.

Non-democratic context

When democratic institutions are not existent or underdeveloped and the government clearly fails to protect human rights, companies need to show a strong sense of moral responsibility. Yet in countries with weak regulation and/or law enforcement, neglect and violation of human rights by companies have been revealed in a number of cases; drastic examples range from forced labour and child labour to

---

2   ESCR are still widely contested, in spite of the adoption of the International Covenant on ESCR by the UN General Assembly in 1966 (see also Nolan & Taylor, 2009).

ecological damage. However, companies are increasingly becoming aware of the moral duty to "do no harm" when legal rules are missing. In case of an authoritarian and oppressive state, a fundamental question for foreign companies should be whether operating in such a context is morally acceptable at all. Companies need to consider to what extent presence requires collaboration with the non-democratic government. For example, in a highly corruptible environment it might be necessary to bribe local authorities in order to start or continue business operations. If a company such as an international hotel chain risks becoming involved in severe human rights abuses through its mere presence and it lacks the power to prevent or mitigate these violations, abstaining from operations in that country is morally requisite. However, such a decision is not always taken or implemented easily. Where a company has been long present in a country with hitherto acceptable human rights standards, long-term investments have been made and financial consequences of the pull-out were high, such a decision is very difficult (see Sorell, 2004). In cases where operations are started or continued in a non-democratic environment, companies have to define how to deal with conflicts between domestic law and international standards. The UN Special Representative John Ruggie recommends that companies should comply with domestic law, but "seek ways to honour the principles of internationally recognized human rights when faced with conflicting requirements" (United Nations, 2011, p. 21). Respecting domestic law safeguards the integrity of the company's own personnel and property, but "civil disobedience" may be required when compliance causes significant human rights violations (Ostas, 2004). Under consideration of the criteria to "do good" (see above), the company should consider urging the government to better fulfil its obligation to protect human rights. Regimes that are internationally isolated and dependent on the wealth created by foreign companies might be particularly responsive to such demands.

Human rights responses: The examples of InterContinental, Hyatt and Shangri-La

Various tools and techniques have been developed to help companies manage human rights obligations and guide decision-making by managers and employees. A due-diligence process aims to "identify, prevent, mitigate and account for" how impacts on human rights are addressed (United Nations, 2011, p. 15). An increasing number of companies that have corporate ethics programmes and human rights policies provide human rights training for employees and report on human rights issues. These efforts are mostly closely aligned with overall CSR policies and actions. For example, the guidelines of the GRI (Global Reporting Initiative), one of the leading standards for CSR reporting, include human rights issues. The respective performance indicators that require companies to report on investment and procurement practices regarding human rights cover employee and security forces training on human rights as well as non-discrimination, freedom of association, child labour, forced and compulsory labour and indigenous rights (see GRI, n.d.).

The following section exemplifies how hotel chains approach their human rights obligations by examining the actions of three large businesses: InterContinental Hotels, Hyatt and Shangri-La. The focus on large chains is based on the notion that size, power and responsibilities are closely connected. InterContinental and Hyatt were chosen after having screened the extent to which the ten largest hotel chains (according to Tourism Review, 2010) have committed to human rights. InterContinental was selected as the largest hotel chain, while Hyatt was chosen as a representative of the upmarket sector where reputation plays a considerable role (which may provide a strong motivation to take human rights issues seriously).[3] In addition, Shangri-La was selected as a hotel chain with a non-Western background based and mainly operating in a non-democratic environment (i.e. Hong Kong/China).

The following section briefly introduces InterContinental Hotels, Hyatt and Shangri-La and describes measures by these companies to meet human rights responsibilities; after that, a critical account of these chains' actions is given.

InterContinental Hotels Group

IHG (InterContinental Hotels Group) was founded in 2003 (although its origins go back to 1777) and has headquarters in Denham, UK. Its 4,600 hotels across over 100 countries employ circa 120,000 employees. IHG is the globally largest hotel group measured by rooms (more than 600,000). Its brands include Candlewood Suites, Crowne Plaza, Even, Holiday Inn, Holiday Inn Express, Hotel Indigo, Hualuxe, InterContinental and Staybridge Suites. The majority of hotels operate under franchise agreements; in addition, circa 650 are managed by the company, but separately owned, and ten are directly owned.

The company emphasizes its strategic approach to CSR and has a "Code of Ethics and Business Conduct" including commitments to health and safety, equal opportunities and environmental protection. IHG issues a comprehensive CSR report (IHG, 2013); the report's section titled "Community" includes human rights issues.

In its "human rights policy", IHG claims to sustain the protection of human rights, particularly the rights of employees, business partners and communities where IHG operates. The company particularly focuses on staff-related issues. It promises to respect the rights to voluntary freedom of association, to provide a safe, healthy working environment, to abstain from forced and compulsory labour or the exploitation of children, to eliminate employment discrimination and to promote diversity. IHG has a whistleblower line and a dedicated website (www.ihgethics.com). Moreover, IHG claims to support fair competition and honest as

---

3 However, this choice does not mean that other chains have not taken measures; large firms such as Hilton have also committed to human rights.

well as integral business conduct in compliance with applicable laws. IHG has developed a "Bribery and Anti-Corruption Policy" and a "Gifts and Entertainment Policy" which apply to all employees. The suppliers' "Vendor Code of Conduct" also includes human rights criteria. To protect local communities, IHG encourages the individual hotels to undertake a social impact assessment before carrying out any building work, to engage regularly with local leaders to identify and resolve any rights issues, to keep the use of resources to a minimum and to support cultural preservation projects through corporate donations or staff volunteering.

IHG has also taken steps regarding international initiatives. In 2010, IHG signed up to the UN Global Compact, i.e. committed to align operations and strategies with the ten universal principles that include commitments to human rights and labour standards. Moreover, the company supports the International Tourism Partnership's position statement on human trafficking which aims to bring together the world's leading international hotel companies to reach collaborative solutions to address the issue of human trafficking.

Key future objectives are the development of a global e-training for human rights, continued work with industry peers and other stakeholders to understand and assess human rights issues and to make progress regarding supply chain diversity. The company plans to roll out a "foundational standard" which requires all IHG hotels to adopt and display a human rights policy at individual property level.

Hyatt Hotels Corporation

Hyatt Hotels Corporation was founded in 1957 and is based in Chicago, Illinois. Hyatt Corporation's worldwide portfolio consists of more than 500 properties in 45 countries with more than 75,000 employees. The company's subsidiaries manage, franchise, own and develop hotels and resorts under various brands such as Hyatt, Park Hyatt, Andaz, Grand Hyatt, Hyatt Regency, Hyatt Place and Hyatt House.

Hyatt has a "Code of Business Conduct and Ethics" and a diversity and inclusion strategy. In addition, the online corporate responsibility platform, Hyatt Thrive (http://thrive.hyatt.com), focuses on four areas: "environmental sustainability", "economic development and investment", "education and personal advancement" and "health and wellness". In addition, the company issues a yearly CSR report (Hyatt, 2013), covering the topics "People", "Community" and "Planet".

In 2010, Hyatt introduced a human rights statement that emphasizes the responsibility to manage "business in a manner that is consistent with fundamental human rights" and promises to foster "similar ideals in those with whom we do business" (Hyatt, 2010).

Hyatt has taken steps to enhance employees' rights and sees itself as a leader in advancing a diverse workforce. It promotes employee network groups based on a common cultural heritage, race, gender, age or interest. The company has been recognized as one of the best companies to work for (according to *Fortune*). The US HRC has awarded the company 100% in the HRC Equality Index for several years.

Hyatt considers elimination of human trafficking a major issue. A global training programme for employees has been developed in conjunction with the Polaris Project, an organization dedicated to combating human trafficking. Hyatt respects all applicable laws prohibiting the use of child labour and supports legislation enacted to prevent and punish the crime of sexual exploitation of children. The "Supplier Code of Conduct" includes the requirement to uphold workers' rights and anti-corruption statements.

One of the company's subsidiaries, Grand Hyatt Cannes Hotel Martinez, is a member of the UN Global Compact.

Shangri-La Hotels and Resorts

Shangri-La Hotels and Resorts was founded in 1971 and is based in Hong Kong. The company currently owns and/or manages more than 80 hotels under the Shangri-La, Kerry and Traders brands, with a room inventory of over 34,000 and circa 40,000 employees. The main focus of activities is in Asia.

Shangri-La has developed a code of conduct and CSR training programmes. The company issues a sustainability report based on the guidelines by the GRI (Shangri-La, 2012). It has introduced a CSR scorecard to guide hotels in balancing economic interests with environmental governance and community involvement.

Shangri-La is committed to human rights, which it claims is underscored in the company values of "humility, courtesy, respect, helpfulness, sincerity and selflessness" (see Shangri-La, 2013, p. 4). The company claims to aim for a fair workplace, in which diversity, equality and equal opportunities are seen as central. Shangri-La promises to protect employees' rights and to abide by national labour codes and laws as well as the Fundamental Conventions of the ILO (see Shangri-La, 2013, p. 4). Regarding business partners, Shangri-La's "Supplier Code of Conduct" makes reference to human rights; it requires suppliers to provide safe and healthy working conditions, use fair hiring practices and adhere to environmentally responsible practices in manufacturing.

Shangri-La declared its endorsement of the UN Global Compact in 2011. The Communication on Progress 2013 has been published (Shangri-La, 2013).

In the future, the company plans to strengthen corporate governance, including training on human rights and anti-corruption measures and to address indigenous rights and negative impacts on communities.

Critical account

As the previous section has shown, InterContinental Hotels, Hyatt and Shangri-La take a range of measures to ensure meeting human rights obligations. However, this description is mainly based on company sources; it reflects the issues and challenges that the companies are themselves aware of. In some areas, the companies admit the need for further improvement, e.g. Shangri-La recognizes a systematic review of risks related to corruption is lacking. However, unsurprisingly, the companies' statements largely focus on positive achievements.

A different view arises if one consults additional external sources. Examples regarding an alleged neglect of negative and positive responsibilities can be found. One example of the negative duty to "do no harm" is the following. Although Hyatt claims to respect employees' rights, in June 2013 hotel workers gathered outside the company's annual shareholders' meeting in Chicago to protest about "long-standing labor abuses" (Stevens, 2013). The protesters were members of Unite Here, a labour union that had reached agreement on wages and benefits with Hyatt years ago, but complained about subcontracting and lack of workplace safety. On the other hand, one could argue that this example still points to the upholding of rights such as the freedom of association. The second example refers to the positive duty to "do good". InterContinental Hotels has recently been confronted with the challenge of taking morally appropriate decisions in a non-democratic environment. In 2013, "Free Tibet" and "Students for a Free Tibet UK" launched an international boycott campaign in protest against plans by the group to build a luxury hotel in Lhasa, Tibet, where the Chinese authorities have been accused of violating human rights. Yet the management did not perceive a contradiction between its human rights responsibilities and the engagement in Tibet. An IHG spokesperson responded to the protests by stating that the company took "great pride" in operating responsibly and this would be no different in Lhasa, as "high operational standards and policies, including the recruiting, training and development of our hotel staff" will be put in place (Harmer, 2013). In this case, reputational concerns obviously were outweighed by other considerations.

The last example must be seen in relation to a neglect in the statements and measures of all three hotel chains in the sample. InterContinental Hotels, Hyatt and Shangri-La emphasize their commitment to comply with the laws and regulations of the countries and jurisdictions in which they operate. But what happens in the case of unjust laws and contradictions between domestic law and international human rights standards? How do the chains deal with the challenges of non-democratic environments? These hotel chains operate worldwide and not only in democratic environments where the state ensures human rights (one, Shangri-La, is based in a country that lack democratic structures); their size and resources give them power and potential to influence. The human rights commitments say nothing about the relations with non-democratic regimes beside (the highly important) strive for anti-corruption measures. If one follows the positive duty to promote human rights and to intervene with an unjust government, the expectations towards these companies become much wider than they acknowledge currently. However, what these companies do recognize is that their responsibility extends to the decisions and behaviours of business partners, as the introduction of suppliers' codes of ethics particularly underlines.

Conclusion

Both the expectations towards businesses and the awareness of companies regarding human rights obligations are currently rising. Measures to meet the negative responsibility to "do no harm" and the positive duty to "do good" are needed. The starting point can be the CSR tools and techniques that have been developed in recent years. In addition, human rights specific instruments are required. Firms should commit to do no harm and to contribute to the advancement of human rights, and they should provide human rights training and include human rights issues in their reports. Human rights obligations and challenges differ to some extent according to the institutional context, whereas balancing local cultural expectations and laws with global human rights standards is not always easy. In a democratic environment, there tends to be little need for an active role for companies to contribute to human rights protection beyond their own activities. The situation is different in non-democratic environments, where following legal requirements is not necessarily in line with international human rights standards.

The chapter considered the responses of three large hotel chains that show awareness regarding human rights obligations in their own operations, and also include relations with business partners. Human rights are at times criticized as a primarily Western idea; however, the example of Shangri-La underlines that human rights are also upheld in other regions of the world. Nevertheless, even InterContinental Hotels, Hyatt and Shangri-La, which have committed to respect human rights, have met with criticism. Besides, the focus of these companies' human rights commitments is largely on obeying the law. However, it might be necessary to define responses for acting in an environment of unjust law, as large chains not only have the responsibility to respect human rights, but also have the power to promote human rights, e.g. by intervening with governments.

References

Arnold, D. G. (2010). Transnational corporations and the duty to respect basic human rights. *Business Ethics Quarterly,* 20(3).

Bohdanowicz, P. & Zientara, P. (2008). Corporate social responsibility in hospitality: Issues and implications. *Scandinavian Journal of Hospitality and Tourism,* 8(4), 271–93.

Cragg, W. (2000). Human rights and business ethics: Fashioning a new social contract. *Journal of Business Ethics,* 27(1), 205–14.

Cragg, W. (2010). Business and Human Rights: A Principle and Value-Based Analysis. In G. G. Brenkert & T. L. Beauchamp (eds). *The Oxford Handbook of Business Ethics,* pp. 267–305. Oxford: Oxford University Press.

Donnelly, J. (1982). Human rights as natural rights. *Human Rights Quarterly,* 4(3), 391–405.

Frankental, P. (2013). Business and human rights – towards global standards. In K. Haynes, A. Murray & J. Dillard (eds). *Corporate Social Responsibility: A Research Handbook* (pp. 221–7). Milton Park: Routledge.

Friedman, M. (1970). The social responsibility of business is to increase its profits. *New York Times Magazine.*

Gond, J.-P., Palazzo, G. & Basu, K. (2009). Reconsidering instrumental corporate social responsibility through the mafia metaphor. *Business Ethics Quarterly*, 19(1), 57–85.

GRI (n.d.). Standard disclosures. Retrieved from https://www.globalreporting.org/standards/G3andG3-1/guidelines-online/G3Online/StandardDisclosures, accessed 28 June 2014.

Harmer, J. (2013, August 5). Tibet activists blockade intercontinental London Westminster hotel. *The Caterer and Hotelkeeper.* Retrieved from http://www.catererandhotelkeeper.co.uk/articles/5/8/2013/349463/tibet-activists-blockade-intercontinental-london-westminster-hotel.htm#sthash.USIVoFPE.dpuf, accessed 1 April 2014.

Hsieh, N. (2004). The obligations of transnational corporations: Rawlsian justice and the duty of assistance. *Business Ethics Quarterly*, 14, 643–61.

Hsieh, N. (2009). Does global business have a responsibility to promote just institutions? *Business Ethics Quarterly*, 19(2), 251–73.

Human Rights & Equal Opportunity Commission (1997, 25 September). Meeuwissen V Hilton Hotels of Australia Pty Ltd, H97/51.

Hyatt (2010). Human rights statement. Retrieved from http://investors.hyatt.com/files/doc_downloads/corp%20gov/HumanRightsStatement.pdf, accessed 5 June 2014.

Hyatt (2013). Corporate responsibility report 2012. Retrieved from http://thrive.hyatt.com/en/thrive/about-hyatt-thrive/reporting.html, accessed 5 June 2014.

IHG (InterContinental Hotels Group) (2013). Corporate responsibility report. Retrieved from http://www.ihgplc.com/index.asp?pageid=718, accessed 30 May 2014.

Kang, K.H., Lee, S., & Huh, C. (2010). Impacts of positive and negative corporate social responsibility activities on companies performance in the hospitality industry. *International Journal of Hospitality Management*, 29(1), 72–82.

Kobrin, S.J. (2009). Private political authority and public responsibility: Transnational politics, transnational companies, and human rights. *Business Ethics Quarterly*, 19(3), 349–74.

Manoharan, A., Gross, M.J., & Sardeshmukh, S.R. (2014). Identity-conscious vs identity-blind: Hotel managers' use of formal and informal diversity management practices. *International Journal of Hospitality Management*, 41(0), 1–9.

Nolan, J. & Taylor, L. (2009). Corporate responsibility for economic, social and cultural rights: Rights in search of a remedy? *Journal of Business Ethics*, 87, 433–51.

Oliveira, I. & Ambrósio, V. (2013). Sexual harassment in the hotel housekeeping department. *International Journal of Management Cases*, 15(4), 180.

Ostas, D.T. (2004). Cooperate, comply, or evade? A corporate executive's social responsibilities with regard to law. *American Business Law Journal*, 41(4), 559–94.

Othman, N.Z. & Hemdi, M.A. (2013). Corporate social responsibility (CSR) activities, brand image and hotel guest retention. In N. Sumarjan, Z.M.S. Mohd & R.S. Mohdet (eds). *Hospitality and Tourism: Synergizing Creativity and Innovation in Research.* London: Taylor & Francis.

Putten, F.-P. v.d., Crijns, G., & Hummels, H. (2003). The ability of corporations to protect human rights in developing countries. In R. Sullivan (ed.), *Business and Human Rights: Dilemmas and Solutions.* Sheffield, UK: Greenleaf Publishing, pp. 82–91.

Quinn, D.P. & Jones, T.M. (1995). An agent morality view of business policy. *Academy of Management Review*, 20(1), 22–42.

Rasche, A. (2012). The United Nations and transnational corporations: How the UN global compact has changed the debate. In J. Lawrence & P. Beamish (eds). *Globally Responsible Leadership. Business According to the UN Global Compact* (pp. 33–49). Thousand Oaks: Sage.

Rawls, J. (1999). The law of peoples. In J. Rawls (ed.). *The Law of Peoples: With "the Idea of Public Reason Revisited"* (pp. 3–128). Cambridge: Harvard University Press.

Sadar, S. (2011). Children working in hotels. *International Journal of Business Economics and Management Research,* 2(1), 56–77.

Santoro, M.A. (2010). Post-Westphalia and its discontents: Business, globalization, and human rights in political and moral perspective. *Business Ethics Quarterly,* 20(2), 285–97.

Schmitz, H.P. & Sikkink, K. (2002). International human rights. In W.-T. Carlsnaes, T. Risse & B.A. Simmons (eds). *Handbook of International Relations* (pp. 517–37). London: Sage.

Shangri-La (2012). Sustainability report 2012. Retrieved from www.shangri-la.com/corporate/about-us/corporate-social-responsibility/sustainability/reports, accessed 5 June 2014.

Shangri-La (2013). Shangri-La hotels and resorts 2013 UN global compact communication on progress. Retrieved from http://www.shangri-la.com/corporate/about-us/corporate-social-responsibility/sustainability/reports, accessed 5 June 2014.

Sloan, P., Legrand, W., & Chen, J.S. (2013). *Sustainability in the Hospitality Industry: Principles of Sustainable Operations.* London: Taylor & Francis.

Sorell, T. (2004). Business and human rights. In T. Campbell & S. Miller (eds). *Human Rights and the Moral Responsibilities of Corporate and Public Sector Organisations.* Dordrecht: Kluwer Academic Publishers, pp. 129–43.

Stevens, H. (2013, 18 June). Housekeepers protest Hyatt's "Longstanding labor abuses". *Triple Pundit.* Retrieved from http://www.triplepundit.com/2013/06/housekeepers-protest-hyatts-longstanding-labor-abuses, accessed 1 June 2014.

Swanson, D.L. (1995). Addressing a theoretical problem by reorienting the corporate social performance model. *Academy of Management Review,* 20(1), 43–64.

Tepelus, C.M. (2008). Social responsibility and innovation on trafficking and child sex tourism: Morphing of practice into sustainable tourism policies? *Tourism & Hospitality Research,* 8(2), 98–115.

Tourism Review (2010). Top 10 largest hotel groups of the world. Retrieved from http://www.tourism-review.com/top-10-world-largest-hotel-groups-news1988, accessed 25 January 2014.

UN Global Compact (2012a). Global Compact Principle Two. Retrieved from http://www.unglobalcompact.org/AboutTheGC/TheTenPrinciples/Principle2.html, accessed 11 January 2013.

UN Global Compact (2012b). The Ten Principles. Retrieved from http://www.unglobalcompact.org/aboutthegc/thetenprinciples/index.html, accessed 11 January 2013.

United Nations (2008a). Clarifying the concepts of "Sphere of influence" and "Complicity". Report of the special representative of the Secretary-General on the issue of human rights and transnational corporations and other business enterprises, John Ruggie. Human Rights Council, Eighth Session, a/Hrc/8/16. Retrieved from http://www.reports-and-materials.org/Ruggie-companion-report-15-May-2008.pdf, accessed 11 January 2013.

United Nations (2008b). Protect, Respect and Remedy: A framework for business and human rights. Report of the special representative of the Secretary-General on the issue of human rights and transnational corporations and other business enterprises, John Ruggie. Human Rights Council, Eighth Session, a/Hrc/8/5. Retrieved from http://www.reports-and-materials.org/Ruggie-report-7-Apr-2008.pdf, accessed 11 January 2013.

United Nations (2011). Report of the special representative of the secretary-general on the issue of human rights and transnational corporations and other business enterprises, guiding principles on business and human rights: Implementing the United Nations "Protect, Respect and Remedy" framework. Human Rights Council Seventeenth Session, a/Hrc/17/31. Retrieved from http://www.business-humanrights.org/media/documents/ruggie/ruggie-guiding-principles-21-mar-2011.pdf, accessed 11 January 2013.

Wettstein, F. (2009). Beyond voluntariness, beyond CSR: Making a case for human rights and justice. *Business and Society Review,* 114(1), 125–52.

Wettstein, F. (2012a). CSR and the debate on business and human rights: Bridging the great divide. *Business Ethics Quarterly*, 22(4), 739–70.

Wettstein, F. (2012b). Silence as complicity: Elements of a corporate duty to speak out against the violation of human rights. *Business Ethics Quarterly*, 22(1), 37–61.

Wettstein, F. & Waddock, S. (2005). Voluntary or mandatory: That is (not) the question: Linking corporate citizenship to human rights obligations for business. *Zeitschrift für Wirtschafts- und Unternehmensethik*, 6(3), 304–20.

Wood, S. (2012). The case for leverage-based corporate human rights responsibility. *Business Ethics Quarterly*, 22(1), 63–98.

2

The relevance of business sustainability in the hotel industry

Zabihollah Rezaee
Fogelman College of Business & Economics, University of Memphis, USA

Eun Kyong (Cindy) Choi
Kemmons Wilson School of Hospitality & Resort Management, University of Memphis, USA

Given the growing attention to business sustainability, this chapter examines the relevance and application of business sustainability for the hotel industry. There are five dimensions of sustainability performance useful to hotels: EGSEE (Economic, Governance, Social, Ethical and Environmental). Standardized sustainability reporting and assurance guidelines are needed to accurately, completely and reliably communicate EGSEE sustainability performance to all stakeholders. Publishing a sustainability performance report along with annual reports will bring benefits to the hotel companies and the EGSEE dimensions of sustainability performance reporting will ensure a more effective and useful report for all hotel stakeholders.

Introduction

Business sustainability has been extensively and inconclusively debated in business literature (Brockett & Rezaee, 2012). Corporations' primary goals have refocused from profit maximization to increasing shareholder wealth. Now, in the light of recent moves towards business sustainability worldwide, those goals are shifting to create shareholder value while fulfilling their social and environmental responsibilities. The hotel industry is not an exception. Many hotels—including chain hotels and private hotels—are adapting sustainability policies and practices to protect the interests of all their stakeholders including shareholders, customers, suppliers, employees, government, the environment and society.[1] Yet a frequently asked question is, "Do hotels have a social responsibility to stakeholders other than shareholders?" The answer is definitely yes. CSR (Corporate Social Responsibility) is an integral component of business sustainability and is particularly relevant when there is a conflict between the corporate objectives of maximizing profits and social goals. This chapter addresses emerging issues in business sustainability in the hotel industry relevant to profit, people and planet and how sustainability programmes and performance can be effectively integrated into business strategies in the hotel industry.

Business sustainability has received considerable attention from policymakers, regulators and the business and investment community for the past decade and is expected to remain an important theme well into the 21st century. Several professional organizations, including the Global Reporting Initiative (GRI, 2013), the International Integrated Reporting Council (IIRC, 2013) and the Sustainability Accounting Standards Board (SASB, 2013), are currently promoting sustainability and providing sustainability performance, reporting and assurance guidelines. Recently, more than 5,000 public companies worldwide have issued sustainability reports on various dimensions of sustainability performance (GRI, 2013). Brockett & Rezaee (2012) discuss five dimensions of sustainability performance, namely EGSEE (Economic, Governance, Social, Ethical and Environmental).

The remainder of this chapter covers: (1) the rise of sustainability performance and integrated reporting; (2) sustainability performance dimensions and their relevance to the hotel industry; (3) sustainability performance reporting and assurance; (4) evolution of sustainability in the hotel industry; and (5) concluding remarks.

The rise of sustainability performance and integrated reporting

Traditionally, business organizations have solely reported economic performance to their shareholders with the main goal of creating shareholder value. However, in

1 For example, Sheraton Hotels & Resorts, a part of the Starwood Corporation, implemented a green participation programme called "Make a green choice". The programme asks guests to become part of green practices and decline housekeeping services by placing a door hanger on the outside of their guestroom door before 2 a.m. If they participate, they receive a $5 food or beverage voucher or 500 points towards their membership points (Starwood Hotels & Resorts Worldwide Inc., 2012).

recent decades stakeholders and the public increasingly scrutinize how business organizations, including hotels worldwide, can maximize their positive impacts and minimize harm resulting from their business activities by paying attention to socially and environmentally responsible initiatives and impacts. In particular, hotels are expected to protect the interests of all stakeholders, including shareholders, customers, suppliers, employees, government, environment and society, and thus should report not only on their economic performance but also on the environmental and social impacts of their business. Multiple bottom-line reporting on EGSEE sustainability performance has recently been considered to ensure the sustainability of businesses and to recognize that a financially profitable business may impose significant external costs on society and the ecosystem (Brockett & Rezaee, 2012). The MBL ("multiple bottom line") complements and completes the conventional bottom line of solely reporting of net income. In addition to measuring financial performance, the MBL also considers the performance of a business in promoting environmental protection and social welfare.

The term sustainability was first defined in the Brundtland report as a development that "meets the needs of the present without compromising the ability of future generations to meet their own needs" (UN, 1987, p. 37). In this context, sustainability is described as a means of conducting activities to meet the needs of society while preserving the environment for future generations. Brockett & Rezaee (2012, p. 4) define sustainability as "conducting business activities to create value for present shareholders while protecting the rights of future shareholders and stakeholders". The term "corporate social responsibility" has evolved and been interchangeably used for business sustainability to measure and report on EGSEE dimensions of business sustainability performance (Brockett & Rezaee, 2012). There are two distinct views of a business organization's focus on sustainability including social and environmental responsibilities. One view is that a business organization exists solely to maximize profits and create value for its shareholders within the realm of law and morality. In this context, a business organization may engage in social or environmental initiatives merely to benefit its public image, prevent government intervention and/or gain government favour, obtain industry leadership, build better reputation or improve market share. Another view is that a business is the property of its owners and not its stakeholders. As such, the owners have the right to decide how to handle their property as they desire as either for profit or for social good, or both. Nonetheless, there has been a move in recent years to a middle ground view of "doing well by doing good" by focusing on achieving high performance on all five EGSEE dimensions of sustainability in creating shareholder value while protecting the interests of other stakeholders.

Currently, sustainability reports are voluntary and audits are based on the company's preference. These reports may bear different names, serve different purposes and vary in terms of structure, format, accuracy and assurance. Some kind of reporting standardization is required to make sustainability reports on EGSEE performance comparable and commonly acceptable. In 1999, the Global Reporting Initiative (GRI, 2013) provided a comprehensive Sustainability Reporting

Framework to enable greater organizational transparency. In 2013, the International Integrated Reporting Council (IIRC, 2013) developed the International Integrated Reporting Framework. IIRC guidelines state that the primary purpose of an integrated report is to explain to providers of financial capital how an organization creates value over time, but that it should benefit all stakeholders interested in an organization's ability to create value over time, including staff, customers, suppliers, business partners, local communities, legislators, regulators and policymakers. The future of sustainability/integrated reporting is based on an ideal of transparency which presumes that the information reported provides the most complete and realistic portrait possible of the positive and negative impacts of corporate activities. It is expected that the future of sustainability reports will reflect all five EGSEE dimensions of sustainability performance, as discussed in detail in the next section, and assurance will be provided on these reports to enhance their credibility and reliability.

Sustainability performance dimensions and their relevance to the hotel industry

Sustainability performance is typically classified into financial and non-financial performance, which is further grouped into five dimensions: E (economic), G (governance), S (social), E (ethical), and E (environmental)—abbreviated as EGSEE by Brockett & Rezaee (2012). Although business sustainability continues to evolve, several dimensions of sustainability performance pertaining to social and environmental initiatives have gained widespread global acceptance. These initiatives include ethical workplace, customer satisfaction, just and safe working conditions, non-discrimination fair wages, workplace diversity, environmental preservation, clear air and water, minimum age for child labour, safe and good-quality products, concern for the environment, and fair and transparent business practices. Each industry—including the hotel industry—has its own set of key financial and non-financial sustainability performance indicators and should carefully identify its own social and environmental responsibilities given the context of the business culture in which it operates. The list of financial and non-financial sustainability KPIs (key performance indicators) depends on a variety of factors including industry, location, customer products, legal regimes, cultural diversity, corporate mission and strategy, corporate culture, political infrastructure and managerial philosophy. Despite these different sustainability performance dimensions and their KPIs, sustainability has become an integral component of business (Brockett & Rezaee, 2012).

This section describes each of the EGSEE sustainability performance dimensions, their KPIs and their relevance to the hotel industry as described in Table 2.1 and further explained in the following subsections.

Table 2.1: **Sustainability performance dimensions and descriptions**

Source: Adapted from Brockett & Rezaee, 2012

Dimension	Description	Key Performance Indicators
Economic sustainability	Financial strengths and concerns of an organization's economic impacts on its stakeholders and society	Direct economic value generated and distributed, local suppliers and non-cash donations
Governance sustainability	A legal perspective of an organization as reforms and mechanisms that ensure compliance with all applicable laws, rules, regulations and standards	The governance structure of the organization, chairman and executive officer, unitary board structure and list of stakeholder groups
Social sustainability	The transformation of social goals into practice that would benefit an organization's stakeholders	Employment, labour/management relations, occupational health and safety, and training and education
Ethical sustainability	An organization's conducting business with ethical responsibility and integrity	Diversity, discrimination, child labour, codes of conduct and codes of ethics
Environmental sustainability	An organization's activities and operations on the environment beyond what is legislated by law	Materials, energy, water, biodiversity, emissions and waste

Economic sustainability performance

The most important and commonly accepted dimension of sustainability is "economic performance". The primary goal of any business organization—including hotels—is to create shareholder value through generating sustainable economic performance. Business organizations should focus on activities that generate long-term corporate profitability rather than short-term performance. The economic dimension of sustainability performance can be achieved when business organizations focus on long-term sustainability performance and improved effectiveness, efficiency and productivity. Long-term economic sustainability performance should be communicated to shareholders through the preparation of high-quality financial reports. In broader terms and in compliance with G4 of the GRI Guidelines, the economic dimension of sustainability should reflect the financial strengths and concerns of an organization's economic impacts on its stakeholders and society by showing how the economic status of stakeholders changes in response to the entity's activities. Economic sustainability performance can be measured directly through financial activities between an organization and its stakeholders or indirectly through non-financial costs and benefits of economic relations with stakeholders. Economic sustainability KPIs relevant to an organization's operating, investing and financing activities should be developed, including long-term ROA (return on assets), ROE (return on equity), market value, growth, quality and quantity of earnings, R&D (research and development) and market share.

Economic sustainability of hotels is important in assuring a desired return on investment for shareholders and in contributing to the local economy and society. Hotels have a direct and indirect impact on a local economy through providing job opportunities, contracting local suppliers and generating taxes from hotel rooms and foods sales. In 2012, the lodging industry generated $39.0 billion in pretax income and employed 1.8 million workers across the United States (AH&LA, 2013). Economic and financial sustainability of hotels not only creates value for shareholders but also generates financial and non-financial rewards for their stakeholders including employees, customers, suppliers, government and society.

Governance dimensions of sustainability performance

The corporate governance landscape has significantly changed in the aftermath of the global 2007–2009 financial crises. Internal and external corporate governance measures have been established by policymakers, regulators and corporations to improve the quality of corporate governance and thus regain stakeholders' trust and confidence in corporate sustainability performance and reporting. Regulatory reforms in the United States such as the Sarbanes-Oxley Act of 2002 (SOX, 2002) and the Dodd-Frank Act of 2010 (DOF, 2010) are designed to improve the quality and effectiveness of corporate governance. Effective corporate governance promotes accountability for the board of directors and executives, enhances sustainable operational and financial performance, improves the reliability and quality of financial information, and strengthens the integrity and efficiency of the capital market, which results in economic growth and prosperity for the nation. The governance dimension of sustainability performance is affected by legal, regulatory, internal and external mechanisms, and best practices to create shareholder value while protecting the interests of other stakeholders. Governance KPIs are board independence, board committees, executive compensation, succession planning, board diversity, codes of business ethics, anti-fraud and corruption policies and practices, and accountability.

The annual report of Millennium & Copthorne Hotels plc (2013) discloses how the hotel is committed to corporate governance and integrity. The board committee meets up to ten times a year and is responsible for setting strategies for growth and ensuring the availability of resources. The board, in particular, approves the following matters: ethics and policies, strategies and long-term plans, annual budgets, capital expenditures, major contracts and proposals, and internal controls and corporate governance. Internal control systems and risk management are among some of the responsibilities that executive management possesses in the hotel's operational performance.

Social dimension of sustainability performance

The social dimension of sustainability performance reflects the transformation of social goals into practice that would benefit an organization's stakeholders. Social performance measures an organization's social mission and its alignment with interests of the society. The social dimension of sustainability performance ranges from offering high-quality products and services to improving customer satisfaction, and ensuring employee health and well-being, and adding a positive contribution to the sustainability of the planet and the quality of life for future generations. Some examples of KPIs of social sustainability include: (1) the number of FTE (full-time employees) dedicated to social investment projects; (2) philanthropy as a percentage of (pretax) profit; (3) the percentage of eligible employees who signed the Code of Conduct and Ethics Policy; (4) public health issues and employee health and safety; (5) total investment in the community, donations and other social expenses; and (6) whistle-blowing policies, programmes and procedures.

Hotels throughout the world have all implemented programmes that are aimed at contributing to social sustainability efforts. Banyan Tree, based in Singapore, has started a programme called Seedlings to provide education for young people in the local community (Banyan Tree, 2007). Scholarships and internships are provided so that adolescents gain experience, preparation and mentorship before their first job. The hotel has also established several schools in the local community that offer programmes that enrich the education of their students. In addition to education, Banyan Tree has also expressed interest in improving the health of the community, especially children's health.

Ethical dimension of sustainability performance

An organization's ethical culture can play an important role in ensuring achievement of goals and sustainability. Effectiveness of ethical sustainability performance depends on corporate culture of integrity and competency and appropriate tone at the top. Characteristics of an ethical organization culture are codes of conduct for directors, officers and employees, a system of responsibility and accountability, and a workplace promoting honesty, mutual respect and freedom to raise concerns. Some important KPIs relevant to ethics are: (1) strong union relation; (2) corporate codes of conduct; (3) employee involvement, retirement benefits and health and safety policies; and (4) human rights strength.

One of the relevant ethical issues facing the hotel industry is discriminatory hiring and workplace practices. Many hotels including IHG (InterContinental Hotels Group) comply with EEO (Equal Employment Opportunity) when hiring new employees in an effort to prevent discrimination based on race, colour, ethnic or national origin, gender, sexual orientation, age, religion, marital status, or disability unrelated to the nature of employment (IHG, 2013). In 2011, Mandarin Oriental Hotel Group developed an employee policy for ethical behaviour to prevent discrimination or harassment at work (Mandarin Oriental Group, 2011). Ethical sustainability can go beyond hiring and diversity. For example, Marriott International created a Business Ethics Bulletin for associates to conduct business with integrity (Marriott International, 2012).

Environmental dimension of sustainability performance

Stakeholders are demanding more transparent information about the impacts of an organization's activities and operations on the environment beyond what is legislated by law (Brockett & Rezaee, 2012). The environmental dimension of sustainability performance includes creating an environmentally safe workplace, reducing carbon footprints and maximizing the positive effects of an organization on natural resources and the environment, including improving the air and water quality. CERES (Coalition for Environmentally Responsible Economies)—the UN environment programme in collaboration with the UN Global Compact—is promoting environmental initiatives (UN, 1987). KPIs for the environmental dimension of sustainability performance include: (1) continuous replacement of non-renewable scare resources; (2) disclosure of initiatives on climate changes; (3) promotion of environmentally safe products; (4) efficient utilization of scarce natural resources; and (5) minimization of the uses of environmentally harmful materials and products.

Three main areas in which environmental sustainability can be implemented in the hotel industry are energy management, water management and waste management (Leonidou *et al.*, 2013). Energy management includes installing energy-efficient lighting and replacing old equipment with energy-efficient equipment. Hotels in the United States spend an average of $2,196 per room on energy every year. Simply reducing energy consumption by 10% would lead to the same financial benefits as increasing the average daily room rate by $0.62 at limited service hotels and by $2.45 at full-service hotels (Energy Star, n.d.). Asking guests to reuse their towels and bed sheets, installing water-efficient fixtures and using environmentally safe detergents are all sustainable water-management practices. Hotels consume an average of 209 gallons of water per occupied room each day, which is 34 more gallons than the typical US household uses (San Antonio Water System, 2012). Hotels can reduce energy, water and chemical use by implementing the towel and linen reuse programme. Hotels also can reduce water usage by about 46% by installing low-flow taps. A low-flow showerhead uses only 50% of water compared to pre-1992 shower heads (Maxwell, 2014). In addition, waste management can make hotels greener by sorting waste in guestrooms, offices and kitchens, donating hotel furniture and leftover food, requiring reusable food containers packaging, and recycling (Bohdanowicz, 2006). Over 1,100 hotel properties across the United States participate in the Global Soap Project, a non-profit organization that re-processes used soaps from hotels and reproduces them into new bars for impoverished countries (Global Soap Project, 2011).

Sustainability performance reporting and assurance

Business organizations have traditionally reported their financial performance through four basic financial statements: (1) the Statement of Financial Position, reflecting the company's performance; (2) the Statement of Comprehensive Income, reporting results of operations that are reflected in net income for the period; (3) the Statement of Cash Flows, disclosing the change in cash flows from operating, investing and financing activities; and (4) the Statement of Changes in Equity (IFRS, 2013). This conventional financial reporting model has been criticized for focusing on historical financial information and for its limitations in accurately reflecting forward-looking financial and non-financial KPIs. Critics have advocated alternative reporting models to provide both financial and non-financial KPIs relevant to all five EGSEE dimensions of sustainability performance (Brockett & Rezaee, 2012). Economic sustainability performance reflected in financial reports is typically measured and recognized in compliance with a set of generally accepted accounting principles, audited by professional auditors and commonly accepted by investors as verifiable, reliable financial information. Other non-financial dimensions of sustainability performance are less quantifiable, more subject to interpretation and are typically not audited. Furthermore, what may seem socially or environmentally responsible for an individual or a group in one situation may be inappropriate to others. Examples of conflicts between corporations and society include environmental issues (e.g. pollution, acid rain and global warming), wage issues when multinational corporations hire workers in poor countries, and child labour issues in developing countries. Tobacco companies may contribute to the nation's economic growth by generating a high return on investment for their shareholders and even engaging in social activities and producing social reports, despite their products being considered detrimental to public health.

The Global Reporting Initiative guidelines

The GRI was launched in 1997 to promote global standardization to sustainability reporting (GRI, 2011). The evolution of GRI guidelines began with the primary focus on environmental performance reporting with its first publication, *Sustainability Reporting Guidelines*, in 2000 and then moved into governance, social and environmental sustainability performance reporting and assurance. In its G4 guidelines, issued in May 2013, the GRI promotes sustainability reporting as a standard practice for disclosing economic, governance, social and environmental sustainability performance (GRI, 2013). The GRI reporting process enables business organizations to disclose sustainability information based on one of the three application levels (A, B or C), depending on the extent of information provided. GRI also recommends that assurance be provided on sustainability reports by external assurance providers by adding a "+"to the application level declared. In April 2014, the European Parliament issued a directive that would require business organizations to report on their economic sustainability as well as environmental, governance, social and diversity (European Parliament, 2014).

Sustainability assurance

Quality, relevance and reliability of sustainability reports can be substantially improved by the assurance provided on these reports. Either external or internal sustainability assurance can be valuable to all stakeholders. Companies may seek assurance on their sustainability reports for a variety of reasons, including improving the trust and credibility in an organization's sustainability reports on all five EGSEE dimensions of sustainability performance, increasing the organization's perceived values for being trustworthy and honest, and strengthening communication with their stakeholders. Internal assurance services can also be provided to improve the credibility of the organization's sustainability reports. Nonetheless, external assurance provided by competent individuals from professional assurance providers, stakeholder panels and other external individuals can be viewed as more objective and independently verifiable. Assurance improves the trust and credibility in an organization's financial statements, which validates that the disclosed information is as accurate as possible. This increases the organization's values for being trustworthy and honest. In addition, it also improves stakeholder communication as some companies use their stakeholders as part of their external assurance. Internal assurance services are implemented to improve the credibility of company statements, but the GRI has suggested that external assurance be employed as well.

Evolution of sustainability in the hotel industry

There has been growing international interest in business sustainability in all five EGSEE sustainability performance dimensions. Business sustainability programmes are designed to minimize conflicts between corporations and society—caused by differences between private and social costs and benefits—and to align corporate goals with those of society. The main focus is on two important aspects of a business sustainability programme, namely the creation of social value through corporate activities (social value-added activities) and the avoidance of conflicts between corporate goals and societal goals (societal consensus). Business sustainability requires business organizations, including hotels, to take initiatives to advance social good beyond their own interests and to be in compliance with applicable regulations. Simply put, business sustainability means enhancing corporations' long-term financial performance, creating positive impacts on the community, environment, employees, customers and suppliers and minimizing harm to society and the environment. The true measure of success for hotels should be determined not only by reported earnings but also by their governance effectiveness, social responsibility initiatives, ethical behaviour and environmental conscience.

Business sustainability affects many aspects of the hospitality industry, from creating long-term financial performance by generating sustainable revenues and reducing operating costs and maximizing RevPAR (revenue per available room), to ensuring customer satisfaction, a safe work environment and fulfilling social and environmental responsibilities. Sustainability practices in hotels include waste management, recycling and waste reduction, air and water quality improvement, conservation, and food and beverage quality.

Hotel sustainability has slowly gained interest and awareness over the decades and has inspired many hotels to take steps towards improving the environmental and social impacts of the hotel industry. Goldstein & Primlani (2012) state that the concept of hotel sustainability is nothing new as it first originated over half a century ago when hoteliers wanted to incorporate elements of nature into the hotel experience to enhance their guests' stay. The Santa Barbara oil spill from the '60s stimulated the origins of the environmental movement by promoting awareness of how pollution affects human health. During 1973–4, the energy crisis impelled hoteliers, the architecture and engineering design community, and hospitality associations to focus on energy conservation strategies on account of the growing concern of utility costs and energy supply (Goldstein & Primlani, 2012). In the 1980s and 1990s, the idea of sustainability came to existence when the United Nations wanted to start a development that would allow the present to use resources responsibility so that it would not deplete those of future generations (Goldstein & Primlani, 2012). In 1992, the IHEI (International Hotels Environment Initiative) was launched by a set of chief executives from international hotel groups to educate environmental issues in the hotel industry and to encourage hotels to implement environmental practices into their properties (UN, n.d.). Since 2000, hotel owners have enhanced their CSR approach by including environmental objectives and have vastly emphasized reducing utility costs after the financial crisis from 2008 to 2009. The new trend of hotel sustainability emphasizes environmental objectives in CSR (Goldstein & Primlani, 2012). For example, hotels put efforts on receiving certifications of going green from public and private environmental organizations such as Green Seal and the United States Green Building Council's LEED (Leadership in Energy and Environmental Design) programme (Millar, n.d.). As of 27 June 2014, there are 273 LEED certified hotel properties (Hasek, 2014) and 83 certified hotels by Green Seal in the world (Hasek, 2013). In 2013, TripAdvisor, the world's largest travel site, launched a programme called "GreenLeaders" which was developed in partnership with US Environmental Protection Agency's ENERGY STAR programme, the US Green Building Council and the United Nations Environment Programme to assist customers to find sustainable lodgings (TripAdvisor, 2013). Travelocity, Orbit and Expedia also incorporated a list of green hotels on their websites (Hasek, 2010).

Drivers of sustainability in the hotel industry

Hotel sustainability has evolved into a movement as people are realizing that sustainability is not a fad. Awareness, consumer expectations, regulations, etc. are just a few drivers that have made hotel sustainability what it is today (Deloitte, 2008). Awareness is heightened through media attention and has influenced the expectations of tourists and travellers. Deloitte's survey found that 95% of respondents believed that hotels should partake in green initiatives, including recycling, using energy-efficient light bulbs and encouraging guests to use their towels and sheets more than once. The survey also found that 74% of respondents had taken steps towards going green by purchasing fluorescent lights or environment-friendly cleaning products and 68% had expressed that they were at least fairly green. These results show that, as consumers are becoming increasingly green, they also expect the same efforts from hotels, driving them to become more sustainable. Information travels fast in this age of technology, and a hotel's reputation can be easily tarnished if guests decide to disclose how that hotel is not environmentally friendly.

Regulations have also increasingly motivated hotels to undertake green initiatives. The City of Los Angeles' 2008 ordinance, which requires projects to meet the LEED standard, and the Kyoto Protocol are examples of these many regulations (Deloitte, 2008). The Audubon Green Globes' Green Leaf Eco-Rating Program inspects facilities to find which companies display best practices in energy efficiency, pollution prevention, environmental management and resource conservation, and issues a Green Leaf seal for promotion to Green Leaf-rated facilities (Eigerman, 2011). American and European governments have been offering tax credits and deductions as well as lower cost financing for those who implement sustainable efforts (Deloitte, 2010).

The more obvious and common incentives to sustainability in the hotel industry are the financial benefits from going green. Assessments have been made to show that most buildings worldwide use more energy than necessary and that cost reduction strategies can be achieved, making sustainability an attractive goal (Goldstein & Primlani, 2012). Luxury hotels that offer swimming pools and spas among other services will be highly affected by the constraint of water supply if prices were to increase. As the prices for these resources rise, it would greatly benefit hotels to implement operational efficiency to decrease bills and increase bottom line financial returns. Many hotels, including Sheraton Hotels & Resorts, have adopted a linen and towel reuse programme which can save costs for them. For example, a hotel with 100 guest rooms with 75% occupancy can save an estimated $25,000 per year through the programme (Brodsky, 2005). Furthermore, guests might choose a hotel that implements sustainability practices over competitors for this reason, which will generate revenue. Some research even indicates that some environmentally conscious guests are willing to pay premium prices to stay at a sustainable hotel (Kuminoff *et al.*, 2010).

In May 2011, Marriott International launched the HCMI (Hotel Carbon Measurement Initiative) to develop, test and refine an industry-wide methodology for calculating carbon footprint. Marriott International has also implemented its EEAP (Energy and Environmental Action Plan) worldwide in 2012, which aims to reduce energy and water consumption. In conjunction with that initiative, Marriott International became the first lodging company to join the Constellation Energy's Project Vulcan. This programme goes along with the MRCx (Marriot Retro-Commissioning) programme. Project Vulcan requires hotels to reduce lighting and air-conditioning usage in common areas and unoccupied rooms, and to optimize cooling cycles during peak energy demand periods.

Best practices of sustainability performance reporting and assurance in the hotel industry

There are several hotel companies supporting sustainable reporting in the world. Marriott International issues its sustainability report using GRI 3.1 and receives a verified C reporting level (IIRC, 2013). Marriott International assigned a large portion of its 10-K filings and sustainable report to green hotel developments. According to the reports, Marriott International is the first in the hospitality industry to have a series of green hotel prototypes approved by the US Green Building Council's LEED. Marriott International described in its 10-K that it launched a programme with IHG and Wyndham Worldwide in 2010 to develop an industry standard for carbon accounting. Not all hotels need to develop their own protocols for sustainability like Marriott International, given that a huge variety of programmes and certifications that are relevant to the hospitality sector already exist. These can be broadly categorized into environmental certification programmes, green building certification programmes and product-specific standards and certification programmes.

Many hotels such as Hilton Worldwide, IHG, Mandarin Oriental Hotel Group and Swissotel Hotels and Resorts follow the GRI guidelines and include its GRI level as well as GRI index. After all, the report for Mandarin Oriental Hotel Group was reviewed by an independent third-party auditor, LRQA (Lloyd's Register Quality Assurance), and the report for Swissotels was audited by the SQS (Swiss Association for Quality and Management System). On the other hand, Marriott International does not include either GRI index or GRI level in its report. The report also does not cover information for governance sustainability. There is no doubt that sustainability is an important factor in hotels being successful. Hotels should find the most effective ways to communicate with their stakeholders regarding their sustainability performance.

Conclusions

Business sustainability has gained considerable attention from regulators, investors and the business community worldwide. Sustainability performance has become a company's branding, reflecting its culture and business strategy of focusing on profit, people and planet. More than 5,000 global public companies are now reporting their EGSEE sustainability performance in disclosing their sustainability activities and performance in creating shareholder value and in protecting interests of other stakeholders. Hotels should also benefit from EGSEE sustainability performance, reporting and assurance issues presented in this chapter. To increase sustainability effectiveness, hotels can consider electing a sustainability committee. The committee's responsibility will be to focus on all five EGSEE dimensions of sustainability performance. The committee should also consider sustainability guidelines (e.g. GRI, IIRC) and hotel industry best practices of sustainability performance, reporting and assurance in developing its sustainability mission, goals, strategies and actions. External stakeholders (e.g. advisory panels) can be an important resource in providing review of the contents and disclosures of sustainability performance reporting and assurance.

Sustainability reporting has evolved from reporting on an organization's CSR to a stand-alone reporting to all five EGSEE dimensions of sustainability performance as discussed in this chapter. Sustainability performance information is now demanded by socially responsible investors, highly recommended and/or required by global stock exchanges and regulators and widely disclosed by business organizations. However, sustainability performance reporting has been mostly voluntary and arbitrary. Integrated and uniform sustainability performance reporting can be achieved when business organizations including hotels focus on satisfying the needs of all stakeholders, including employees, customers, environment, society and investors. Sustainability reporting can be promoted in three ways: (1) through market forces of the demand for and interests in EGSEE performance reporting by investors and financial markets; (2) through mandatory sustainability reporting by regulators and listing standards of stock exchanges; and (3) through a combination of mandatory and voluntary initiatives. Further promotion of business sustainability in general and sustainability reporting in particular demands integration of sustainability into business strategic planning and decisions and disclosure of both financial and non-financial KPI information to all stakeholders.

References

AH&LA (American Hotel and Lodging Association) (2013). 2013 lodging industry profile. Washington DC: AH&LA. Retrieved from http://www.ahla.com/content.aspx?id=35603, accessed 14 July 2014.

Banyan Tree (2007). Banyan Tree announces new initiatives in corporate social responsibility. Retrieved from hhttp://www.banyantreeglobalfoundation.com/wp-content/uploads/2015/06/banyan_tree_sr_2007_en.pdf, accessed 10 May 2014.

Bohdanowicz, P. (2006). Environmental awareness and initiatives in the Swedish and Polish hotel industries-survey results. *International Journal of Hospitality Management*, 25(4), 662–82.

Brockett, A. & Rezaee, Z. (2012). *Corporate Sustainability: Integrating Performance and Reporting.* New Jersey, USA: Wiley, p. 336.

Brodsky, S. (2005). Water conservation crucial to energy savings. Skokie. *Hotel & Motel Management.* Retrieved from http://infohouse.p2ric.org/ref/43/42990.pdf, accessed 12 May 2014.

Deloitte (2008). The staying power of sustainability: Balancing opportunity and risk in the hospitality industry. Retrieved from http://www.expoknews.com/wp-content/uploads/2010/02/us_cb_sustainability_1906081.pdf, accessed 10 May 2014.

Deloitte (2010). Hospitality 2015: Game changers or spectators? Retrieved from http://www.fairtrade.travel/uploads/files/Hospitality_2015_Deloitte_report.pdf, accessed 10 May 2014.

DOF (2010). Dodd-Frank Wall Street Reform and Consumer Protection Act of 2010. *Public Law*, 111–203. Retrieved from http://www.gpo.gov/fdsys/pkg/PLAW-111publ203/pdf/PLAW-111publ203.pdf, accessed 28 July 2014.

Eigerman, J. (2011). Trends in sustainability regulation. Retrieved from http://dfllp.com/wp-content/uploads/2011/10/Trends-in-Sustainability-Regulation-chapter-2011.pdf, accessed 10 May 2014.

Energy Star (n.d.). Hotels: An overview of energy use and energy efficiency opportunities. Retrieved from http://www.energystar.gov/sites/default/files/buildings/tools/SPP%20Sales%20Flyer%20for%20Hospitality%20and%20Hotels.pdf, accessed 8 May 2014.

European Parliament (2014). Disclosure of non-financial and diversity information by certain large companies and groups. Text approved Part V (April 2014), 312. Retrieved from http://www.europarl.europa.eu/sides/getDoc.do?pubRef=-//EP//NONSGML+TA+20140415+SIT-05+DOC+PDF+V0//EN&language=EN, accessed 28 July 2014.

Global Soap Project (2011). Hotels. Retrieved from http://www.globalsoap.org/hotels, accessed 10 May 2014.

Goldstein, K.A. & Primlani, R.V. (2012). Current trends and opportunities in hotel sustainability. Gurgaon: Hospitality Valuation Services. Retrieved from http://www.hvs.com/Content/3218.pdf, accessed 10 May 2014.

GRI (Global Reporting Initiative) (2011). G3.1 sustainability reporting guidelines. Retrieved from https://www.globalreporting.org/resourcelibrary/G3.1-Guidelines-Incl-Technical-Protocol.pdf, accessed 10 May 2014.

GRI (2013). G4 exposure draft 2013. Frequently asked questions about the G4 exposure draft and the second G4 public comment period. Retrieved from https://www.globalreporting.org/resourcelibrary/G4-FAQ.pdf, accessed 10 May 2014.

Hasek, G. (2010). Online travel agencies step up efforts to promote green hotels. Retrieved from http://www.greenlodgingnews.com/Online-Travel-Agencies-Step-Up-Efforts-Promote-Green-Hotels, accessed 26 July 2014.

Hasek, G. (2013). Green seal, with 83 certified hotel properties, moves toward GS-33 update. Retrieved from http://www.greenlodgingnews.com/green-seal-with-83-certified-hotel-properties-moves, accessed 26 July 2014.

Hasek, G. (2014). Number of LEED certified hotel projects approaches 300. Retrieved from http://www.greenlodgingnews.com/number-of-leed-certified-hotel-projects-approaches, accessed 26 July 2014.

IFRS (International Financial Reporting Standards) (2013). Financial statement presentation. Retrieved from http://www.ifrs.org/Meetings/MeetingDocs/Other%20Meeting/2007/April/25th/AP3-Financial-Statement-Presentation-Phase-B.pdf, accessed 14 July 2014.

IHG (InterContinental Hotels Group) (2013). Corporate responsibility report. Retrieved from http://www.ihgplc.com/index.asp?pageid=741, accessed 8 May 2014.

IIRC (International Integrated Reporting Council) (2013). Integrated financial and sustainability reporting in the United States. Retrieved from http://irrcinstitute.org/pdf/FINAL_Integrated_Financial_Sustain_Reporting_April_2013.pdf, accessed 10 May 2014.

Kuminoff, N., Zhang, C., & J. Rudi (2010). Are travelers willing to pay a premium to stay at a "green" hotel? Evidence from an Internal Meta-Analysis of Hedonic Price Premia. *Agricultural and Resource Economics Review* 39(3), 468–84.

Leonidou, L.C., Constantinos N.L., Fotiadis, T.A., & Zeriti, A. (2013). Resources and capabilities as drivers of hotel environmental marketing strategy: Implications for competitive advantage and performance. *Tourism Management*, 35 (April), 94–110.

Mandarin Oriental Hotel Group (2011). 2011 sustainability report. Retrieved from http://files.mandarinoriental.com/sustainability/files/inc/50014369.pdf, accessed 8 May 2014.

Marriott International (2012). 2011–2012 sustainability report. Retrieved from http://www.marriott.com/Multimedia/PDF/CorporateResponsibility/MarriottSustainabilityReport_2011and2012condensed4MB.pdf, accessed 10 May 2014.

Maxwell, J. (2014). Not a drop in the bucket. Retrieved from http://www.asianhospitality.com/trends-nissues/Not+a+drop+in+the+bucket/1800, accessed 10 May 2014.

Millar, M. (n.d.). Five important benefits of green certification. Retrieved from https://hotel-executive.com/business_review/2857/five-important-benefits-of-green-certification, accessed 14 July 2014.

Millennium & Copthorne Hotels plc (2013). Annual report and accounts 2013. London: Millennium & Copthorne Hotels plc. Retrieved from http://www.millenniumhotels.com/content/dam/Millennium/CIR/RNS-News/2013/01012014_annual_report_2013.pdf, accessed 10 May 2014.

San Antonio Water System (2012). Commercial water saver hotel program. Retrieved from http://www.saws.org/Conservation/CaseStudies/docs/WaterSaverHotelProgram_20120510.pdf, accessed 10 May 2014.

SASB (Sustainability Accounting Standards Board) (2013). Conceptual Framework of the Sustainability Accounting Standard Board. San Francisco: SASB. Retrieved from http://www.sasb.org/wp-content/uploads/2013/10/SASB-Conceptual-Framework-Final-Formatted-10-22-13.pdf, accessed 25 July 2014).

SOX (Sarbanes-Oxley Act 2002) (2002). The public company accounting reform and investor protection act. Retrieved from http://www.sec.gov/about/laws/soa2002.pdf, accessed 28 July 2014.

Starwood Hotels & Resorts Worldwide Inc. (2012). Make a green choice. Retrieved from http://www.starwoodpromos.com/sheratongreenchoice/?EM=VTY_SI_GREENCHOICE_PROMOTION, accessed 21 July 2014.

TripAdvisor (2013). TripAdvisor GreenLeaders™ programme highlights eco-friendly hotels to help travelers plan greener trips. Retrieved from http://www.tripadvisor.com/PressCenter-i5903-c1-Press_Releases.html, accessed 26 July 2014.

UN (United Nations) (1987). *Report of the World Commission on Environment and Development: Our Common Future.* New York: Oxford University Press, 36–51.

UN (n.d.). CSD-7: Sustainable development success stories. Retrieved from https://sustainabledevelopment.un.org/content/dsd/dsd_aofw_mg/mg_success_stories/csd7/tour6.htm, accessed 12 May 2014.

3

Strategic decision elements for hotel managers embarking on a sustainable supply chain management initiative

Susan M. Tinnish

Kendall College, USA

With nearly 51,000 lodging properties in the United States alone, hotels have an important role to play in the hospitality industry's efforts towards greater sustainability. Many hotels have taken steps to create programmes focused on sustainability. These programmes have focused on environmental consumer-facing efforts (e.g. towel reuse programmes), as well as operational initiatives (e.g. reducing energy use or water usage). Some hotels have concentrated on the social aspect of sustainability (e.g. Wyndham Hotel Group, Carlson Companies and Hilton Worldwide, which have signed a code of conduct against human [child] trafficking). Many businesses realize they no longer compete as solely autonomous entities, but rather as supply chains; this represents a significant paradigm shift in business management and thinking. As hotels consider their next focus in sustainability initiatives, industry leaders can consider options with the company's supply chain. This chapter will allow managers to think more purposefully about the role of SSCM (Sustainable Supply Chain Management) in a hotel. The chapter theorizes that hotels must consider different decision criteria from manufacturing organizations in choosing sustainable supply chain alternatives.

Introduction

Many hotels have taken steps to create programmes focused on environmental sustainability. These programmes have concentrated on consumer-focused efforts (e.g. towel reuse programmes) as well as operational initiatives (e.g. reducing energy use or water usage). In some cases, hotels have targeted the social aspect of sustainability (e.g. Wyndham Hotel Group, Carlson Companies and Hilton Worldwide, which have all signed a code of conduct against human [child] trafficking).

As hotels consider their next target for sustainable initiatives, they may concentrate on their supply chain. Supply chain activities focus on product development, sourcing, production and logistics, as well as the information systems needed to coordinate these activities (Handfield, 2011). SCM (Supply chain management) focuses on the management of supply chain activities to help create more value (benefits or cost reductions) to allow both purchaser and supplier to attain a sustainable competitive advantage (Simchi-Levi *et al.*, 2000). Carter & Rogers (2008, p. 368) define SSCM (sustainable supply chain management) as the strategic achievement and integration of an organization's social, environmental and economic goals through the systemic coordination of key interorganizational business processes to improve the long-term economic performance of the individual company and its value network.

In industrial segments like manufacturing or retail, the greatest opportunity for improving sustainability performance such as reducing carbon emissions, water use, toxic chemicals and addressing social and human rights concerns occurs in global SSCM. For example, up to 60% of a manufacturing company's carbon footprint is in its supply chain. For retailers, close to 80% of their carbon footprint is in the supply chain; this sector's supply chain also faces exposure to human rights and social issues (CERES, n.d.). Like other industrial sectors, the lodging industry can move its sustainability efforts forward through expansion of initiatives to global supply chains.

Many fields have contributed to an understanding of SCM and SSCM including purchasing; logistics and transportation; operations management; marketing; management information systems; organizational theory; and strategic management. Using the lens of organizational theory, change management and strategy, this chapter will propose additional strategic elements for hotels choosing options for implementing SSCM programmes.

Literature review

Supply chain management and sustainable supply chain management

The topics in supply chain management have shifted in academic literature demonstrating the evolution of SCM. Topics include production planning and control for remanufacturing, reverse logistics, inventory, logistics network design and management issues (Lambert & Cooper, 2000). Technology and the internet have transformed SCM activities and this change is reflected in the literature. Attaran & Attaran (2007) address topics such as e-business; CPFR (Collaborative Planning, Forecasting and Replenishment); VMI (Vendor-Managed Inventory); CRP (Continuous Replenishment Programmes); ECR (Efficient Consumer Response); and EDI (Electronic Data Interchange). Attaran & Attaran conclude that collaborative SCM practices, especially CPFR, are firmly established as the way forward for successful and sustainable business operations. More recent articles have covered topics on various nuances of sustainable supply chain including green design, green manufacturing, environmental SCM and the broad issue of sustainability. Mejias & Padro (2013) completed a literature review of logistic journals articles from 1990 and 2011 highlighting best practices for effective SCM. Srivastava (2007) completed a comprehensive view of published literature on aspects and facets of Green SCM; he categorized the literature in three groups: supply chain design; the importance of GrSCM (green supply chain management) or green design; and green operations. Beamon (2008) describes the challenges and opportunities facing the supply chain of the future and describes the various effects these issues have on supply chain design, management and integration. Seuring & Müller (2008) researched pressures and incentives for sustainable SCM, identifying and measuring impacts on sustainable SCM, supplier management and generic cross-company issues related to SCM.

Research conducted specifically in the hospitality industry is less significant. Odoom (2012) wrote his dissertation on logistics and SCM in the hotel industry. His research focused on defining logistics and SCM and how various practices reduce costs and the competitive advantage of logistics and supply chain in the hotel industry. He concluded with a discussion on how logistics and SCM practices can be implemented across the hotel industry. More research is found in the area of tourism. Zhang *et al.* (2009) define tourism SCM and examine its components. Further, they explore the critical issues associated with tourism and propose a research agenda. Gomes da Costa & Carvalho (2011) studied the village of Palmela in Portugal to examine the sustainability of the tourism supply chain. Font *et al.* (2008) examined UK and European tour operators to identify examples of good practice across the entire supply chain and made recommendations for more widespread engagement. Their article also addressed the complexity and differences inherent in the tourism supply chain. In Maloni & Brown's (2006) study on food chain issues, they detailed unique CSR applications in the food supply chain including animal welfare, biotechnology, environment, fair trade, health and safety, and labour and human rights.

Drivers to engage in SSCM

According to PwC, a consulting firm, more than two-thirds of supply chain executives (N=500) state sustainability will play an important role in how they manage their supply chains through 2015 (Delay *et al.*, 2014, p. 5).

The business case justifying SSCM is based on similar categories for substantiating other sustainable initiatives including economic, environmental and social benefits such as cost savings; reputation management; access to capital; tax breaks and credits; new innovation in products and services; employee engagement; environmental gains; social advances (all cited by Green Hotelier, 2012; Ashton, n.d.); quality; continuity of supply; revenue increases; customer experience improvements; supply chain resilience/risk management; strategic value (Tillon *et al.*, n.d.); and reputation management.

Strategic importance of SCM

Supply chain management has migrated from a purchasing function to a higher-level, value-added one within corporations. SCM involves operational, tactical and strategic decision-making. SSCM involves three levels of decision-making (Simchi-Levi & Simchi-Levi, 2003 as cited in Zhang *et al.*, 2009):

- *Strategic*: Involves decisions concerning long-term issues such as demand planning, strategic alliances, new product development, outsourcing, supplier selection, pricing and network configuration decisions

- *Tactical*: Involves medium-term decisions such as inventory control, production/distribution coordination, material handling and equipment selection

- *Operational*: Involves weekly or daily events such as vehicle scheduling, routing, workforce allocation and process planning

Various researchers have examined SCM and SSCM from these three perspectives: SCM as a competitive strategy to enhance organizational productivity and profitability using performance measurement and metrics (Gunasekaran *et al.*, 2004); the importance of strategic supply chains using well-integrated suppliers (Tomas *et al.*, 2004); and a systems perspective on supply chain measurements (Holmberg, 2000).

Organizational readiness for SSCM

The literature includes three themes related to organizational readiness: diffusion of innovation; strategy; and organizational capacity and competencies.

So *et al.*'s (2012, pp. 6–7) work used Rogers' Innovation-Decision Process (IDP); the decision process to adopt sustainability in supply chain activities encompasses five stages: knowledge; persuasion; decision; implementation; and confirmation. They summarize the process as a temporal event "through which an adopter passes from first knowledge of an innovation, to forming an attitude towards the innovation, to a decision to adopt or reject, to implementation of the new idea, and to confirmation of this decision" (So *et al.*, 2012, p. 5). The researchers mention various implementation challenges in stages 4 and stage 5 of Rogers' IDP.

Young & Dhanda (2013) outline a five-stage process that reflects the varying ways organizations react to sustainability. Although these responses do not always occur in a strict progression, Young & Dhanda present them as stages on the path to sustainability (Young & Dhanda, 2013, p. 16):

- Stage 1 is *non-compliance* where an organization is fined for not complying with local emission regulations

- Stage 2 is *compliance* where, perhaps in a reaction to external pressure from NGOs and regulators, organizations begin to comply but the actions are primarily aimed at compliance so as not to incur fines or taxes

- Stage 3 is *beyond compliance*. Organizations discover that savings and payoffs of going further than compliance can far outweigh the initial investments. This reinforces the win–win scenario wherein reinvestment of initial savings leads to positive gains including an improvement in brand value and reputation

- Stage 4 is where *sustainability is fully integrated* into strategy. This occurs when organizations decide to proactively integrate sustainability into every aspect of business strategy. In addition, sustainability is also factored into the investment and decision-making process across the organization

- Stage 5 is a stage where organizations *advance*, without passing through other stages; this is usually due to a change in mission

Similarly, the second annual Sustainability & Innovation survey, conducted by Boston Consulting Group and the MIT Sloan Management Review, created a similar typology with *Cautious adopters* and *Embracers* (Haanaes *et al.*, 2011). *Cautious adopters* tend to view sustainability initiatives as being important simply in terms of risk management, as well as cost savings through improvements in efficiency. *Embracers*, however, see sustainability as a competitive advantage.

Amit & Schoemacher (1993, p. 35) examine specific competencies/capabilities for firms in supplying "green products" (as cited in Pampanini & Martino, 2012). They define a capability as "a firm's capacity to deploy resources, usually in combination, using organizational processes, to affect a desired end". The allocation, coordination and deployment of the resources towards execution of SSCM are key attributes of capabilities.

Operating a sustainable supply chain management

Companies have choices about how and what to implement in regards to their SCM activities including: supply chain partners; internal functions and levels of the organization; external efforts through collaboration with other players in the industry (Tillon *et al.*, n.d., p. 5); what type of technology to introduce; and what type of organizational practice to adopt (Sarkis, 2002, p. 397).

Various researchers have studied how organizations operate SSCM. Lia *et al.* (2006) use empirical data to examine SCM practices, competitive advantage and organizational performance. Ketchen & Giunipero (2004) utilize a platform of participants, social structure, goals and technology to examine how supply chain practices shape firm outcomes.

Sarkis (2002) identified primary strategic and operational elements to aid managers in evaluating SSCM alternatives. He utilized ANP (analytical network process) to identify the multi-criteria decision elements and relationship between the various parts to document decision variables. The ANP technique relies on pairwise comparisons and matrices built by comparison questions like "how much more important is procurement than production operations in the introductory phases of a product's life cycle?" The answers measure the relative weights of the elements. ANP structures solutions as a network between a goal, decision criteria and alternatives. In an SSCM scenario, organizations have the goal to develop improved green supply chains. The goal is influenced by the five elements: product life-cycle influence; operational life cycle; environmentally influential organizational practices; organizational performance requirements; and green supply chain alternatives. Elements may be clustered together and interrelated. Through calculation of a super matrix where the comparisons are built from sub-matrices of sub-priorities, the ANP creates a structure that is described by the clusters, the elements, their connections and their interdependencies.

His research offers managers a tool to weigh elements of a multidimensional problem to allow them to make decisions in a complex environment. By identifying the five elements, he creates a framework for decision-makers to prioritize or select systems that will aid in managing sustainable supply chains. His five elements are detailed below.

Product life-cycle influence

Sarkis (2002, p. 398) describes a typical product life cycle as comprising four phases: "a product introduction phase that is characterized by investment in product R&D, a growth phase characterized by increasing production capacity and logistics channels, a maturity phase, where process and cost efficiencies are typically implemented, and a decline phase where the focus is on product divestment". During the early stages of a product's life cycle, the product can be influenced by the design, which in turn affects the SSCM decisions like purchases of raw materials. In contrast, during the mature and decline stages, process re-engineering and implementing an efficient reverse logistics system will impact the supply chain.

Operational life cycle
The operational life cycle will typically include procurement, production, packaging, distribution and reverse logistics. While slightly more tactical, operational decisions do impact SSCM choices. For example, the procurement decisions affect the purchase of materials that are either recyclable or reusable, or have already been recycled. Or the selection of vendors is an important decision. If systems and processes preexist and are designed for the prevention of waste, then different SSCM decisions will be made (Sarkis, 2002, p. 399).

Environmentally influential organizational practices
The five practices Sarkis (2002, p. 399) focuses on include reduction (reduce), reuse, remanufacture, recycle and disposal alternatives. Reduction impacts inputs into the supply chain; the other four practices affect production processes.

Organizational performance requirements
Sarkis (2002, p. 400) delineates the specific organizational performance requirements of cost, quality, time and flexibility. While not directly related to SCM or SSCM, these requirements are necessary to identify how well various alternatives can perform to support the business.

Green supply chain alternatives
Sarkis (2002, p. 400) identifies several SSCM supply alternatives including TQEM (total quality environmental management), ISO 14000 (environmental management system) or ISO 9000 (QMS/Quality Management Standard) certification, or EDI.

Theoretical model

Sarkis's model was built using the ANP technique. While the lodging industry can learn from efforts of manufacturers or retailers like Amazon, Hewlett-Packard and Wal-Mart, this chapter seeks to show that the SSCM decision variables differ for a hotel. This chapter extends Sarkis's framework through the addition of elements that might be warranted for consideration before a chain or hotel undertakes any SSCM initiative. Additional elements are introduced to reflect the uniqueness and complexity of the lodging industry.

Thus the author advances five new strategic elements to Sarkis's framework to theoretically construct a more useful framework (see Figure 3.1). This extension of the Sarkis model is called the HLSE (Hotel and Lodging Strategic Elements) model and includes these additional five variables:

• Business model (organizational structure and consumer preferences)

Figure 3.1 **HLSE (hotel and lodging strategic elements) model**

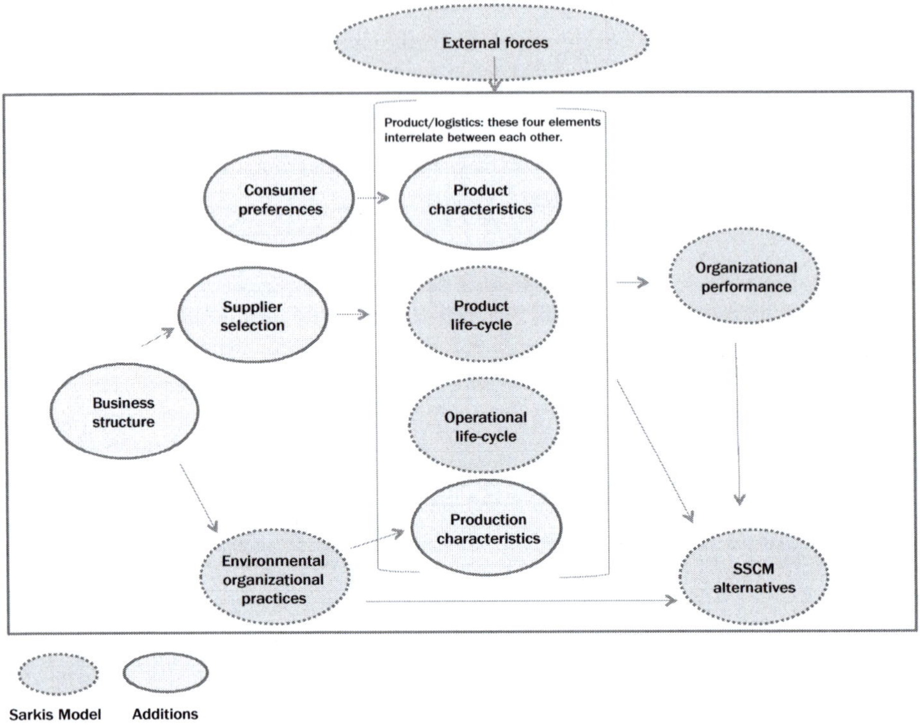

Sarkis Model   Additions

- Product characteristics
- Supplier selection
- Production characteristics
- External forces

Whereas Sarkis's model actually computes preferences for SSCM alternatives through the use of paired comparisons, matrices and calculation of the super matrix, the HLSE are derived from literature and ethnographic observations of the author.

The model depicts that business structure (franchised hotel versus managed versus owned) influence supplier selection and the use of environmentally influential organizational processes. In turn, consumer preferences also affect product characteristics. Like Sarkis's model, an interrelationship exists between Product Life Cycle stages and Operational Life Cycle. In addition, that interrelationship now also includes Product Characteristics and Production Characteristics. These four elements constitute the Product/Logistics sub-process. Organizational Performance Criteria and the Product/Logistics combined with Environmentally Influential Organizational Processes drive SSCM alternatives. The next section provides justification for the inclusion of these elements while noting differences between manufacturing and the lodging industry.

Business model

The HLSE model encapsulates two differences from a manufacturing environment which impact SSCM: business organization structure (franchise, multiple outlets, management companies, ownership); and consumer demands/requirements/expectations.

Business organization structure

At the most fundamental level, the hotel industry is typified by a varied and complex level of ownership, responsibility and motivations. The role of owners, management companies, brands and franchise-operated outlets cannot be minimized. Tony Nieves, who was the senior vice president of supply management for Hilton, noted the company mandates much of the product for its owned properties and tries to "direct its managed and franchised hotels" (Nessler, 2006). Hotel companies (flags such as Marriott and Sheraton) set brand standards but as they do not necessarily control all outlets (hotels), the companies must rely on influence to accomplish any SSCM initiatives.

Consumer demands/requirements/expectations

Consumer demands influence the product offered by hotels. Desire for local or organic food influences supply chain decisions. Luxury accommodations face a specific set of sustainability challenges; in fact, a specific standard (STEP: Luxury Eco-Certification) was designed to help hoteliers balance guest expectations with a desire for sustainability. Hoteliers have debated the topic of luxury versus sustainability with the sustainability "camp" working to convince guests that sustainability can be glamorous (Chesters, 2014). Every consumer also has expectations about their hotel experience. Expectations about room service, the room amenities and bedding influence SSCM. These expectations are formed around basic travel motivations. Pechlaner & Fisher (2006) and Gnoth (1997) have studied tourism motivations (e.g. escapism, social contact, relaxation, excitement and physical activity) as well as the importance of certain destination features (scenery, good value for money, diversity, quaintness, etc.). Many goods and services at hotels support feelings of luxury, rarity or escapism. The revenue associated with these goods and services can create inherent disincentives to choose more sustainable choices. Something as simple as bottled water exemplifies this issue. Ongoing revenue streams from bottled water often create a disincentive to eliminate legacy products like bottled water. The Institute of Hospitality produces a guide, *Making Drinking Water Part of Your CSR Policy*, and Whole World Water has launched a campaign to unite the hospitality and tourism industry in eradicating the use of bottled water.

Product characteristics

The nature of the product is unique; in general, tourism products are heterogeneous, complex in nature and composite. The lodging industry's product is a tightly interwoven bundle of tangible products and intangible services. Seven differences exist between a hotel product and a manufactured product:

- *Intangibility*: Elements of the "product" are intangible including service, ambience, luxury and rarity
- *Inseparable*: The product and service are basically inseparable from each other
- *Heterogeneity*: The "product" is not easily standardized; restaurants and food and beverage outlets in hotels prepare multiple menu items with some flexibility and the menu (or product) frequently changes
- *Malleability*: The customer often influences the look and feel of the final product. Meetings and social events held at hotels are customized products where the customer has great input on what are the "inputs" to the final product
- *Perishability*: The product is perishable; if a hotel room goes unsold, the "product" cannot be inventoried for future use
- *Usability*: The product is consumed where it is purchased (*in situ*); a hotel customer must be present to receive the "product"
- *Simultaneity*: The complete product cannot normally be examined prior to their purchase (Kotler *et al.*, 2014, p. 37; Parasuraman *et al.*, 1985, p. 42; Zeithaml *et al.*, 1985, pp. 33–5)

Supplier selection

Like a retailer, hotels must deal with a number of outlets. However, unlike retailers, a hotel's purchases include perishables, subject to local taste and demand. This shapes the number of suppliers, ability to consolidate among suppliers, and choice of suppliers. These constraints, in turn, influence the sophistication of suppliers and their potential to meet specific SSCM requirements. On one hand, the ability to buy local creates inherent advantages for SSCM. Hotels often choose (or may be driven by consumer demand) to purchase locally. This often allows reduction of the ecological footprint related to transport and contributes to the establishment of links with local communities. However, local purchasing does limit the size, scale and may restrict capabilities of the supplier. Local sourcing presents a different choice for hotels versus manufacturing concerns.

Godts *et al.* (2012) provide a comprehensive list and series of questions to ask when evaluating the suppliers and their capabilities. Their list includes: financial health; reliability; avoiding corruption and fraud; use of child labour; use of forced labour/human rights violations; discrimination; safety; employment contracts (minimum wage, full-time versus part-time employees, social security, poor human resources practices like termination due to illness, pregnancy or disability); working hours and overtime; impact on the local communities (assessing positive and negative economic, environmental and social impacts on the local community covering issues like health, pollution, development, respect for culture and ideas of indigenous people); freedom of association and collective bargaining; energy use; waste; use of toxic materials; and risk management.

By evaluating internally controlled operations and external suppliers against the hotel's value chain, a hotel can make a sound decision about strategic options for SSCM. Porter (Hill & Jones, 2008) defines the value chain as containing these elements:

- Inbound logistics include the receiving, warehousing and inventory control of input materials

- Operations which transform the inputs into the final product

- Outbound logistics activities are required to get the finished product to the customer, including warehousing, order fulfilment, etc.

- Marketing and sales activities are associated with buyers purchasing the product, including channel selection, advertising, pricing, etc.

- Service activities maintain and enhance the product's value including customer support, repair services, etc.

Production characteristics

The discussion of production characteristics will examine production in two veins: sustainability and logistical. Production characteristics support sustainability from the three perspectives of environmental, economic and social. From a logistical perspective, production characteristics can be viewed as controlled operations, upstream suppliers and downstream ones.

Environmental production

Hotels have economic incentives to decrease natural resource usage. In the United States alone, hotels represent more than 5 billion square feet of space, nearly 5 million guest rooms, and close to $4 billion in annual energy use (USGBC, 2009). Hotels are also water-intensive: hotel guests use between 620 and 820 litres of water (Tuppen, 2013).

Social and economic production

Sustainability by the hotel industry focuses primarily on environmental concerns to the exclusion of the social or economic concerns. "Reporting on social performance is infrequent and inconsistent within hospitality and the wider context of the tourism industry" (Darcy *et al.*, 2010 cited in Melissen, 2013). Neither the hotel industry nor its partners has received the same level of negative press that pressured other industry into changing (i.e. retailers like Nike) (Tillon *et al.*, n.d., p. 10). Measures of economic and social sustainability include whether employment opportunities are economically viable, offer upward mobility and are available within the surrounding community (commuting time). Very closely related is outsourcing of jobs. Lower-skilled jobs like housekeepers, stewards, dishwashers and laundry attendants are a source of production for hotels. Issues around a living wage and outsourcing have received negative attention in recent years (Chase, 2009; Mulady, 2012).

Another social and economic issue is human trafficking. Victims of trafficking may work against their will in hotels or motels for long hours for little or no pay. Labour exploitation rises to the level of labour trafficking when the victim is made to believe, through the use of force, fraud or coercion that he or she cannot quit and has no other choice but to continue to work. The trafficker may be hotel management or a labour recruiter/labour broker which subcontracts to the hotel to provide the labour supply. While documentation of human trafficking among the 1.8 million workers in the accommodation sector is unknown (Bureau of Labor Statistics, 2014), industry associations pose formal policies and statements. The AH&LA (American Hotel & Lodging Association) has a formal statement opposing human trafficking and offers training and educational materials on the issue to its members. The Green Hotelier (Tuppen, 2013) has developed a *Know How Guide* to assist hoteliers in understanding human trafficking and forced labour.

Companies have an influence over their supply chain through their purchasing power and choice of suppliers, as well as through operations, product and service design, marketing and engagement with customers. From a logistical perspective, production characteristics can be viewed in three streams:

- Controlled operations

- Upstream suppliers

- Downstream

Controlled operations

The controlled operations are those directly under the hotel's jurisdiction and include catering, housekeeping, reservations, front desk, catering, restaurants, room service, security and grounds keeping. Using the production capacity of an organization through its operational activities will transform raw materials into semi-finished and finished products. The controlled operation of a hotel creates products such as a clean room (from a dirty room) or a meal.

Hotels can readily address issues relating to their own operations. However, the production process is distinctly different between a hotel and a manufacturer. When a housekeeper fails to "honour" a customer's request to reuse towels and then the housekeeper removes the towels, the housekeeper's action will not "disrupt" the production process. While "quality" defects may be more apparent in a manufacturing line, these deviations are not easily recognized in hotels. Training and unlearning are part of the implementation of SSCM. A case study of Hilton's WeCare! Programme in 70 hotels in continental Europe from 2006 to 2008 demonstrates how engaging employees was necessary to produce behaviour changes (Bohdanowicz *et al.*, 2011).

Furthermore, different from other industries, part of a hotel's costs are directly linked to consumer behaviour, e.g. how much water or electricity guests use. Likewise, back-of-house operations can control waste. However, downstream activities by customers will influence diversion rates for recycling. Thus, the issue of incentives is critical for hotels. Incentives to reduce natural resource use can create a paradox as hotel guests seek luxury, escapism and relaxation (and don't want to do "extra work").

Upstream suppliers
Upstream suppliers are those vendors from which the hotel buys goods or services. From the broad categories of FF&E (Furniture, Fixture and Equipment), OS&E (Operating Supplies and Equipment) and MRO (Maintenance, Repair and Operations), hotels purchase the following items:

- Banquet equipment: holding cabinets, portable bars, proof cabinets, buffet stations, quick chillers

- Bathroom fixtures

- Beverage equipment: dispensers, soda systems, bar equipment, coffee grinders/brewers, espresso equipment

- Beverages

- Cleaning and housekeeping supplies

- Cooking and steam equipment: ranges, ovens, fryers, griddles, boilers, combi-ovens, sanitizing equipment

- Energy and lighting

- Food

- Food preparation equipment: slicers, choppers, mixers, worktables, food processors

- Hotel systems: alarm, fire, PBX, UPS
- In-room technologies
- Items for direct customer use (shampoo, bathrobes)
- Liquor
- Office furniture
- Office supplies: paper, personal computers
- Public space materials
- Refrigeration and ice machines: reach-ins, walk-ins, blast chill coolers, ice dispensers/makers, refrigerated display cases
- Services: printing, distribution
- Sleeping room/guest room: mattresses and box springs, bed frames and bases, "top of the bed" (bedspreads, coverlets and comforters), wall mounts, carpeting, lamps and light fixtures, in-room safes, mini bars, indoor and outdoor furniture, wall coverings, artwork, mirrors, silk plants/flowers, and accessories
- Transportation vehicles
- Uniforms and work wear
- Warewashing: dishwashers, disposers, burnishers

Downstream operations and stakeholders

"Downstream" in typical SCM refers to movement in the direction of the customer or consumer. Managing a supply chain downstream relates to transactions, materials, information and financial data and information between an organization and its customers. Downstream represents the hotel's guests. In hotels, the "product" is both produced and consumed in place; this *in situ* nature of the hotel business influences decisions about SSCM. A simplistic typology is to group customers as leisure travellers, groups and business travellers. Hotels must work with a diverse range of customers on the treatment of the product downstream.

The example cited earlier about towel reuse shows how hoteliers lose control over their downstream operations to customers. Another example is recycling. While a manufacturer can train and mandate recycling on their plant, a hotel cannot demand guests recycle. While hoteliers have control over back-of-house operations, they have little to no control over front-of-house (customer-facing) activities.

External forces

The pressure on sustainability can be conceptualized in terms of elaboration of SCM. Mejias & Padro (2013) point out that government, stakeholders and customers can pressure companies to focus on their SSCM. External pressure is not unique to hotels; other industries are subject to external forces, an element missing from Sarkis's model. A holistic, strong analysis of strategy must include both internal and external environmental issues (Hill & Jones, 2008). Sarkis's model recognizes that SSCM extends beyond an organization's borders, but he does not recognize the importance of external stakeholders as well as changes in the competitive landscape driven by a competitor's behaviour or shifting consumer values preferences.

External pressure may come from competitors or from efforts launched by a hotel brand which raises the bar for each individual hotel within that chain. Another source of external pressure could come from consumers. Sirakaya-Turk *et al.* (2013) demonstrate the connection between consumers' personal values and sustainable purchasing behaviour. Prud'homme & Raymond (2013) explored the correlation between sustainability and customer satisfaction and retention (a positive connection was shown).

A third source of external pressure is from NGOs. A recent development in the hotel industry demonstrates this activity. A group representing brands, hotel suppliers, architecture firms, purchasing companies and sustainability experts created the Hospitality Sustainable Purchasing Consortium in 2011. The Consortium, led by MindClick SGM™, will work collaboratively to facilitate greening the FF&E supply chain for hotels, create an industry-wide purchasing index (HSPI) that measures and reports on the sustainability performance of suppliers' collaborate to establish consistent measures of sustainable purchasing and establish key performance (Green Lodging News, 2011).

Discussion

This extension of Sarkis's framework to include five additional strategic elements allows hotel managers to consider a variety of approaches to pursue around SSCM (see Table 3.1). Porter & Kramer (2006) advise managers to think of CSR as an extension to each firm's strategy, and this is also true for SSCM (Porter & Kramer, 2011). By addressing the business model implications for SSCM, this model is inextricably linked to the unique strategy of a hotel company. Examining differences in the hotel product versus a manufactured product gives credence to the need for an alternative model. Supplier selection offers its own unique perspective for hotels as they manage large-scale relationships with distributors and small local relationships. Considering both the supplier and the lodging company's own value chain allows adds the "whole system perspective" necessary for addressing sustainability. This element allows a firm to consider upstream and downstream considerations.

Table 3.1 **Comparison of strategic elements**

Sarkis strategic decision framework	Hotel and lodging strategic elements
--	Business model
--	Product characteristics
--	Supplier selection
Product life-cycle influence: product introduction phase, growth phase, maturity phase and decline phase	Product life-cycle influence
--	Production characteristics
Operational life cycle: value chain of organization including procurement, production, distribution and reverse logistics	Operational life cycle
Environmentally influential organizational practices: reduce, reuse, remanufacture, recycle and disposal alternatives	Environmentally influential organizational practices
Organizational performance requirements: cost, quality, time and flexibility	Organizational performance requirements
Green supply chain alternatives: TQEM, EDI	Green supply chain alternatives
--	External forces

By introducing external forces, the model becomes more robust and fully representative of the strategic forces at play on the lodging industry (Porter, 1998). Porter & Kramer (2006) focus on inside-out linkages (where a company impacts society through its operations) and outside-in linkages (where external social conditions also influence an enterprise's activities).

Giving consideration to the new HLSE allows managers to view SSCM more strategically and with more specificity for the lodging industry. It allows a hotel to think about its SSCM in one of five ways:

- Compliance

- Process re-engineering

- Restructuring

- Innovation

- Progression

In doing so, the hotel can spur the creation of value and innovation. Beyond the cost savings that smart SSCM can achieve, value is created through better collaboration with the suppliers. The purchasing function is increasingly considered a part of value creation. With a greater focus on sustainable products and services, SSCM may contribute to innovation and promote the creation of new opportunities. Customers are increasingly attracted to sustainable products and services. Access to capital may also be facilitated as financial markets value companies that manage their social, environmental and economic risks and benefits.

Limitations

From a theoretical perspective, the extension of the Sarkis model allows lodging managers to think more strategically about the role of SSCM. However, the new elements are entirely theoretical and have not been empirically tested. This extended framework should be regarded as a starting point for additional empirical and theoretical research. Future models and developments can provide additional insight. The limited research in the area of hospitality and SSCM identifies existing gaps and recognizes that significantly more work needs to be completed in this field.

Conclusion

The HLSE model allows hoteliers to think more purposefully about the role of SSCM in a hotel. The inclusion of additional elements establishes that hotels are different from manufacturing organizations.

Managers have the opportunity to act more strategically by aligning their organizations with the trend towards sustainability. In doing so, they can protect their organization's reputation, help build a stronger brand and differentiate their company. SSCM offers opportunities for re-engineering without sacrificing quality or supply chain resilience/risk management. As more hotels make efforts to save money and reduce operational efficiencies, lagging hotels will find themselves under external pressure to become more competitive. As a driver of organizational change, SSCM can affect vendor selections and sourcing practices both internally and with the hotel's supplier. Ultimately, SSCM can drive innovation and creativity and, potentially, save costs.

References

Ashton, N. (n.d.). In Focus: Is there a business case for sustainable tourism? TUI Travel. Retrieved from http://www.tuitravelplc.com/sustainability/in-focus/business-case-sustainable-tourism, accessed 26 October 2015.

Attaran, M. & Attaran, C. (2007). Collaborative supply chain management: The most promising practice for building efficient and sustainable. *Business Process Management Journal*, 13(3), 390–404.

Beamon, B. (2008). Sustainability and the future of supply chain management. *Operations and Supply Chain Management*, 1(1), 4–18.

Bohdanowicz, P., Zientara, P., & Novotna, E. (2011). International hotel chains and environmental protection: An analysis of Hilton's we care! programme (Europe, 2006–2008). *Journal of Sustainable Tourism*, 19(7), 797–816. doi: 10.1080/09669582.2010.549566.

Bureau of Labor Statistics (2014). Accommodation: NAICS 721. Retrieved from http://www.bls.gov/iag/tgs/iag721.htm#workforce%20, accessed 30 May 2014.

Carter, C. & Rogers, D. (2008). A framework of sustainable supply chain management: Moving toward new theory. *International Journal of Physical Distribution and Logistics Management*, 38(5), 360–87.

CERES (n.d.). Sustainable supply chains. Retrieved from http://www.ceres.org/issues/supply chain, accessed 4 January 2014.

Chase, K. (2009). A hard ending for housekeepers. Retrieved from http://www.boston.com/business/articles/2009/09/17/housekeepers_lose_hyatt_jobs_to_outsourcing, accessed 30 May 2014.

Chesters, C. (2014). Sustainability doesn't mean compromising on luxury. Retrieved from http://www.hoteliermiddleeast.com/20516-sustainability-doesnt-mean-compromising-on-luxury, accessed on 30 May 2014.

Delaye, N., Householder, N., & Thatcher, J. (n.d.). Sustainable supply chains: Making value the priority. PwC and APICS. Retrieved from http://www.pwc.com/us/en/operations-management/publications/assets/sustainable_supply_chain.pdf, accessed 29 May 2014.

Font, X., Tapper, R., Schwartz, K., & Kornilaki, M. (2008). Sustainable supply chain management in tourism. *Business Strategy and the Environment*, 17, 260–71. doi: 10.1002/bse.527.

Gnoth, J. (1997). Tourism motivation and expectation formation. *Annals of Tourism Research*, 24(2), 283–304.

Godts, C., Graham, G., & Haché, V. (eds) (2012). *Sustainable Purchasing and Supply Chain Management*. Brussels: The Business & Society Belgium.

Gomes da Costa, M. & Carvalho, L. (2011). The sustainability of tourism supply chain: A case study research. *TOURISMOS: An International Multidisciplinary Journal of Tourism*, 6(2), 393–404.

Green Hotelier (2012). Responsible procurement. Green hotelier.com, 27 January. Retrieved from http://www.greenhotelier.org/our-themes/responsible-procurement, accessed 13 November 2015.

Green Lodging News (2011). Hospitality leaders launch sustainable purchasing consortium. Retrieved from http://www.greenlodgingnews.com/hospitality-leaders-launch-sustainable-purchasing, accessed 30 May 2014.

Gunasekaran, A., Patel, C., & McGaughey, R. (2004). A framework for supply chain performance measurement. *International Journal of Production Economics*, 87, 333–47.

Haanaes, K., Balagopal, B., Kong, M.T., Velken, I., Arthur, D., Hopkins, M., & Kruschwitz, N. (2011). The "embracers" seize advantage. *MIT Sloan Management Review Magazine* (Spring). Retrieved from http://sloanreview.mit.edu/article/new-sustainability-study-the-embracers-seize-advantage, accessed 1 November 2014).

Handfield, R. (2011). What is supply chain management? Retrieved from http://scm.ncsu.edu/scm-articles/article/what-is-supply chain-management, accessed 24 February 2014

Hill, C. & Jones, G. (2008). *Strategic Management: An Integrated Approach* (2008 ed.). Boston, MA: Houghton-Mifflin.

Holmberg, S. (2000). A systems perspective on supply chain measurements. *International Journal of Physical Distribution & Logistics Management*, 30(10), 847–68.

Ketchen, D. Jr & Giunipero, L. (2004). The intersection of strategic management and supply chain management. *Industrial Marketing Management*, 33, 54.

Kotler, P., Bowen, J., & Makens, J. (2014). *Marketing for Hospitality and Tourism*. Boston, MA: Pearson.

Lambert, D. & Cooper, M. (2000). Issues in supply chain management. *Industrial Marketing Management*, 29(1), 65–83.

Lia, S., Ragu-Nathan, B., Ragu-Nathan, T.S., & Rao, S. (2006). The impact of supply chain management practices on competitive advantage and organizational performance. *Omega*, 34, 107–24.

Maloni, M. & Brown, M. (2006). Corporate social responsibility in the supply chain: An application in the food industry. *Journal of Business Ethics*, 68(1), 35–52.

Mejias & Padro (2013). Best practices in sustainable supply chain management: A literature review. Book of Proceedings of the 7th International Conference on Industrial Engineering and Industrial Management—XVII Congreso de Ingeniería de Organización, July.

Melissen, F. (2013). Sustainable hospitality: A meaningful notion? *Journal of Sustainable Tourism*, 21(6), 810–24. doi: 10.1080/09669582.2012.737797.

Mulady, K. (2012). Hotel Grinch lays off workers as living wage law takes effect. Retrieved from http://www.equalvoiceforfamilies.org/hotel-grinch-lays-off-workers-as-living-wage-law-takes-effect/#sthash.BkWX9Xrm.dpuf, accessed 30 May 2014.

Nessler, D. (2006). Major hotel brands tout benefits of supply chain management for owners cost efficiencies, distribution of product are primary advantages. *Hotel Business* (7 February), 34.

Odoom, C. (2012). Logistics and supply chain management in the hotel industry: Impact on hotel performance in service delivery. *UNLV Theses/Dissertations/Professional Papers/Capstones*. Paper 1339.

Pampanini, R. & Martino, G. (2012). Contributing to the analysis of the sustainability management in the organization of the green procurement: Theoretical elements and empirical evidence from a case study. Retrieved from http://ageconsearch.umn.edu/bitstream/121994/2/2-Pampanini-Martino.pdf, accessed 30 May 2014.

Parasuraman, A., Zeithaml, V., & Berry, L. (1985). A conceptual model of service quality and its implications for future research. *The Journal of Marketing*, 49(4), 41–50.

Pechlaner, H. & Fischer, E. (2006). Alpine wellness: A resource-based view. *Tourism Recreation Research*, 31(1), 67–77.

Porter, M. (1998). *Competitive Advantage: Creating and Sustaining Superior Performance* (1998 ed.). New York, NY: Free Press.

Porter, M. & Kramer, M. (2006). Strategy and society: The link between competitive advantage and corporate social responsibility. *Harvard Business Review* 84(12), 78–92. Retrieved from http://efnorthamerica.com/documents/events/ccc2008/Mark-Kramer-Keynote/Strategy-Society.pdf, accessed 27 February 2014.

Porter, M. & Kramer, M. (2011). Creating shared value. *Harvard Business Review*, 89(1/2), 62–77.

Prud'homme, B. & Raymond, L. (2013). Sustainable development practices in the hospitality industry: An empirical study of their impact on customer satisfaction and intentions. *International Journal of Hospitality Management*, 34, 116–26.

Sarkis, J. (2002). A strategic decision framework for green supply chain management. *Journal of Cleaner Production*, 11, 397–409.

Seuring, S. & Müller, M. (2008). Core issues in sustainable supply chain management—a Delphi study. *Business Strategy and the Environment*, 17, 455–66. doi: 10.1002/bse.607.

Simchi-Levi, D., Kaminsky, S., & Simchi-Levi, E. (2000). *Designing & Managing the Supply Chain Concepts, Strategies and Cases*. New York, NY: McGraw-Hill.

Sirakaya-Turk, E., Baloglu, S., & Mercado, H.U. (2013). The efficacy of sustainability values in predicting travelers' choices for sustainable hospitality businesses. *Cornell Hospitality Quarterly*. Retrieved from http://cqx.sagepub.com/content/early/2013/08/29/1938965513499822.abstract, accessed by 30 May 2014.

So, S., Parker, D., & Xu, H. (2012). A conceptual framework for adopting sustainability in the supply chain. Proceedings of the 10th ANZAM Operations, Supply Chain and Services Management Symposium, Melbourne, VIC, 14–15 June 2012.

Srivastava, S. (2007). Green supply chain management: A state-of-the-art literature review. *International Journal of Management Review*, 1460–8545. doi: 10.1111/j.1468–2370.2007.00202.x.

Tillon, A., Chiang, E., Connors, M., Crawford, S., & de Sousa-Shields, T. (n.d.). Improving sustainable supply chain efforts among retail leader. Retrieved from http://mitsloan.mit.edu/actionlearning/media/documents/s-lab-projects/RILA-report.pdf, accessed 30 May 2014.

Tomas, G., Hult, M., Ketchen, D., & Slater, S. (2004). Information processing, knowledge development and strategic supply chain performance. *Academy of Management Journal*, 47(2), 241–53.

Tuppen, H. (2013). Addressing human trafficking in the hospitality industry. Retrieved from http://www.greenhotelier.org/know-how-guides/addressing-human-trafficking-in-the-hospitality-industry, accessed 30 May 2014.

USGBC (2009). LEED and the Hospitality Industry, FAQs. Retrieved from http://www.usgbc.org/Docs/Archive/General/Docs5301.pdf, accessed 21 October 2015.

Young & Dhanda (2013). *Sustainability: Essentials for Business*. Los Angeles, CA: Sage Publishing.

Zeithaml, V., Parasuraman, A., & Berry, L. (1985). Problems and strategies in services marketing. *Journal of Marketing*, 49(2), 33–46.

Zhang, X, Song, H., & Huang, G. (2009). Tourism supply chain management: A new research agenda. *Tourism Management*, 16(3), 345–58. doi: 10.1016/j.tourman.2008.12.010.

4

Exotic tourism in very fragile locations

Sustainable value creation in environmentally and socially fragile locations

Duane Windsor

Jones Graduate School of Business, Rice University, USA

This chapter examines the theory and practice of sustainable value creation—defined as sustainably shared value creation—for environmentally and socially fragile locations attracting increasing exotic tourism. The chapter explains how stakeholder management theory and TBL (triple bottom line) performance theory should be combined with environmental stewardship for sustainable exotic tourism. Businesses have special responsibility independent of general criticisms of corporate social responsibility to practise environmental stewardship for nature at such sites. Such businesses must generate sustainably shared value creation—including nature and local communities—or exotic tourism is a failure. Most sites will be linked to hotel or resort lodging and draw employees and resources from local communities. The chapter points to examples in the Maldives and on the Serengeti Plain of businesses managing sustainable value creation. Absence of global standards for exotic tourism makes assessment difficult, but customer, government and community demand for sustainable exotic tourism will probably grow.

Introduction

This section explains the general background and motivation for this chapter, and key definitions used. The chapter assesses the theory and practice of sustainable value creation in environmentally and socially fragile locations attracting increasing exotic tourism. In this context, sustainable value creation must be multidimensional value creation shared sustainably among multiple stakeholders. Businesses must organize this sustainably shared value creation process through combining environmental stewardship with stakeholder management practices and TBL performance. Otherwise, exotic tourism will be a failure. Fragile locations are easily harmed. These sites must be very carefully managed by businesses, governments and local communities. These sites are often located in developing countries where local capacities for such management are typically less than adequate.

The motivation for this chapter is that extant literature on exotic tourism focuses largely on environmental and social damage risks, and on consumer willingness to pay and on motives for travel. Shared value creation is a relatively new concept for business management that has not yet been fully applied to exotic tourism. Business responsibility for sustainable value creation is an underdeveloped topic. This chapter addresses that key gap in literature. This responsibility involves shared value creation for a business and multiple stakeholders that is sustainable through conservation and improvement of the natural and social environments of a particular exotic tourism site. The management issue is always in the detail. The business is typically a hotel, resort or lodge (on which this chapter focuses) or a site tour operator. The key business stakeholders include customers, employees, local vendors and local communities.

All these people—the business and its key stakeholders—have shared responsibility for stewardship of specific sites which they affect. While some authors argue that nature is or should be treated as if a primordial stakeholder (Driscoll & Starik, 2004; Starik, 1995), stewardship (Davis *et al.*, 1997) is the more relevant status here because of the special fragility of exotic tourism sites. Primordial stakeholder status tends to connote massive climate change, and thus the planet as a whole. Environmental stewardship seems more appropriate for specific fragile sites whose loss or damage should be avoided as irreplaceable. Massive climate change is one of the external conditions within which site stewardship must be exercised. Sustainable site stewardship must be collaborative among multiple stakeholders (Fliervoet *et al.*, 2013; Ross *et al.*, 2010). That requirement does not prevent or resolve potential conflicts among those stakeholders. A key role of effective stakeholder management by business is addressing such potential conflicts. Such conflicts make sustainable value creation more difficult but not automatically impossible.

Exotic tourism defines a very special subcategory of what is commonly termed ecotourism or sometimes sustainable tourism. Some appropriate distinction can be drawn between ecotourism and sustainable tourism (Diamantis & Ladkin, 1999). This chapter focuses on exotic tourism as a very special subcategory and thus is not especially concerned with the higher-level distinction issue. Exotic tourism locations involve significant risk of negative impact on environmentally fragile (and often unique) locations and any adjacent communities. If exotic tourism practices degrade rather than help preserve environmentally and socially fragile locations, then the whole concept of exotic tourism will need to be reappraised.

Recent loss of life among Sherpas serving as guides on Mt Everest illustrates possible risks to employees and local communities. Because of the commercialization of climbing, a key source of income for Nepal, the mountain had become littered with corpses and debris resulting in stronger government regulations and clean-up efforts (Burke, 2010).

The remainder of this chapter is organized as follows. The next section provides a literature review demonstrating a gap concerning sustainable value creation among multiple stakeholders. Addressing this gap is the motivation for this chapter. The subsequent section identifies four key points about how stakeholder management theory and TBL theory can contribute to informing better stewardship and responsibility for environmentally and socially fragile sites. The next section explains sustainable value creation as a special case of the more general shared value creation approach to CSR. The penultimate section identifies instances from the hotel (or resort) industry in order to illustrate these points more clearly. The industry, seeking to create sustainable value at environmentally and socially fragile locations, is an important setting for assessing stakeholder management theory and TBL theory. The conclusion emphasizes the contributions of this chapter to understanding sustainable value creation at environmentally and socially fragile tourist locations.

Literature review

This literature review is not a systematic survey of the very substantial number of books and academic journals concerning the tourism industry (Buckley, 2012a; Jackson *et al.*, 2011; Keating & Kriz, 2008). That broad and growing literature has expanded to address ecotourism and exotic tourism (Buckley, 2006, 2010; Manhas, 2012; Swarbrooke *et al.*, 2003), including impacts on environment and society (Buckley, 2004). The emphasis here is on the key gap in extant literature in which sustainable value creation remains underdeveloped. This chapter addresses that significant gap.

The extant literature has tended to focus on environmental and social damage risks and consumer willingness to pay, in addition to consumer motivations and behaviour (Correia *et al.*, 2007). While there is a literature on tourism management (Buckley, 2009), sustainable and shared value creation is a relative concept that consequently has not been as well developed in the literature on exotic tourism.

While simple isolation arguably would be better for preservation of fragile sites, isolation is unlikely within the framework of sustainable development (how to increase economic wealth for local populations) and growing demand for exotic tourism by both consumers and local communities. WTTC (World Travel & Tourism Council) (2009, p. 6) estimated that 2008 overall travel and tourism, at about US $5.8 trillion, was close to 10% of total global GDP (gross domestic product).

Exotic tourism around the world is increasingly important to the hotel industry, affluent tourists, and the preservation of environmentally and socially fragile locations. Ecotourism or sustainable tourism is essentially tourism that typically involves education about the natural environment and ideally is conducted in such a way as to be ecologically sustainable through low impact and small scale at a particular site. Relatively conventional ecotourism would include biking in British Columbia or New Zealand (Freeman & Thomlinson, 2014; Reis *et al.*, 2014). Interacting with snow leopards (Deemer, 2014) or elephants in the wild (Okello *et al.*, 2014) is quite a different matter.

One can engage in ecotourism and sustainable tourism in parts of Canada or New Zealand, but those locations typically do not qualify as exotic tourism as defined in this chapter.

Exotic tourism involves especially fragile locations, typically in remote areas of developing countries with weak infrastructure and government. At these locations, ecological and social sustainability are likely to prove most difficult. A framework combining environmental stewardship with stakeholder management and TBL performance is required.

Understanding the fragility of exotic tourism sites is not well advanced. (Santos Lobo *et al.*, 2013 is a study of fragility with respect to the tourism carrying capacity of a Brazilian show cave.) While ecotourism is widely embraced as a positive value, whether ecotourism can be conducted sustainably or is simply an "eco-facade" is disputed (Butcher, 2005; Diamantis & Ladkin, 1999). Ecotourism or sustainable tourism must work at exotic sites, or exotic tourism is a failure. The role of community-based tourism (Reimer & Walter, 2013) remains under investigation (Salazar, 2012; Taylor & Davis, 1997).

Risks of harm from exotic tourism

There are grave risks of tourism harm to nature and society. The United Nations Environment Programme (UNEP) reports that "Tourism's Three Main Impact Areas" are increased consumption of scarce resources (illustrated by water for golf courses), pollution in various forms and physical impacts such as especially the degradation of fragile ecosystems such as alpine regions, rainforests, wetlands, mangroves, coral reefs and sea grass beds. These fragile ecosystems are highly attractive to tourists and businesses.[1] Local governance systems may not be adequate for protection (Qiu, 2013).

1   http://www.unep.org/resourceefficiency/business/sectoralactivities/tourism/factsand-figuresabouttourism/impactsoftourism/environmentalimpacts/tourismsthreemainim-pactareas/tabid/78776/default.aspx, accessed 9 August 2014.

Drawing on other sources cited in the online report (see the UNEP website for these sources), UNEP estimated that more than 250,000 pilgrims, 25,000 trekkers and 75 mountaineering expeditions annually climb to the Gangotri Glacier in the Himalayas, which is the source (sacred to Hindus) of the Ganges River—with resultant damages to forests and vegetation. UNEP estimated there are about 109 countries with coral reefs, with 90 of those countries experiencing reef damage from anchors, sewage, tourist pilfering and commercial harvesting. Damage to coral reefs can be long-lived. In the Caribbean region, according to 1999 information cited by the UNEP report, there were then annually 63,000 port calls from ships with most of the environmental impacts coming from cruise ships. While much of this information is now dated with respect to specific counts, the main points remain reasonably valid today.

An interesting instance of the impact of increased tourism, and associated economic development, is represented by conditions in Shangri-La County, China (Dong *et al.*, 2014). As recently reported by those authors, Shangri-La is one of the three counties in DTAP (Diqing Tibetan Autonomous Prefecture) of Yunnan Province, located in south-western China bordering Burma (Myanmar), Laos and Vietnam and also Tibet. Yunnan has rich natural resources for mining, plant biodiversity and population diversity (ethnic, cultural, linguistic and religious). The terrain varies from mountainous to tropical. Yunnan is probably the most biologically and ethnically diverse province in China. The Yangtze, Pearl, Mekong, Red, Salween and Irrawaddy rivers have sources or upstream tributaries in Yunnan. The authors discuss the strategic measures involved in promoting both ecotourism and protection of ethnic cultures for a process of sustainable development.

Consumer willingness to pay for conservation and improvement

Consumers of such exotic tourism services tend to be relatively affluent, with disposable income. Such consumers may have preferences favouring environmental preservation and enhancement, and also local community collaboration and enhancement. The consumers as well as the hotel industry have a strong responsibility for environmentally fragile locations, employees and adjacent communities.

There is evidence of consumers' willingness to pay a premium for ecotourism both on the basis of attractiveness of products and services and attitudinal support for conservation (see Cheung *et al.*, 2014). One recent study found such evidence for a sample of 2,352 Italian travellers (Lu *et al.*, not yet published). Some consumers evince interest in physically and emotionally strenuous adventures (Fletcher, 2014). The majority of ecotourists are reportedly white and upper-middle-class Westerners (Fletcher, 2014), for whom ecotourism arguably may be a kind of transcendent wilderness experience involving resonation with their cultural values and a temporary escape from modern society.

Many exotic tourism sites are located in developing countries, a circumstance raising additional issues of government pressure for economic development (Jamali & Mirshak, 2007). The government of Malaysia has actively promoted rural tourism as economic diversification. A survey of respondents residing in Sarawak (on the island of Borneo), part of Malaysia, found that local communities wished to conserve cultural heritage and sustainable resources (Lo *et al.*, 2014), which increased tourism might threaten. There are strong pressures for tourism.

Some well-known examples of such locations include mountain and plain preserves in East Africa, rainforests in Costa Rica, the Great Barrier Reef off Australia, the Maldives and the Seychelles in the Indian Ocean, resort islands near Tahiti and mountaineering in the Himalayas. Honey (2008) provides case studies on the impacts of increasing tourism—on indigenous populations and ecosystems—in six countries: the Galápagos Islands (politically part of Ecuador), Costa Rica, Tanzania, Zanzibar, Kenya and South Africa. It is important to note that the countries foster ecotourism for purposes of economic development.

Stakeholder management theory and triple bottom line theory

The focus of this chapter is on marshalling and applying what stakeholder management theory (Norrish *et al.*, 2014) and TBL theory (Elkington, 1994, 1997) can contribute to a useful process for addressing the stewardship responsibility which is shared among the hotel industry (and site tour operators) and the consumers and local communities. The resulting framework combines environmental stewardship, stakeholder management practices and TBL performance. As a first step in this contribution, the chapter suggests four key points for design and functioning of the proposed framework.

First, in principle, stakeholder management theory and TBL theory should be compatible on the issue of sustainable luxury hospitality. A resort or hotel facility should satisfy consumers, minimize negative impact on the local environment and adjacent communities (including human rights issues), and provide benefits for employees and communities. In reality, both theories embed two different concepts and thus may not be fully compatible. One idea is a positive or at least constant outcome for all dimensions. In this, minimization of damage is sufficient. (All jet aircraft generate air pollution.) The other concept is about trade-offs among dimensions. Economic and environmental outcomes might come at some cost to social outcomes in TBL, but the aggregate value is positive. Sustainable value is thus not, as yet, well defined for management guidance.

Second, the conduct of effective stakeholder dialogue is not a well-developed practice—despite growing literature on this topic (see Welpa *et al.*, 2006 on science-based dialogue especially relevant to exotic tourism sites). One reason is that dialogue tends to be negotiation, whether conducted directly or indirectly. In relationship to the first point above, one form of dialogue is concurrence on sustainability. All parties to the dialogue may share a sustainability view as all benefit,

perceptually or actually, from such sustainability. The other form of dialogue is discussion of the myriad details, including employee compensation and community
benefits and prices to consumers. The last, probably affluent in this instance, are
less price sensitive but probably more environmentally sensitive. How to connect
these two forms of dialogue is not well explored as yet. As a result, there is considerable scope for potential conflict among stakeholders. Such possible disagreement
is in providing a limit for a theoretical framework seeking to combine stakeholder
management, TBL performance and environmental stewardship. How to practise
stewardship in conditions of conflict is not as yet well studied. But the limitation is
not automatically fatal, as whose cooperation matters will vary by specific location.

Third, handling of these differences—between theories and dialogue
approaches—is a problem for managerial value creation at each location. What to
do in the Seychelles is, in considerable detail, different from what to do in the Maldives as well as in Costa Rica. There are different conditions, communities, employees and, to some extent, consumers. This reality is a partial reinforcement of the
new development in stakeholder literature concerning the role and mechanics of
entrepreneurial value creation in which economics and ethics are not separable
(Freeman *et al.*, 2004; Surie & Ashley, 2008). The managerial process is entrepreneurial precisely because each location has a different set of considerations. The
case studies assessed towards the end of this chapter illustrate location-specific
conditions.

Fourth, there is a gap between the present state of global standards for the whole
hospitality industry (including hotels, tour operators and entertainers) and the
managerial value creation process at each location. Global standards are still largely
abstract: meet consumer expectations, protect community and human rights, protect the natural environment (or at least minimize negative impacts of tourist), and
operate an economically sustainable business (WTTC, 2009). The value creation
process is in the details at each location. One approach is to craft a solution in consultation with employees and adjacent communities and present the resulting bill
to the consumers. Another approach is to involve consumers, in some way, in such
dialogue. The hospitality industry is at the beginning of how to design and work
such processes.

The key idea of sustainable value creation is that environmental and social conservation should work in combination with economic development. Making the
key idea work is the function of stakeholder management practices and TBL performance. Figure 4.1 illustrates how significant groups—principally businesses
and their key stakeholders, but also guardian organizations—interface with the
dimensions of the TBL performance framework. The figure shows customers on
the left and locations on the right, with dimensions of the TBL in between. The
customers in this instance are fragile location tourists. Arrows show direction of
influence. Customer demand for exotic tourism generates negative environmental
and social impacts, but also positive revenue contributions. Businesses and their
vendors and employees have a responsibility to minimize the negative impacts on
fragile sites sufficient to ensure long-term conservation and preferably to eliminate

Figure 4.1 **How key actors interface with the triple bottom line performance framework**

Customers   Dimensions of the triple bottom line   Locations

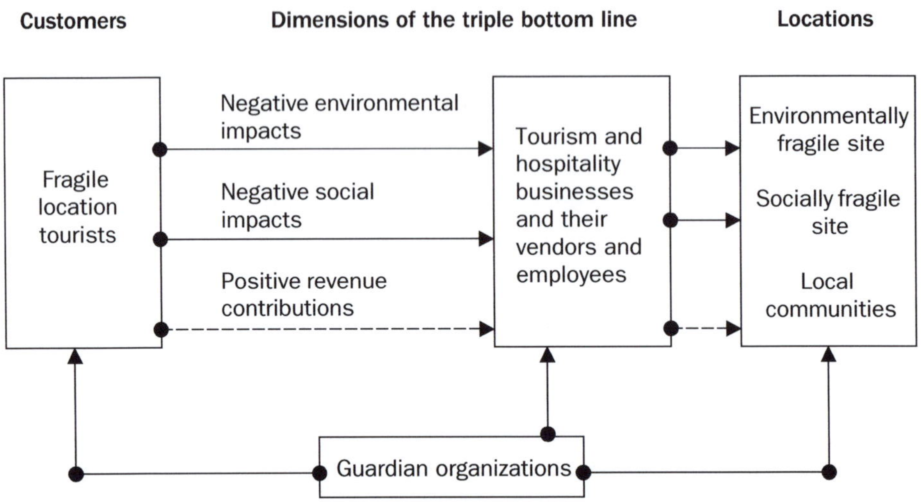

such impacts; and to share positive revenue contributions, in various forms such as employment and subsidies, with local communities. The latter are then involved in stewardship directly. Funding for site protection increasingly comes from revenue contributions (Buckley, 2012b).

Guardian organizations provide guidance and monitoring in various forms to tourists, businesses and local communities. Some examples of such organizations' guidance include issuances by the Adventure Travel Trade Association (2013), the South African Department of Environmental Affairs and Tourism (2002) and the World Tourism Organization (1999). There are also pro-environment and pro-local community NGOs (Agarwal, 2008; Horwich *et al.*, 2010).

Exotic tourism directly illustrates the TBL performance framework introduced by Elkington (1994, 1997). TBL has three dimensions of business performance: social, environmental and financial—also known as the three Ps for people, planet and profits (see Slaper & Hall, 2011). Typically occurring in environmentally and socially fragile locations, exotic tourism involves issues for local communities, local environmental sites and the profit-oriented business and its employees and customers. The theory is that a business should attempt win–win–win strategies for sustainable development (Elkington, 1994). Such management must occur in exotic tourism or the approach fails at the particular site.

Potential conflicts among stakeholders raise significant problems for successful stewardship, but do not automatically prevent sustainable value creation. Stakeholder management issues are illustrated by a reported conflict among stakeholders over how to enhance links between rail tourism and rail trail biking tourism in the Otago region of the south island of New Zealand (Reis *et al.*, 2014). The authors surveyed train passengers and rail trail visitors and interviewed key tourism and community stakeholders. The individuals surveyed or interviewed generally concurred that enhanced linkage of the two tourism products would benefit region tourism stakeholders. But there was a division between current beneficiaries and other stakeholders. Beneficiaries of the current links expressed hesitation over community growth management. Other stakeholders supported enhanced linking. The authors conclude that issue attitudes are influenced by real and expected outcomes for individuals and communities. A multi-stakeholder setting is complicated to address, especially in a rural area where stakeholders weight benefits and costs of tourism development strongly.

Shared value creation in a stewardship framework

The chapter has developed the argument for placing shared value creation in a stewardship framework for exotic tourism. This combination then involves stewardship, stakeholder management and TBL performance. Assessing success or failure at specific sites is the more difficult and underdeveloped methodology. Social responsibility reporting is now well-established practice in the hotel industry, although there is no standardized approach and the reporting tends to be general rather than detailed. One study (Holcomb *et al.*, 2007) applied content analysis to the websites, annual reports and CSR reports of the top ten hotel companies (as listed in *Hotels* magazine). The study found that eight of the companies reported charitable donations, six had a diversity policy, and four included some mention of social responsibility in vision or mission statements. However, the study also found that environmental considerations and vision and values were the least reported dimensions. A much larger study (de Grosbois, 2012) subsequently applied content analysis to the websites and online reports of the top 150 hotel companies in the world in summer 2010. Although a large number of the companies report CSR goals, a much smaller number provide details of specific initiatives and even fewer report actual performance results. The author also found a marked absence of uniformity across the companies in methodologies, measures and scope of reporting.

Recent literature on CSR has involved two developments relevant here. One is a strategic approach to CSR in substitution for more traditional philanthropy or corporate citizenship. Another is a proposed shift away from CSR to focus on CSIR (corporate social irresponsibility). This chapter draws on both developments.

One development, in a sequence of articles by Porter & Kramer (2002, 2006, 2011), has emphasized what can be characterized as first strategic philanthropy and then strategic CSR. In this strategic perspective, corporate activities in philanthropy and CSR should be directed at strengthening the competitive advantage, reputation and sustainable financial performance of a business rather than simply providing altruism to particular non-shareholder stakeholders. Strategic CSR is the umbrella within which falls strategic philanthropy. Both approaches might operate to the firm's advantage without conveying benefits to others. The 2011 article promotes the idea of shared value creation, or win–win outcomes in which both the shareholders and other stakeholders gain. Sustainable value creation, in the context of exotic tourism, is a special case within the more general idea of shared value creation. Some authors have criticized the shared value creation theory as essentially financial performance in disguise (see Beschorner, 2013; Crane *et al.*, 2014). However, conceptually shared value creation lies at the core of the TBL win–win–win approach. Such multidimensional performance is either feasible or not feasible: the outcome at fragile sites is the most conservative evidence, in the sense that success at such sites tends to support shared value creation in difficult conditions. If successful, shared value creation is the apex of the strategic philanthropy and strategic CSR approaches. If there is not shared value creation, then exotic tourism is a failure, and harm is imposed on the local natural environment and adjacent communities. In the specific instance of exotic tourism, both environment and local society must be improved.

Such harm directs attention to the second development in the CSR literature. The irresponsibility literature argues that avoidance of harm to the environment and non-shareholder stakeholders is more likely to improve social welfare than is corporate philanthropy (whether strategic or altruistic). Windsor (2013b) distinguishes among strict legal and ethical compliance, irresponsibility and corporate citizenship as three dimensions of CSR. In this formulation, CSR is not restricted to voluntary and thus definitionally altruistic actions (or philanthropy) at the expense of shareholders, contrary to some authors (see Lantos, 2002). The restriction effectively treats CSR beyond any legal compliance as diversion of shareholders' private property, while conceding that such diversion in the short run can occur if strategic for the long run.

If CSR is not to be purely strategic in orientation, then the motive for CSR should be moral in some way. That is, the business executive should espouse CSR beyond legal compliance as a voluntary moral duty. (Legal compliance can itself be viewed as a voluntary moral duty of citizenship.) However, this conception of moral duty is general as well as voluntary; and no limit to voluntary CSR is defined. Lantos (2002) argues that corporate altruism is from all major ethical perspectives—utilitarianism, rights, justice and care—immoral for a publicly held corporation. Voluntary CSR should be undertaken only for strategic reasons. Altruism is restricted to private firms and individuals. Lantos's line of argument requires, however, that the motive be strictly altruistic. Such a pure motive seems unlikely in a publicly held company. Reputational and strategic considerations may be the dominant motives. Even the executive discussion at Merck regarding distribution of a treatment for river blindness involved, in part, strategic considerations. That distribution cannot be regarded as purely altruistic given tax treatment of corporate donations. Motive raises the question of authenticity in ecotourism (Honey, 2008). Motive may not be as important as application of best practices, which might occur for strategic reasons (Windsor, 2013a).

The present author proposes, in the context of sustainable value creation in environmentally and socially fragile locations, a theory or concept of special responsibility in the form of stewardship for nature and responsibility to local communities. While a general theory of responsibility would of course apply, that general theory is disputed (see Lantos, 2002). The circumstances of fragile locations unavoidably place the business in a position of stewardship for the natural environment and responsibility to local communities. (The business is not necessarily in a position of stewardship for the local community, which more desirably should be a partner in the stewardship process.) A business should not exploit fragile locations for profit. Rather profit should flow from care for the environment and attentiveness to the local community. Sustainable profit is dependent on sustainable environment and sustainable community in a way that fits shared value creation and TBL performance. A reported instance in which such a relationship is not at work concerns the Pacific Islands (Brodie *et al.*, 2013) in which biodiversity and local communities are under stress. Reducing this harm would, in accordance with the theory of CSIR, be a very significant improvement. Reducing harm is more important than practising philanthropy, whether strategic or altruistic.

Examples from the hospitality industry

Singapore-based Banyan Tree hotel group operates some 30 luxury resorts and hotels, together with spas and galleries and three golf courses, in various Asia Pacific countries as well as in Mexico and the United Arab Emirates, and plans to expand to other regions.[2] Banyan operates in the Maldives and the Seychelles, and at Sanya, China (see Qiu, 2013), for instance. Ho Kwon Ping, founder and executive chair, has explained the case for shared value creation. In his view, there is no necessary dichotomy between shareholder value and stakeholder value (Cho, 2010). Ping attributes the widely perceived dichotomy to the difficulty that measuring shareholder return is very simple while measuring stakeholder return is very vague. He founded Banyan Tree (a reference to the shade and shelter of the tree for travellers) on a core value of sustainable development reflecting a TBL orientation. In Ping's view, success depends on strategic brand building that emotionally resonates with the customer. Banyan Tree maintains a marine lab at its resort in the Maldives to study environmental conservation. Ping's views indicate that sustainable value creation is as much a strategy option as an academic theory.

Shared value creation analysis

A variant of shared value creation—benefit for society and competitive advantage for tourist hotels—was formulated analytically in Tsai *et al.* (2010). Experts identified cost and differentiation advantage criteria for CSR programme candidates.

2 http://www.banyantree.com/en/corporate_information/, accessed 10 August 2014.

A formal method was then used to build a network of relationships among cost and differentiation advantage criteria. Dependencies among criteria were identified using a different process. The authors then used a goal programming approach to identify the optimal CSR programme portfolio for limited resources and other constraints. Activity-based costing was used to calculate costs of the chosen CSR programmes. The authors concluded that image improvement was the major driver for the international tourist hotel to implement CSR goals. Multidimensionality of CSR initiatives generates problems for analysis of the relationship between CSR and financial performance (Kang *et al.*, 2010). One study (Inoue & Lee, 2011) disaggregated CSR into five dimensions of voluntary activities directed at different stakeholder issues (employee relations, product quality, community relations, environmental issues and diversity issues) across four tourism industries (airline, casino, hotel and restaurant). The authors found different effects for short-term and future profitability across dimensions and industries.

Three hotel examples

Table 4.1 provides a comparison of three hotel examples in which TBL implementation is practised in combination with stakeholder management and stewardship responsibility. The table is organized into three columns. The first column provides the hotel company or location: Marriott hotel group, Soneva Group in the Maldives and Serengeti Serena Safari Lodge in the Serengeti Plain (in Tanzania). The second column lists key stakeholders, including nature as a primordial stakeholder, in alphabetical order. The third column indicates how the company or location addresses TBL implementation. Marriott illustrates generally the corporate policy approach not adapted to any specific site. Soneva in Maldives shows environmental benchmarking efforts on a specific island and coral reef site. Serengeti Serena illustrates environmental and social initiatives on a specific vast animal reserve setting.

Most hotel chains now have CSR or sustainability policies and practices at some level of implementation. A reasonable model of such an approach can be found for Marriott, one of the leading hotel chains, without getting to the very special conditions of exotic tourism. Marriott policies and practices are very instructive.[3] The Marriott website includes information and policy statements on "purpose, values and principles of responsible business through policies on employment, human rights, environment, supply chain and in the conduct we uphold and expect of others". The company maintains a Global Green Council, co-chaired by the global officer of Global Operations Services, the executive vice president and the chief communications and public affairs officer, to set goals and policies and to review performance. The co-chairs report to the president and CEO. The council includes various global officers and senior executives, including for sustainability and CSR.

---

3   http://www.marriott.com/corporate-social-responsibility/corporate-responsibility.mi, accessed 8 August 2014.

Table 4.1 **Stakeholders and triple bottom line implementation in the three examples**

Example	Stakeholders (*in alphabetical order*)	TBL Implementation
Marriott—illustration of general corporate policies without specific fragile site application	Customers Employees Local communities Nature Shareholders Vendors	*Policies in alphabetical order* Conduct of others Employment Environment Human rights Supply chain
Soneva Group in the Maldives Nature comprises island and coral reef	Customers Employees Local communities Nature Shareholders Vendors	*Environmental benchmarking for* Chemicals Energy Paper Water
Serengeti Serena Safari Lodge in the Serengeti Plain (Tanzania) Nature comprises a large animal preserve with marked biodiversity	Customers Employees Local communities Nature Shareholders Vendors	*Environmental and social initiatives for* Energy conservation Local produce sourcing Subsidized community services

Marriott formally accepts an obligation to mitigate its impact on the natural environment, comply with laws and improve sustainable futures for communities.

Like many hotel chains, Marriott supports and endorses the action agenda of the WTTC. The WTTC (2009) report on "Leading the Challenge on Climate Change" outlines sustainability policies and commitments captured into five themes: accountability and responsibility; local community sustainable growth and capacity building; educating customers and other stakeholders; greening supply chains; and innovations, capital investment and infrastructure. The WTTC (2009) report provided recommendations for industry dialogue and increased private–public partnerships, removal of restrictions on trade and intellectual property rights impeding green investments, using the market to support innovation in climate change mitigation and adaptation, investment in low-carbon operations, and communication to consumers and empowerment of citizens.

As reported in WTTC (2009, p. 32), the Six Senses Spa and Soneva Fushi Resort in the Maldives is designed to implement the Soneva Group's sustainable practices. The Maldives resort uses environmental benchmarking to compare monthly consumption rates for energy, water, paper and chemicals. The resort planned to become carbon neutral by 2009 and carbon free by 2010. The various resorts within the chain were to be decarbonized by 2020. Under that standard, the various resorts will not emit any significant amount of CO_2 and use only renewable energy to be shared with surrounding communities so as to provide a zero carbon emission power source. The effort has multiple implications for the resort: timber usage, natural ventilation, cooling and lighting, local material and organic produce sourcing, increased use of bicycles and battery-powered vehicles, and various energy-saving measures (e.g. deep sea water water-cooling, heat recovery, thermal storage and solar powering). The resort is reportedly designed and operated to minimize impact on the island and coral reef.

The Serengeti Serena Safari Lodge is located near the world famous Ol Duvai Palaeolithic site and the wildlife Serengeti National Park in Tanzania, East Africa. The website provides a statement on "Responsibility for the Community in Which We Exist".[4] The lodge, part of a chain Serena Hotels, draws on the local community for staff, guides, dancers and entertainers. The website reports on the provision of subsidized medical care services and employee wellness programmes, reforestation planting, park road maintenance, jobs for the local community and on local cultural tourism. The lodge implements a code of responsible practice concerning energy conservation, waste recycling, sewage disposal, and reduction of air pollution, pesticides, noise pollution and visual pollution. The lodge emphasizes local produce sourcing.

Conclusion

This chapter examines the theory and practice of sustainable value creation in exotic tourism, defined as tourism to sites that are especially fragile environmentally and also especially attractive to some tourists. The chapter makes the following contribution to scholarly and managerial understanding of sustainable value creation in these relatively extreme conditions. It combines environmental stewardship, stakeholder management theory and TBL performance theory to show how the shared value creation idea provides the foundation for a concept of sustainable value creation. An exotic tourism site must provide such sustainable value creation for businesses and other stakeholders (customers, employees and local communities) as well as conservation and preferably improvement of the natural environment—or be counted as a failure. Whatever general criticisms have been made of shared value creation and CSR, those concepts must work in exotic tourism, which should be regarded each site as a very special case.

The chapter argues that the appropriate idea for exotic tourism is not treating nature as a primordial stakeholder but rather practising environmental stewardship by people who affect nature. The responsible people are the stakeholders associated with each specific location having environmentally and socially fragile conditions. The stakeholders include tourists, local communities, tourism and hospitality businesses and their employees—together with guardian organizations. The founder and executive chair of Banyan Tree group explains the case for shared

---

4   http://www.serenahotels.com/serenaserengeti/ecotourism-en.html, accessed 8 August 2014.

value creation. Policies and practices at Marriott, and specific instances of exotic tourism for the Maldives and the Serengeti Plain, are highlighted for purposes of illustration.

References

Adventure Travel Trade Association (2013). ATTA values statement. Retrieved from http://cdn.adventuretravel.biz/wp-content/uploads/2013/02/Values-Statement-Trade-English.pdf, accessed 29 November 2014.

Agarwal, A. (2008). Role of NGOs in the protection of environment. *Journal of Environmental Research and Development*, 2(4), 933–8.

Beschorner, T. (2013). Creating shared value: The one-trick pony approach—a comment on Michael Porter and Mark Kramer (2011). *Business Ethics Journal Review*, 17(1), 106–12. Retrieved from http://businessethicsjournalreview.com/2013/09/08/beschorner-on-porter-kramer-on-creating-shared-value, accessed 8 August 2014.

Brodie, G., Pikacha P., & Tuiwawa M. (2013). Biodiversity and conservation in the Pacific Islands: Why are we not succeeding? In N.S. Sodhi, L. Gibson, & P.H. Raven (eds), *Conservation Biology: Voices from the Tropics*, New York, NY: John Wiley, pp. 181–7.

Buckley, R. (ed.) (2004). *Environmental Impacts of Ecotourism*. Wallingford, UK: CAB International.

Buckley, R. (ed.) (2006). *Adventure Tourism*. Wallingford, UK: CAB International.

Buckley, R. (2009). *Adventure Tourism Management*. London, UK: Routledge.

Buckley, R. (2010). *Conservation Tourism*. Wallingford, UK: CAB International.

Buckley, R. (2012a). Sustainable tourism: Research and reality. *Annals of Tourism Research*, 39(2), 528–46.

Buckley, R.C. (2012b). Tourism, conservation and the Aichi targets. *Parks*, 18(2), 12–19.

Burke, J. (2010, April 19). Team sets out to clear bodies from Everest's death zone: Sherpa expedition plans to climb some 8,000 metres to remove bodies of dead mountaineers and clear tonnes of rubbish. *The Guardian*. Retrieved from http://www.theguardian.com/world/2010/apr/19/mount-everest-death-zone-clean, accessed 10 August 2014.

Butcher, J. (2005). The moral authority of ecotourism: A critique. *Current Issues in Tourism*, 8(2–3), 114–24.

Cheung, L.T.O., Fok, L., & Fang, W. (2014). Understanding geopark visitors' preferences and willingness to pay for global geopark management and conservation. *Journal of Ecotourism*, 13(1), 35–51. doi: 10.1080/14724049.2014.941848.

Cho, K. (2010, May 14). "Idealism and business are not incompatible", says Banyan Tree founder [Ho Kwon Ping]. Retrieved from http://knowledge.insead.edu/csr-banyan-tree-100510.cfm?vid=413, accessed 9 August 2014.

Correia, A., do Valle, P.O., & Moço, C. (2007). Why people travel to exotic places. *International Journal of Culture, Tourism and Hospitality Research*, 1(1), 45–61.

Crane, A., Palazzo, G., Spence, L.J., & Matten D. (2014). Contesting the value of "creating shared value". *California Management Review*, 56(2), 130–49.

Davis, J.H., Schoorman, F.D., & Donaldson, L. (1997). Toward a stewardship theory of management. *Academy of Management Review*, 22(1), 20–47.

de Grosbois, D. (2012). Corporate social responsibility reporting by the global hotel industry: Commitment, initiatives and performance. *International Journal of Hospitality Management*, 31(3), 896–905.

Deemer, E. (2014). In search of the snow leopard: A new take on conservation-based ecotourism for natural habitat adventures. *Journal of Ecotourism*, 13(1), 71–7. doi: 10.1080/14724049.2014.937439.

Diamantis, D. & Ladkin, A. (1999). Sustainable tourism and ecotourism: A definitional and operational perspective. *The Journal of Tourism Studies*, 10(2), 35–46.

Dong, M., Wu, D., Fu, X., Deng, H., & Wu, G. (2014). Regional-scale analysis on the strengths, weaknesses, opportunities, and threats in sustainable development of Shangri-La county [Yunnan Province, China]. *International Journal of Sustainable Development & World Ecology*, 22(2), 171–7. doi: 10.1080/13504509.2014.943330.

Driscoll, C. & Starik, M. (2004). The primordial stakeholder: Advancing the conceptual consideration of stakeholder status for the natural environment. *Journal of Business Ethics*, 49(1), 55–73.

Elkington, J. (1994). Towards the sustainable corporation: Win–win–win business strategies for sustainable development. *California Management Review*, 36(2), 90–100.

Elkington, J. (1997). *Cannibals With Forks: The Triple Bottom Line of 21st Century Business*. Oxford, UK: Capstone.

Fletcher, R. (2014). *Romancing the Wild: Cultural Dimensions of Ecotourism*. Durham, NC: Duke University Press.

Fliervoet, J.M., Van den Born, R.J.G., Smits, A.J.M., & Knippenberg, L. (2013). Combining safety and nature: A multi-stakeholder perspective on integrated floodplain management. *Journal of Environmental Management*, 128(15), 1033–42.

Freeman, R. & Thomlinson, E. (2014). Mountain bike tourism and community development in British Columbia: Critical success factors for the future. *Tourism International Review*, 18(1–2), 9–22.

Freeman, R.E., Wicks, A.C., & Parmar, B. (2004). Stakeholder theory and "the corporate objective revisited". *Organization Science*, 15(3), 364–9.

Holcomb, J.L, Upchurch, R.S., & Okumus, F. (2007). Corporate social responsibility: What are top hotel companies reporting? *International Journal of Contemporary Hospitality Management*, 19(6), 461–75.

Honey, M. (2008). *Ecotourism and Sustainable Development: Who Owns Paradise?* (2008 ed.). Washington, DC: Island Press.

Horwich, R.H., Islari, R., Bose, A., Dey, B., Moshahary, M., Dev, N.K., Das, R., Lyon, J. *et al.* (2010). Community protection of the Manas biosphere reserve in Assam, India, and the endangered Golden Langur Trachypithecus geei. *Oryx*, 44(2), 252–60. doi: 10.1017/S0030605310000037.

Inoue, Y. & Lee, S. (2011). Effects of different dimensions of corporate social responsibility on corporate financial performance in tourism-related industries. *Tourism Management*, 32(4), 790–804.

Jackson, M., Smith, D., & Inbakaran, R. (2011). Qualitative literature review and quantitative analysis of tourist typologies. *Tourism Development Journal*, 9(1), 14–22.

Jamali, D. & Mirshak, R. (2007). Corporate social responsibility (CSR): Theory and practice in a developing country context. *Journal of Business Ethics*, 72(3), 243–62.

Kang, K.H., Lee, S., & Juh, C. (2010). Impacts of positive and negative social responsibility activities on company performance in the hospitality industry. *International Journal of Hospitality Management*, 29(1), 72–82.

Keating, B.W. & Kriz, A. (2008). Outbound tourism from China: Literature review and research agenda. *Journal of Hospitality and Tourism Management*, 15(2), 32–41.

Lantos, G.P. (2002). The ethicality of altruistic corporate social responsibility. *Journal of Consumer Marketing*, 19(3), 205–32.

Lo, M.-C., Ramayah, T., & Hui, H.L.H. (2014). Rural communities perceptions and attitudes towards environment tourism development. *Journal of Sustainable Development*, 7(4), 84–94.

Lu, A.C.C., Gursoy, D., & Del Chiappa, G. (not yet published). The influence of materialism on ecotourism attitudes and behaviours. *Journal of Travel Research.* doi: 10.1177/0047287514541005.

Manhas, P.S. (ed.) (2012). *Sustainable and Responsible Tourism: Trends, Practices and Cases.* New Delhi, India: PHI Learning Private Limited.

Norrish, L., Sanders, D., & Dowling, R. (2014). Geotourism product development and stakeholder perceptions: A case study of a proposed geotrail in Perth, Western Australia. *Journal of Ecotourism*, 13(1), 52–63. doi: 10.1080/14724049.2014.938654.

Okello, M., Njumbi, S.J., Kiringe, J.W., & Isiiche, J. (2014). Prevalence and severity of current human-elephant conflicts in Amboseli ecosystem, Kenya: Insights from the field and key informants. *Natural Resources*, 5(9), 462–77.

Porter, M.E. & Kramer, M.R. (2002). The competitive advantage of corporate philanthropy. *Harvard Business Review*, 80(12), 56–68.

Porter, M.E. & Kramer, M.R. (2006). Strategy and society: The link between competitive advantage and corporate social responsibility. *Harvard Business Review*, 84(12), 78–92.

Porter, M.E. & Kramer, M.R. (2011). Creating shared value. *Harvard Business Review*, 89(1/2), 62–77.

Qiu, W. (2013). The Sanya coral reef national marine nature reserve, China: A governance analysis. *Marine Policy*, 41 (September), 50–6.

Reimer, J.K. & Walter, P. (2013). How do you know it when you see it? Community-based ecotourism in the Cardamom mountains of southwestern Cambodia. *Tourism Management*, 34 (February), 122–32.

Reis, A.C., Lovelock, B., & Jellum, C. (2014). Linking tourism products to enhance cycle tourism: The case of the Taieri gorge railway and the Otago central rail trail, New Zealand. *Tourism Review International*, 18(1–2), 57–69.

Ross, A., Sherman, K.P., Snodgrass, J.G., Delcore, H.D., & Sherman, R. (2010). *Indigenous Peoples and the Collaborative Stewardship of Nature Knowledge Binds and Institutional Conflicts.* Walnut Creek, CA: Left Coast Press.

Salazar, N.B. (2012). Community-based cultural tourism: Issues, threats and opportunities. *Journal of Sustainable Tourism*, 20(1), 9–22.

Santos Lobo, H.A., Trajano, E., de Alcântara Marinho, M., Bichuette, M.E. *et al.* (2013). Projection of tourist scenarios onto fragility maps: Framework for determination of provisional tourist carrying capacity in a Brazilian show cave. *Tourism Management*, 35 (April), 234–43.

Slaper, T.F. & Hall, T.J. (2011). The triple bottom line: What is it and how does it work? *Indiana Business Review*, 86(1), 4–8.

South African Department of Environmental Affairs and Tourism (2002). National responsible tourism development guidelines for South Africa. Retrieved from http://www.capetown.gov.za/en/tourism/Documents/Responsible%20Tourism/Tourism_RT_SA_Responsible_Tourism_Guidelines_2002.pdf, accessed 29 November 2014.

Starik, M. (1995). Should trees have managerial standing? Toward stakeholder status for non-human nature. *Journal of Business Ethics*, 14(3), 207–17.

Surie, G. & Ashley, A. (2008). Integrating pragmatism and ethics in entrepreneurial leadership for sustainable value creation. *Journal of Business Ethics*, 81(1), 235–46.

Swarbrooke, J., Beard, C., Leckie, S., & Pomfret, G. (2003). *Adventure Tourism: The New Frontier.* Burlington, MA: Butterworth-Heinemann.

Taylor, G. & Davis, D. (1997). The community show: A mythology of resident responsive tourism. In M.J. Stabler (ed.), *Tourism and Sustainability: Principles to Practice.* Wallingford, UK: CAB International, 323–34.

Tsai, W.-H., Hsu, J.-L., Chen, C.-H., Lin, W.-R., and Chen, S.-P. (2010). An integrated approach for selecting corporate social responsibility programs and costs evaluation in the international tourist hotel. *International Journal of Hospitality Management*, 29(3), 385–96.

Welpa, M., de la Vega-Leinerta, A., Stoll-Kleemann, S., & Jaegera, C.C. (2006). Science-based stakeholder dialogues: Theories and tools. *Global Environmental Change*, 16, 170–81.

Windsor, D. (2013a). Authenticity, greenwashing, and institutionalization of CSR best practices. *Proceedings of the International Association for Business and Society*, 23, 70–90.

Windsor, D. (2013b). Corporate social responsibility and irresponsibility: A positive theory approach. *Journal of Business Research*, 66(10), 1937–44.

World Tourism Organization (1999). Global code of ethics for tourism. Retrieved from http://dtxtq4w60xqpw.cloudfront.net/sites/all/files/docpdf/gcetpassportglobalcodeen.pdf, accessed 29 November 2014.

WTTC (World Travel & Tourism Council) (2009). *Leading the Challenge on Climate Change*. London, UK: WTTC. Retrieved from http://www.cisl.cam.ac.uk/publications/publication-pdfs/leading-the-challenge-on-climate-change.pdf, accessed 11 October 2015.

http://www.unep.org/resourceefficiency/business/sectoralactivities/tourism/factsandfiguresabouttourism/impactsoftourism/environmentalimpacts/tourismsthreemainimpactareas/tabid/78776/default.aspx, accessed 9 August 2014.

http://www.banyantree.com/en/corporate_information, accessed 10 August 2014.

http://www.marriott.com/corporate-social-responsibility/corporate-responsibility.mi, accessed 8 August 2014.

http://www.serenahotels.com/serenaserengeti/ecotourism-en.html, accessed 8 August 2014.

5

The role of leadership and organizational competencies in corporate social responsibility programmes

Susan M. Tinnish
Kendall College, USA

Kevin D. Lynch
Benedictine University, USA

Using a narratives study, this chapter offers a detailed contextual view into the role of leadership and organizational competencies in a global CSR programme. The authors look specifically at one hotel's efforts to embed sustainability and social responsibility across a global chain through the CSR programme. Using a model supported by numerous case examples, the authors apply specific organizational competencies to a hotel. Five supported competencies emerge as key to the process of constructing a global CSR platform. By studying a hotel, the authors extend the literature to include a service-based organization. Further, the authors demonstrate that bilateral organizational collaboration and sensemaking contribute to the process, and this may also improve CSR cognition and support implementation and practice across the entire industry.

Introduction

Sustainability has become a critical part of many organizations today (Epstein & Buhovac, 2010). The hotel and lodging sector in the hospitality industry, like other industries, has embraced the need to include CSR policies and practices into its business model. In response, research has focused on how hotel chains have delivered on CSR promises (Font *et al.*, 2012; Peng *et al.*, 2013), communication channels and the scope of reported information (de Grosbois, 2012), organizational identity (Martínez *et al.*, 2014) and perception of benefits, importance and performance (Levy & Sun-Young, 2011).

However, given the geographic diversity of hotels, their operating structure with general managers responsible for the operations of individual hotels and their varying ownership/management structures, hotel chains face formidable challenges in implementing CSR programmes across the entire chain. This raises the question of key leadership and organizational competencies required to embed sustainability into a culture and create sustainable CSR programmes. Adams & Petrella (2010) suggest that most enterprises accept the need to be more socially and environmentally responsible, but lack technical know-how and leadership. Collaboration with stakeholders and re-examination of prevailing assumptions are critical to sustainability becoming more robust and embedded within organizations (Worley *et al.*, 2010).

Ludema *et al.* (2012) suggest that organizational leaders are shifting their perspective on sustainability from seeing it as an obligation to seeing it as an opportunity. These leaders and organizations are focused on a process of technological and organizational innovation along with a competitive market positioning to unify social, environmental and economic objectives into a single value creation process. Ludema *et al.* conclude that, to accomplish this opportunity, sustainability is being embedded into every aspect of the organization including leadership, mission and vision, strategy formulation and execution, stakeholder dialogue, employee engagement, innovation and organizational design and learning; this conclusion is consistent with the strategy literature, which links sustainability to business strategy (Porter & Kramer, 2006, 2011; Figge *et al.*, 2002; Brady *et al.*, 1999; Esty & Winston, 2009; Lubin & Esty, 2010).

Using a hotel case study, the authors sought evidence of key leadership and organizational competencies to extend existing research to a hospitality organization's CSR platform. Other researchers have explored CSR from a similar perspective including Bohdanowicz *et al.* (2011) and work in Brazil by da Silva *et al.* (2014). In both cases, they characterize their work as operating through a HRM (human resource management) lens. Njite *et al.* (2011) note that few studies have examined how managers, especially those in the service-oriented environment like hospitality industry, have operationalized CSR.

Given the authors' interest in leadership and organizational change, this chapter explores themes of leadership and organizational competencies displayed in the construction of a global CSR platform. Ludema *et al.*'s framework based on organizational competencies and organizational change was adopted as a way to examine the role of leadership, explore the process of introducing genuine change and engage the support of employees. The article contributes by improving CSR cognition and supporting implementation and practice across the entire industry.

Literature review

Corporate social responsibility programmes

For this chapter, the authors choose to define CSR based upon the work of Maon *et al.* (2009, p. 72) who define it as a "stakeholder concept that extends beyond the organization's boundaries and is driven by an ethical understanding of the organization's responsibility to the impact of its business activities; thus, seeking in return society's acceptance of the legitimacy of the organization". Since CSR emerged in the 1950s (De Bakker *et al.*, 2005), it has moved from an ideology to voluntary and relatively uncoordinated practices to a reality in today's contemporary business practices. Theories used to analyse and explain CSR include stakeholder theories (Jamali *et al.*, 2008), instrumental theory (Frooman, 1997; Griffin & Mahon, 1997; Key & Popkin, 1998; Waddock & Graves, 1997), social contracts theory (Donaldson, as cited in Garriga & Melé, 2004), legitimacy theory (Donaldson & Dunfee, 1999; Suchman, 1995; Lindblom, 1994), corporate citizenship theory (Altman & Vidaver-Cohen, 2000), issues management/social responsiveness (Wartick & Rude, 1986), ethical theories including human rights (Cassel, 2001) and common good approach (Mahon & McGowan, 1991; Velasquez, 1992).

Actualization of corporate social responsibility programmes

Many global hotel companies have formal CSR programmes. More companies are reporting on CSR programmes through sustainability reporting mechanisms like the GRI's Sustainability Reporting Framework (including companies such as Coca-Cola, British American Tobacco and Marriott) (GRI, 2012). The hotel industry has likewise followed suit. Ernst & Young (2008) notes in its report "Sustainability in hospitality" that, "The hospitality industry is no exception, and finally, the concept of sustainability has begun to gain momentum in this sector." Hotel companies are increasingly encouraging environmentally friendly practices and embracing sustainability through both developmental and operational strategies prompted by rising energy costs, government pressure, consumer expectations and the competitive landscape. Moon (2011) notes, "The largest hotel companies have all launched sustainability or corporate responsibility programmes." This is borne out by a review of major hotel chains and their programmes in Table 5.1.

Table 5.1 **Major hotel chains and their CSR programmes**

Company	Programme name
Accor	PLANET 21
Fairmont Hotels & Resorts	The Fairmont Green Partnership
Hilton	We Care!
Hyatt	Hyatt Thrive/Hyatt Earth
IHG	Green Engage
Kimpton Hotels	EarthCare
Marriott	Spirit to Preserve
Scandic	--
Starwood	Global Citizenship
Wyndham	WyndhamGreen

Embedding sustainability

Embedding sustainability is more than creating a programme or publishing a report. Lubin & Esty note that CSOs (Chief Sustainability Officers) will be essential to moving companies through the sustainability stages by visualizing goals and aligning vision with business strategy. C-level leadership is necessary for forward progress on strategic sustainability initiatives (Lubin & Esty, 2010).

This requirement for senior level leadership supports the HRM perspective which focuses on the strategic use of the human capital of the firm. CSR programmes can help hotels recruit and retain ecologically minded employees. CSR programmes can boost employees' motivation, job satisfaction and, by extension, organizational commitment (Bohdanowicz et al., 2011, p. 800; Bohdanowicz & Zientara, 2009, p. 150). Bohdanowicz et al. (2011, p. 800) classify these as positive externalities. This is particularly important for hospitality, which offers a challenging employment environment (long hours, high staff turnover and emotional labour).

In analysing Hilton's We Care! programme by demonstrating the close links between CSR and HRM in hotels, Bohdanowicz et al. (2011) seek answers about the character of the interaction between HRM and CSR, managerial changes in implementing CSR projects (change management), change management strategies, and the role of employee empowerment in the implementation process.

Ludema et al. (2012, p. 286) examine the topic of sustainability using an organization development lens. They maintain that sustainability requires five core organizational capabilities: commitment to a bold mission; fierce resolve on the part of senior leadership; vigorous stakeholder engagement; shared leadership at every level; and a culture of learning and innovation.

Methodology section

Lynch (2011) calls for the development of a sustainability strategy via engagement with stakeholders through the use of the polyvocal citizenship perspective. In doing so, organizations and their leaders are better enabled to comprehend the organizational context in which the CSR agenda can be operated. Using a comparative case study approach, Lynch developed the Collaborative Organizational Sustainability Cycle (see Fig. 5.1). This framework suggests that senior leaders, as well as stakeholders, should engage in a continuing process of personal education, internal collaboration, broad collaboration, brainstorming, document drafting and detailed collaboration. Further, the Collaborative Organizational Sustainability Cycle is

Figure 5.1 **The collaborative organizational sustainability cycle**

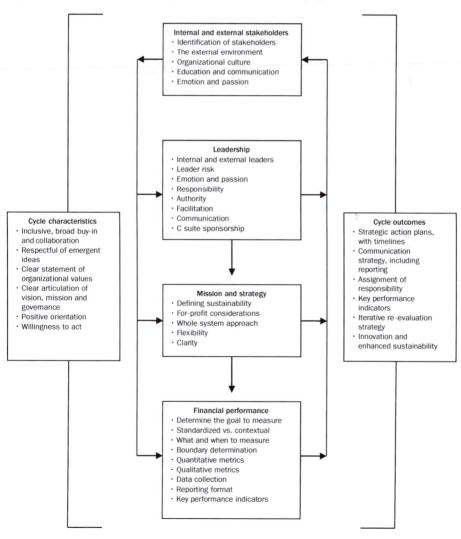

premised upon the idea of full collaboration with organizational stakeholders. Any one stakeholder may have a single agenda. It is the co-mingling of all stakeholder perspectives that creates a collective, sophisticated stakeholder community that allows the organization to innovate and self-organize within its specific context. To exclude all, or even a portion, of the organizational stakeholders would potentially result in managerial capture of the sustainability process, risking greenwashing or worse.

Ludema *et al.* (2012) extend Lynch's framework by identifying organizational and leadership competencies necessary to successfully embed a sustainability agenda in an organization. Their work on organizational competencies is supported by case examples.

In order to further explore and extend our knowledge regarding the organizational and leadership competencies necessary to embed a corporate responsibility and sustainability agenda, the authors completed a series of interviews with the vice president of corporate responsibility of a global hospitality chain. The company is an internationally recognized hospitality organization with over 50,000 employees worldwide, which owns and manages hotels under multiple brands around the world. The interviews were conducted for more than a year, during which the organization unveiled a new fully integrated CSR and sustainability programme. The organization initiated environmental and social programmes designed to enhance the company's sustainability performance. This effort originated with an environmentally oriented programme and eventually added a social orientation one, to create an integrated sustainability platform. The major milestones are presented in Table 5.2.

Subsequent to the roll-out, the integrated programme has evolved into a world-class effort garnering multiple awards including:

- Finalist in the 2013 *Condé Nast Traveller* World Savers Awards

- Environmental Excellence Award through Microsoft's Preferred Supplier Program

Table 5.2 **Major milestones**

Event
1 Identify need to create environmental initiatives and hire a leader for the initiative
2 Hold preliminary meetings to set priorities and agree upon strategy
3 Announce the environmentally oriented programme
4 Implement the environmentally oriented programme
5 Conceptualize the socially oriented programme
6 Announce the socially oriented programme and integrate the two plans into a single sustainability platform
7 Launch training for integrated sustainability platform
8 Implement integrated sustainability platform
9 Issue first sustainability report

- Best Places to Work for LGBT Equality, Human Rights Campaign

- Top 25 Diversity Council Honours Award, Association of Diversity Councils

- 25 Noteworthy Companies, *DiversityInc* Magazine

- Top 50 Employers, Readers' Choice *CAREERS & the disABLED* Magazine

- ADA Hospitality Award, ADA National Network

- 25 Noteworthy Companies, *DiversityInc* Magazine

- Top 100 Employers, *The Black Collegian* Magazine

- Top 3 sustainable seafood restaurants in the UK by fish2fork.com

- Recognition for achievements in reducing water and energy consumption from the government of Dubai

- Award from Hong Kong Awards for Environmental Excellence

- Environmentalist Level from the California Green Lodging Program

The interviews and associated analysis represent a narrative approach to qualitative research, which is rooted in the social disciplines (Daiute & Lightfoot, 2004). Corbin & Strauss suggest that "there are many reasons to do qualitative research, but perhaps the most important is the desire to step beyond the known and enter into the world of participants, to see the world from their perspective and in doing so make discoveries that will contribute to the development of empirical knowledge" (Corbin & Strauss, 2008, p. 16). They further suggest that qualitative research is appropriate when "all of the concepts pertaining to a given phenomenon have not been identified, or aren't fully developed, or are poorly understood and further exploration on a topic is necessary to increase understanding" (Corbin & Strauss, 2008, p. 25).

Creswell supports this, stating that qualitative research should be conducted when an issue needs to be explored, when the issue requires a complex, detailed understanding and because we want to understand the contexts or settings in which participants in the study address the issue (Creswell, 2007).

Finally, qualitative research has a distinctive role in theory building relating to expression of subjective reality more than clarification of an objective reality (Ahrens & Chapman, 2006). Ahrens & Chapman (2006) suggest that, for qualitative field researchers, the methodological and theoretical task is to express the field as social reality, and not simply to describe or clarify the field as part of a given nature. Thus, they suggest that qualitative field studies are not simply empirical but a profoundly theoretical activity.

Qualitative researchers gather information by observing and by talking with and listening carefully to the people who are being researched. They obtain data through participant observation and qualitative interviewing (Rubin & Rubin, 2005). According to Rubin & Rubin (2005), qualitative interviewing projects are particularly useful for describing social processes and how and why things change. Furthermore, they contend that interviewers that are engaged in theory elaboration can pick a specific issue to examine and from that study can pull out themes that have some broader significance.

According to Creswell (2007), narrative research is a qualitative method that begins with the experiences as expressed in lived and told stories of individuals. The procedures for implementing narrative research consist of focusing on studying one or two individuals, gathering data through the collections of their stories, reporting individual experiences and ordering the meaning of those experiences. Creswell states that narratives studies may have a specific contextual focus such as stories told about organizations. Methodologically, stories are collected from the individual, and the stories are situated within the interviewee's personal experiences, their culture and the historical time and place. These stories are then analysed and "restoried" (Creswell, 2007) into a framework that makes sense. Finally, Creswell states that one challenge of narrative research is the need to collect extensive information about and from the interviewee. For purposes of this research, interviews with the participant were conducted over the course of more than one year in order to gain a full understanding of the context of the individual's experiences.

The research data consists of multiple personal interviews with the senior leader of the sustainability initiative; each interview was recorded, transcribed and converted to text documents and coded within *Atlas.ti* software for qualitative analysis. Open coding was utilized to avoid predisposing findings to any particular theme or area. Interviews were coded independently by both researchers and, subsequently, validated through a group of PhD students who also individually coded one of the interviews. The results were analysed to examine themes and patterns specifically associated with organizational and leadership competencies. The analysis and coding were performed in accordance with Corbin & Strauss (2008). This analytical cycle allowed the authors to extract themes and concepts (Rubin & Rubin, 2005). Upon review of themes and concepts, the authors revisited the literature and identified alignment of our findings with the organizational competencies identified by Ludema *et al.* (2012).

Case study

The company in this case study is a global hospitality organization with over 50,000 employees, which owns and manages hotels under multiple brands. Over a period of four years, the organization initiated environmental and social programmes designed to enhance the company's sustainability performance. Eventually, the company added a social orientation programme, to create an integrated sustainability platform.

The authors interviewed the senior manager who was charged with the development and evolution of both programmes. Both programmes are referenced as the "initiative" and the senior manager as the "leader" throughout this chapter.

Findings

In the spirit of qualitative research, the authors maintained no predetermined ideas. Through open coding conducting by multiple individuals and cross-checked, support was found for the ideas from Ludema *et al.* (2012), who propose that embedding sustainability requires five core organizational capabilities. This section provides representative illustration of these five organizational capabilities.

Commitment to a bold mission

Organizations seeking to embed sustainability use a broad scope of outcomes and a future-oriented time horizon (Ludema *et al.*, 2012, p. 286). The leader describes how his/her manager launched their role by saying, "But literally, the day I started, there was no looking back." And, in fact, the timeline on the development of the initiative became tighter, demonstrating the company's need for bold action:

> **LEADER**: And he said … originally we were talking about having something … an employee engagement strategy together by [date six months from now]. And he said, "I want the whole thing done by [date]", and we're presenting it on [date] at the general manager's meeting in Dubai in front of everybody. So we're launching the whole thing then.

Fierce resolve on the part of senior leadership

Lynch (2011) in his study of 11 senior leaders from global firms in four industries (real estate, computer manufacturing, consumer products and consulting) found that fierce resolve on the part of the senior-most leader was essential to the success of an embedded sustainability strategy. Beer *et al.* (2011) captured a similar concept when studying 36 CEOs. In their work, they referred to it as *sisu*, a Finnish word meaning courage, will, perseverance, endurance and inner strength:

> **LEADER**: I had to make the business case for my role. Right. I fought pretty hard for it, and I think it took a little while, but it was a pivotal moment for [name of company].

Vigorous stakeholder engagement

Our case study presents an interesting contrast to Ludema *et al.*'s (2012) view of stakeholder engagement because, initially, the only stakeholder involved in this sustainability initiative was internal employees:

> **LEADER**: ... this is about employees ... We're not going to talk about this as a company. We're doing it for the right reasons, and that's it. It's not about PR, it's not about marketing.

The following quote demonstrates both the fierce resolve of senior management and also the need for employee engagement:

> **LEADER**: [Senior Leader's Name] knew from the start that the key to what we had to do was to engage employees, like he was certain of that from the get-go. And so I knew that was the direction that I needed to go as well as figuring out how to make this a priority in a hugely decentralized organization.

Another aspect of engagement that surfaced through the interviews was the recognition that engagement is not accomplished through a one-size-fits-all strategy. The leader told a story of a Brazilian hotel:

> LEADER: How do you engage people who may be taking a bus two hours to work who make, I don't know what it is, $2 a week if that? ... How do you engage the housekeeper or the gardener, whoever it is, around this message when what they're most worried about is putting food on their table? And God knows in what kind of circumstances they live. And so they came upon this sort of metaphor, if you will, of sustainability by talking about batteries, and, you know, what happens when you throw a battery away? [*The metaphor*] had such an overwhelming response. [*The issue is*] you just have to find what makes people tick.

Maon *et al.* (2009, p. 81) notes the importance of having employees serve as ambassadors, advocates and sources of new ideas. This began with the organization's environmental workshop, where cross-organizational collaboration and stakeholder engagement were fostered. The leader notes:

> **LEADER**: Well, what we've done is ... taken those people that are already very passionate and engaged and have made it okay for them to be passionate and engaged and given them a way to start to influence other people. There's some hardcore people out there, and they find themselves on the fringe. And if you give them a legitimate platform and a way to exercise this passion and then slowly but surely they, it's an amoeba thing. You focus on the circle, and then slowly it broadens as opposed to trying to do this and do this to start with [*nothing*].

Shared leadership at every level

The actual development of the sustainability initiative came not from a centralized, isolated activity but from a whole-systems collaborative effort fostered through the organization's environmental workshop. The leader describes the importance of the environmental workshop in creating shared leadership in three critical ways: creating evangelists; generating ideas for initiative; and creating co-constructed ideas.

> **LEADER**: And what we did in that four days that I think was so important was, first and foremost, we kind of put the big picture out there, why is this important in the big sense, right? … And then we took it down to, these are the impacts that we have at our hotels. And then the third component of that was, well, what do you think we can, what are the opportunities that we have to try to minimize this impact, and, four, what specifically are we going to be doing about it? So we kind of took it from the top level [and] funneled it down … from big picture to, this is how it impacts [*company name*], to this is the opportunity that you have, and then this is what we're going to do about it. And the reason why it was important was because it gave me 45 people that were bought in from the start. I had 45 evangelists, because everybody left really excited and inspired. Forty-five evangelists that just … said really good things about what we were trying to do. I engaged people and had them tell me what we needed to do rather than me sitting in my office [thinking it up on my own].

The leader describes the logistical process of the environmental workshop as follows:

> **LEADER**: And then we had everybody break out into groups and come up with what we're going to do. And then we took those ideas, refined them, and then we, at the end, we had executive leadership. So it was everyone, it was [*CEO name*], it was [*name*], it was [*name*]. It was, everybody in the company showed up on that last day for an hour, and we all presented to them … what we came up with.
>
> [I]t lended some real importance to what we were trying to do. And … again, it wasn't me coming up with the ideas. And I took literally all the information that came out of that and the goals that we set, and we defined the next two years for [*company name*] from that information.

A culture of learning and innovation

Training is mentioned by Maon *et al.* (2009) as a conduit to learning. The leader instituted web-based training developed in-house and focused on all employees to develop a culture of learning and innovation. Training was introduced via the green teams and was determined to be mandatory or voluntary on a property-by-property basis recognizing some of cultural differences. The green teams were self-organized groups established at individual hotels. The leader mentioned, "Our international hotels mandated [*the training*], our North American hotels said, nice to have, and do it if you can …" The training focused on broad issues and concepts:

> **LEADER**: We have the basic overlying issues and concepts that we've put into place, but we've made it, all the training very localized, which is, I'm not going to teach 85,000 people about global warming and the technical issues around that. It's more like … what is it that is "sustainability" for you here? In Santiago, it's all about the pollution there. I think that's what seems to get people fired up so great, so that's the thing that you can see and you can touch and that you can feel an impact. Maybe in California, it's the water issue.

The formation of green teams at the hotel level was instrumental in rolling out training and in the success of the overall initiative. The green teams galvanized interest and action within hotels. Ninety-nine percent of the green teams demonstrated a willingness to introduce new ideas and best practices into their property. The green teams also embodied the notion of shared leadership.

In addition to training, the leader created a virtual community to link the autonomous and geographically dispersed hotels with each other:

> **LEADER**: So my thought was … a hotel in Singapore is so disconnected from a hotel in London. A hotel in Singapore is probably really disconnected from the hotel in the next country and maybe even the hotels in Chicago are somewhat disconnected.
>
> And so what I wanted to create was a shared sense of purpose or responsibility and this idea that we're all in this together.
>
> And then I created this little [community], it looks just like Facebook. And so it's an online channel … and it's only [*for*] green team, it's for our green teams to get together. Shortly thereafter [after we told them to form a green team], we followed up with this website. We put all of their names, all of the hotels in there and every little green team had a place where they could upload what they were doing. What we turned it into was a way for green teams to collaborate with each other.

The importance of community was not overlooked and a by-product was new innovation about the sustainability effort.

Discussion

This case adds a richness of detail about the process embedding sustainability into an organization through a CSR programme. The findings confirmed three of the five core organizational capabilities were present in this case: commitment to a bold mission; shared leadership at every level; and a culture of learning and innovation. Two organizational capabilities—fierce resolve on the part of senior leadership and vigorous stakeholder engagement—were nuanced in ways not previously detailed by Ludema *et al.* (2012).

Commitment to a bold mission

Senior management was both bold and audacious when they told the leader, "I want the whole thing done by [date], and we're presenting it on [date] at the general manager's meeting in Dubai in front of everybody. So we're launching the whole thing then." The focus on action was apparent and bold. The decision to quickly launch to all middle management demonstrated the commitment.

Fierce resolve on the part of senior leadership

This organization engaged quickly and without a major commitment of resources to create an aligned, corporate-wide CSR programme. The lack of resource commitment, on one hand, could be perceived as a lack of organizational resolve. On the other hand, the leader related stories of how he/she was predisposed to action and had a propensity to build programmes from scratch. Ultimately, in this case, the resolve and resourcefulness of the leader were sufficient to offset a lack of "fierce resolve" by senior management as indicated by allocating resources.

Vigorous stakeholder engagement

The first observation about stakeholder engagement is the limitation of initial, far-reaching stakeholder engagement. The only stakeholder initially involved was employees. This is in sharp contrast to other CSR academic literature (Pedersen, 2006; CSR Quest, n.d.) and practitioner guidance (Morris & Baddache, n.d.; CSR Quest, n.d.) which suggests the importance of engaging with external stakeholders. The findings are supported by Greenwood's (2007) work where she differentiates between the role and importance of various stakeholders.

The second observation about the level of vigour from the employees relates to their ability to shape and define the programme. Employee engagement created emergent outcomes and the leader was open to these unpredicted outcomes. This is not to suggest the leader lacked leadership or vision, only that his/her view of the programme was shaped by the efforts already in place. Instead, sensemaking was present and occurred multi-directionally, causing both the leader and employees to continue to evolve in their view of the platform.

Sensemaking involves the ongoing rationalization of what people are doing. Explicit efforts at sensemaking tend to occur when the current state of the world is perceived to be different from the expected state of the world, or when there is no obvious way to engage the world (Weick *et al.*, 2005). Sensemaking was not only about the stakeholders creating situational awareness and understanding about the efforts of the company management. Sensemaking, in this case, occurred as management (the leader) considered the subtle, the existing efforts and the relational in making decisions. Finally, sensemaking was a motivated, continuous effort to understand connections (which can be among people, places and events) in order to anticipate their trajectories and act effectively (Klein *et al.*, 2006a, 2006b).

Shared leadership at every level

The case demonstrated that employees throughout the organization accepted leadership responsibilities in a variety of ways from serving as leaders on green teams to accepting leadership responsibility during or following the environmental workshop. Employees were expected to recruit additional people, encourage participation in training, develop ideas and implement ideas at their individual hotels. The culture of this company is highly autonomous, with each hotel functioning as its own business and requires shared leadership to create sustained change.

A culture of learning and innovation

Creating a culture of learning and innovation relies in part on organizational collaboration. The CSR platform roll-out was rife with examples of organizational collaboration. Organizational collaboration (Sharma & Kearins, 2010) allows stakeholders to share experiences and expectations with the aim of developing better relationships, responding to various pressures for sustainable development, and balancing trade-offs (local and regional, political interest, organizational interests) inherent in the ideological foundations of sustainable development context. Sharma & Kearins (2010) elucidate the potential benefits of organizational collaboration include learning, relationship-building, joint problem-solving, joint innovation and value creation, efficiency, resource sharing, cost saving, capacity building and survival.

The high level of organizational collaboration supports a culture of learning. Learning occurred between the consultants and the leader. Learning occurred between employees in the hotels and the leader. In turn, strong relationships formed respecting various perspectives ("this is how we view sustainability") and recognizing different pressures and trade-offs (pollution in Santiago or water in California). Through shared leadership, actual practices and behaviour changed in the hotels, resulting in innovation.

The relationships formed through the environmental workshop created ambassadors for the initiative. The workshop also formed the foundation for joint problem-solving, joint innovation and value creation. The leader did not exclusively focus on his/her relationship with the hotels' staffs. The leader also focused on connecting the hotels staffs with each other, which allowed informal networks to develop within the organization. Throughout the communication, the leader always went back to the basics asking "What are we trying to achieve?" Sensegiving by leaders and stakeholders affect strategic decision-making. The pattern of leader and stakeholder sensegiving in combination has been shown to shape the processes and outcomes of organizational sensemaking, which is the process of social construction in which individuals attempt to interpret and explain sets of cues from their environments (Maitlis, 2005). This effort at sensemaking promoted an effective and efficient shared understanding of what sustainability meant to the company.

Organizational competencies exist across a company and support the execution of any organizational initiative. In a CSR platform, the organization as a whole must perform and move, if not synchronously, at least in an aligned manner. Otherwise, the CSR platform will fall short of its mission. This case study supports organizational competencies particularly around commitment, shared leadership and culture. In the case, the leader had support from senior leadership, yet the support ("fierce resolve") was moderated by limited resources. In that way, the case demonstrates that strong middle leadership (in this case, leading the CSR platform) and innovation can, to some degree, offset a lack of resources. Vigorous stakeholder engagement was nuanced in ways not previously detailed by Ludema *et al.* (2012).

Conclusion

Building upon Ludema *et al.*'s (2012) framework of five organizational competencies, the authors saw clear evidence of commitment to a bold mission, shared leadership at every level, and a culture of learning and innovation in this case. The organizational competency of fierce resolve was not as strongly evident in this case, although not to the detriment of the CSR roll-out or platform. The case demonstrates how organizational collaboration, sensemaking and employee engagement supports stakeholder engagement. Limited stakeholder engagement, versus widespread, whole-systems stakeholder dialogue, contributed positively to organizational collaboration and sensemaking and is enhanced when the process operates multi-directionally.

References

Adams, C. & Petrella, L. (2010). Collaboration, connections and change. *Sustainability Accounting, Management and Policy Journal*, 1(2), 292–6.

Ahrens, T. & Chapman, C. (2006). Doing qualitative field research in management accounting: Positioning data to contribute to theory. *Accounting Organizations and Society*, 31, 819–41.

Altman, B. & Vidaver-Cohen. D. (2000). Corporate citizenship in the new millennium: Foundation for architecture of excellence. *Business and Society Review*, 105(1), 145–69.

Beer, M., Eisenstat, R., Foote, N., Fredburg, T., & Norgren, F. (2011). Higher ambition: How great leaders create economic and social value. *Harvard Business Review*.

Bohdanowicz, P. &. Zientara, P. (2009). Hotel companies' contribution to improving the quality of life of local communities and the well-being of their employees. *Tourism & Hospitality Research*, 9(2). 147–58. doi: 10.1057/thr.2008.46.

Bohdanowicz, P., Zientara, P., & Novotna, E. (2011). International hotel chains and environmental protection: An analysis of Hilton's We care! programme (Europe, 2006–2008). *Journal of Sustainable Tourism*, 19(7), 797–816. doi:10.1080/09669582.2010.549566.

Brady, K., Henson, P., & Fava, J. (1999). Sustainability, eco-efficiency, life-cycle management, and business strategy. *Environmental Quality Management*, (8)3, 33–41.

Cassel, D. (2001). Human rights business responsibilities in the global marketplace. *Business Ethics Quarterly*, 11(2), 261–74.

Corbin, J. & Strauss, A. (2008). *Basics of Qualitative Research* (2008 ed.). Thousand Oaks, CA: Sage.

Creswell, J.W. (2007). Qualitative enquiry and research design: Choosing among five approaches (2007 ed.). Thousand Oaks, CA: Sage.

CSR Quest (n.d.). Stakeholder engagement. Retrieved from http://www.csrquest.net/default. aspx?articleID=13168, accessed 30 May 2014.

da Silva, D.L.B., Ferreira, L.B., & da Cruz Andrade, D.A. (2014). Corporate social responsibility (CSR) in the hospitality industry: Challenges and practices in São Luís, Maranhão, Brazil. *Journal of Tourism and Hospitality Management*, 2(2), 85–95.

Daiute, C. & Lightfoot, C. (2004). Theory and craft in narrative inquiry. *Narrative analysis: Studying the development of individuals in society*, 111–34.

De Bakker, F., Groenewegen, P., & Den Hond, F. (2005). A bibliometric analysis of 30 years of research and theory on corporate social responsibility and corporate social performance. *Business & Society*, (44)3, 283–317.

De Grosbois, D. (2012). Corporate social responsibility reporting by the global hotel industry: Commitment, initiatives and performance. *International Journal of Hospitality Management*, 31(3), 896–905.

Donaldson & Dunfee (1999). When ethics travel. *California Management Review*, 4(4), 45–62.

Epstein, M.J. & Buhovac, A.R. (2010). Solving the sustainability implementation challenge. *Organizational Dynamics*, 39, 306–15.

Ernst & Young (2008). Sustainability in hospitality. Retrieved from http://www.irei.com/uploads/marketresearch/128/marketResearchFile/hospitality_insights_DF0052.pdf, accessed 1 May 2012.

Esty, D. & Winston, A. (2009). *Green to Gold: How Smart Companies Use Environmental Strategy to Innovate, Create Value, and Build Competitive Advantage*. Hoboken, NJ: Wiley.

Figge, F., Hahn, T., Schaltegger, S., & Wagner, M. (2002). The sustainability balanced scorecard—linking sustainability management to business strategy. *Business Strategy and the Environment*, 11, 269–84.

Font, X., Walmsley, A., Cogotti, S., McCombes, L., & Häusler, N. (2012). Corporate social responsibility: The disclosure–performance gap. *Tourism Management*, 33(6), 1544–53.

Frooman, J. (1997). Socially irresponsible and illegal behaviour and shareholder. *Business and Society*, 36(3), 221–50.

Garriga, E. & Melé, D. (2004). Corporate social responsibility theories: Mapping the territory. *Journal of Business Ethics*, 53, 51–71.

Greenwood, M. (2007). Stakeholder engagement: Beyond the myth of corporate responsibility. *Journal of Business Ethics*, 74, 315–27. doi: 10.1007/s10551–007–9509-y.

GRI (2012). Sustainability reporting guidelines, G3. Retrieved from http://www.globalreporting.org, accessed January 2012.

Griffin, J. & Mahon, J. (1997). The corporate social performance and corporate financial performance debate. *Business & Society*, 36(1), 5.

Jamali, D., Safieddine, A., & Rabbath, M. (2008). Corporate governance and corporate social responsibility synergies and interrelationships. *Corporate Governance: An International Review*, 16(5), 443–59.

Key, S. & Popkin, S.J. (1998). Integrating ethics into the strategic management process: Doing well by doing good. *Management Decisions*, 36(5), 331–8.

Klein, G., Moon, B., & Hoffman, R.F. (2006a). Making sense of sensemaking I: Alternative perspectives. *IEEE Intelligent Systems*, 21(4), 70–3.

Klein, G., Moon, B., & Hoffman, R.F. (2006b). Making sense of sensemaking II: A macrocognitive model. *IEEE Intelligent Systems*, 21(5), 88–92.

Levy, S.E. & Sun-Young, P. (2011). An analysis of CSR activities in the lodging industry. *Journal of Hospitality & Tourism Management*, 18(1), 147–54.

Lindblom, C. (1994). The implications of organizational legitimacy for corporate social performance and disclosure. Paper presented at the Critical Perspectives on Accounting Conference, New York.

Lubin, D. & Esty, D. (2010). The sustainability imperative. *Harvard Business Review*, 88(5), 42–50.

Ludema, J., Laszlo, C., & Lynch, K. (2012). Embedding sustainability: How the field of organization development and change can help companies harness the next big competitive advantage. In A. Shani, R. Woodman & W. Pasmore (eds), *Research in Organizational Change and Development*. Bingley, UK: Emerald Group Publishing, 20, 265–99.

Lynch, K.D. (2011). Measuring corporate sustainability performance: Influence and issues to consider in metric conceptualization. Doctoral dissertation available from ProQuest dissertation and thesis database (UMI #887094961).

Mahon, J. & McGowan, R. (1991). Searching for the common good: A process-oriented approach. *Business Horizons*, 34(4), 79–87.

Maitlis, S. (2005). The social processes of organizational sensemaking. *Academy of Management Journal*, 48(1), 21–49.

Maon, F., Lindgreen, A., & Swaen, V. (2009). Designing and implementing corporate social responsibility: An integrative framework grounded in theory and practice. *Journal of Business Ethics*, 87: 71–89.

Martínez, P., Pérez, A., & Rodríguez del Bosque, I. (2014). Exploring the role of CSR in the organizational identity of hospitality companies: A case from the Spanish tourism industry. *Journal of Business Ethics*, 124(1), 47–66. doi: 10.1007/s10551–013–1857–1.

Moon, J. (2011). Hospitality industry needs to expand sustainability program. Retrieved from http://greenresearch.com/2011/12/23/hospitality-industry-needs-to-expand-sustainability-program-participation, accessed May 2014.

Morris, J. & Baddache, F. (n.d.). Back to basics: How to make stakeholder engagement meaningful for your company. Retrieved from http://www.bsr.org/reports/BSR_Five-Step_Guide_to_Stakeholder_Engagement.pdf, accessed 30 May 2014.

Njite, D., Hancer, M., & Slevitch, L. (2011). Exploring corporate social responsibility: A manager's perspective on how and why small independent hotels engage with their communities. *Journal of Quality Assurance in Hospitality & Tourism*, 12(3), 177–201. doi: 10.1080/1528008X.2011.541833.

Pedersen, E. (2006). Making corporate social responsibility (CSR) operable: How companies translate stakeholder dialogue into practice. *Business and Society Review*, 111(2), 137–63.

Peng, X., Wei, J., & Li, Y. (2013). Corporate social responsibility practices in Chinese hotel industry: A content analysis of public CSR information of top 15 Chinese hotel-management companies. *Tourism Tribune*, 28(3), 52–61. doi: 10.3969/j.issn.1002–5006–2013.03.007.

Porter, M. & Kramer, M. (2006). Strategy and society: The link between competitive advantage and corporate social responsibility. *Harvard Business Review*, 84(12), 78–92.

Porter, M. & Kramer, M. (2011). Creating shared value. *Harvard Business Review*, 89(1/2), 62–77.

Rubin, H. & Rubin, I. (2005). *Qualitative Interviewing* (2005 ed.). Thousand Oaks, CA: Sage.

Sharma, A. & Kearins, K. (2010). Interorganizational collaboration for regional sustainability: What happens when organizational representatives come together? *The Journal of Applied Behavioural Science*, 47(2), 168–203.

Suchman, M. (1995). Managing legitimacy: Strategic and institutional approaches. *Academy of Management Review*, 20(3), 571–610.

Velasquez, M. (1992). International business, morality and the common good. *Business Ethics Quarterly*, 2(1), 27–40.

Waddock, S. & Graves, S. (1997). The corporate social performance-financial performance link. *Strategic Management Journal*, 18(4), 303–20.

Wartick, S. & Rude, R. (1986). Issues management: Corporate fad or corporate function? *California Management Review*, 29(1), 124–32.

Weick, K., Sutcliffe, K., & Obstfeld, D. (2005). Organizing and the process of sensemaking. *Organization Science*, 16(4), 409–21.

Worley, C.G., Feyerherm, A.E., & Knudsen, D. (2010). Building a collaboration capability for sustainability: How GAP Inc. is creating and leveraging a strategic asset. *Organizational Dynamics*, 39, 325–34.

6

Effective delivery of the finance function and sustainable business in hotels in the British Isles

Ruth Mattimoe

DCU Business School, Republic of Ireland

This chapter reviews the professional accountancy literature to gain an overview of extant definitions of sustainability and value, starting with the Brundtland report and the TBL report on "people, planet and profit". Sustainability or social accounting is traced up to the most recent IR (integrated reporting) initiative. The accountability framework called Enterprise Governance devised by the IFAC (International Federation of Accountants) is discussed. The two dimensions of conformance or governance and performance are explained, and the value creation imperative is shown to rest within the performance dimension. Using recent literature, the debate moves on to show that value is created through the business model of the organization and the six capital sources and is retained through knowing when to change the model to avoid erosion of value in the face of a fast-changing world. Using academic and professional literature, the key role of the finance function in sourcing, delivering and retaining value is discussed. To unlock, measure and maximize the value from sustainable business models is a challenge. Some Irish case evidence of sustainable business models and environmental practices is presented. The chapter concludes by noting that sustainability is about smart business as well as about social conscience. The importance of people, in particular the finance professional, in creating value is noted.

Sustainability: Looking beyond the checkbox and "eco-bling"

In this section, the origin of and the importance of sustainability in the context of a world population that will grow from seven billion people in 2012 to nine billion in 2050 is explained (IFAC, 2014). The creation of value and, moreover, the need for sustainability issues to be embedded in the core business strategy of the business and for a culture of integrated thinking, is outlined, so avoiding the "checkbox" approach to this issue.

The term sustainable development rose to significance after it was used by the Brundtland Commission in its 1987 report "Our Common Future" (Brundtland Commission, 1987). In the report, the commission coined what has become the most often-quoted definition of sustainable development: "development that meets the needs of the present without compromising the ability of future generations to meet their own needs" (Brundtland Commission, 1987, p. 41).

Sustainable development is the organization's response to the social, ethical and environmental agenda and what it does, as a business, to embed that within their organization (St Paul's Institute & CIMA, 2014). In simple terms, sustainability is the ability to make something last for a long time or indefinitely, and the term was popularized by Elkington (1997) to describe a way of doing business that does not erode the firm's relationship with the environment or with society (Killian, 2012). A sustainable global economy should therefore combine long-term profitability with ethical behaviour, social justice and environmental care (Elkington, 1997). From an environmental and social perspective, sustainability issues are transforming the competitive landscape, forcing organizations to change the way they think about products, technologies, processes and business models. From a financial perspective, the primacy of shareholders as owners has given way to a more enlightened view of maximizing wealth creation that incorporates *wider stakeholder perspectives* and issues into decision-making.

According to stakeholder theory (Freeman, 1998), the business entity should be used as a vehicle for coordinating stakeholder interests, instead of maximizing shareholder (owner) profit. Business and society are interdependent. This means that reporting to stakeholders other than shareholders is necessary. Because of increasing globalization and scarce resources, the concept of a company having a responsibility beyond the purely legal or profit-related has gained new impetus. The company's actions and activities have an effect on the environment, consumers, employees and other stakeholders. Defined by the European Commission (2001) as the integration by companies of social and environmental concerns in their business operations and in the interaction with their stakeholders on a voluntary basis, CSR is about managing companies in a socially responsible manner. It marked an evolution from the concept of sustainable development. Since 2000, the CSR concept has pushed further and further up the corporate agenda as business strives to act responsibly towards people, planet and profit (the so-called "3Ps").

Companies must strive to be profitable, and also minimize negative environmental impacts and act in conformity with societal expectations. The definition of CSR "is not static" (Killian, 2012, p. 9) and the evolution in the story of CSR is discussed in a later section.

Social accounting (also called sustainability accounting, social and environmental accounting, corporate social reporting and non-financial reporting) is the reporting aspect of CSR and originated in the early 1980s (Tilt, 2007). Considered to be a subcategory of financial accounting, it discloses non-financial information about the social and environmental effects of a company's economic actions to particular interest groups within society and to society at large. In practice ... "many firms, in reporting their CSR activities, include them in a sustainability report" (Killian, 2012, p. 7). She also notes, from a review of CSR reports, that branding using CSR activities contributes to the overall trust of the public in the brand. She gives the example of The Body Shop, which built a brand based on marketing their natural products and their ethical production with no testing on animals, etc. (Killian, 2012, p. 8).

Given the expected increase in world population noted above, it is apparent that this growth will increase demand for scarce natural resources that cannot be met, if production and consumption remain as they are today (IFAC, 2014). Therefore, there are major challenges ahead and sustainability is a significant issue, not just in terms of the tangible benefits of initiatives in the area, but also because it leads to improved brand reputation, creating a competitive advantage (CGMA, 2012a, p. 4).

Value is said to be created when a business earns revenue (a return on capital) that exceed its expenses (the cost of capital) (ACCA, 2011, p. 12). Increasingly, the "value" of an organization is related to intangible non-financial factors. However, this chapter will argue that to create value, companies must create a culture and instil a mindset of *integrated thinking* rather than just checkbox compliance (such as the inclusion, for example, of a separate sustainability report in the annual report). For a company to do more than "box-ticking", its annual report must provide a coherent account of the business model, explaining how value is created and must show how sustainability is not a stand-alone strategy, but is increasingly integrated into the core business strategy.

As Douglas Johnston, Partner (Climate Change and Sustainability Services, Ernst & Young) is quoted as saying:

> a move [is needed] from what's typically been termed "CSR"—which is largely about box-ticking, risk management and a little bit of "eco-bling" on the side—to something that is a lot more embedded within the business (St Paul's Institute & CIMA, 2014, p. 5).

Given the focus on social accounting, value creation and the business model, which fall into the domain of the accountant, the role of the finance function must now be explored. A link is made between value creation, the business model, the finance function and the entire accountability framework of the organization.

The finance function, enterprise governance and value creation

IFAC (2013) categorizes professional accountants as creators, enablers, preservers and reporters of sustainable value for their organizations. ACCA (2011, pp. 6–7) also concurs with these ideas, mentioning value being sourced in professional accountants' talents, delivering value through their financial analysis and risk management skills and value being sustained through their ethical behaviours and professionalism.

There is also a specific mention in the ACCA (2011, p. 7) report of a heightened role for professional accountants "in sustainability and CSR issues". A final concluding comment on the importance of the accountant in helping the value creation effort is noted by ACCA (2011, p. 48):

> The next decade presents an enormous opportunity for the finance profession. In all sectors, in all economies around the world, professional accountants will be using their skills and talents across organisations to help create and sustain long-term value.

The context of value creation resides within an overarching accountability framework conceived by CIMA (Chartered Institute of Management Accountants) and called Enterprise Governance. Enterprise Governance is defined by CIMA and IFAC (CIMA & IFAC, 2004, p. 12) as a framework covering both the corporate governance and the business governance aspects of an organization. Therefore, it covers the internal workings of the organization (business governance or performance) as well as the outward-facing aspects (corporate governance or conformance).

Figure 6.1 **The Enterprise Governance framework**

Source: ACCA (2011). *The Value Creation Model for Business: 2010 and Beyond.* London: ACCA, p. 5. Copyright permission from ACCA gratefully acknowledged.

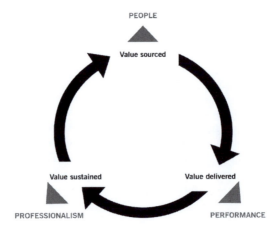

Figure 6.2 **The Enterprise Governance framework**

Source: This figure is an extract from *Enterprise Governance: Getting the Balance Right* of the Professional Accountants in Business (PAIB) published by IFAC (International Federation of Accountants) in February 2004 and used with the permission of IFAC. Any views or opinions that may be included in this publication are solely those of the author, and do not express the views and opinions of IFAC or any independent standard setting body supported by IFAC.

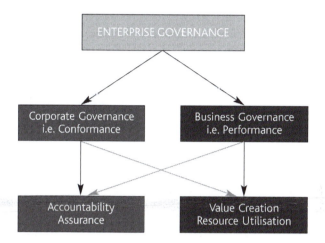

Figure 6.2 illustrates the fact that Enterprise Governance covers the entire accountability framework of the organization. The conformance dimension takes an historic view of the firm, whereas the performance dimension is forward-looking. Companies must balance conformance with performance. The finance function can be involved in both dimensions. The lines in the diagram show that, although conformance feeds directly to accountability and performance to value creation, conformance can also feed to value creation while performance can feed to assurance.

The separation of ownership (the shareholders or principals) and control (by the directors as agents of the shareholders) in listed companies creates the agency problem. An agency, in general terms, is the relationship between two parties, where one is a principal and the other is an agent to whom work is delegated and who engages in corporate transactions with third parties. The goals of the principal and agent may be in conflict and the two may have different attitudes to risk (Eisenhardt, 1989).

The dominance of the shareholder in agency theory "has engendered shareholder-centric definitions of corporate governance" (Brennan & Solomon, 2008, p. 886). Conformance is also called "corporate governance" and covers issues such as board structures, roles and executive remuneration. A statement in the annual report of a public company stating its compliance with the latest Stock Exchange Combined Code of Corporate Governance[1] together with the external audit

---

1   The UK Corporate Governance Code has been instrumental in spreading best boardroom practice throughout the listed sector since it was first issued in 1992. It operates

process and the presence of an in-house audit committee, ensure this dimension is addressed. Therefore, the conformance dimension has the focus on the shareholder, but this covers only part of the accountability issue.

By contrast, the performance (or management of performance) dimension focuses on strategy and value creation—helping the board to make strategic decisions, understand risk and identify key drivers of performance. Value creation is shown in Figure 6.2 to be clearly part of the performance dimension of the Enterprise Governance framework. The definition of "business model" and its relationship to value creation was developed by the CGMA (Chartered Global Management Accountancy; formerly CIMA) profession as "the chosen system of inputs, business activities, outputs and outcomes that aims to create value over the short, medium and long-term" (CGMA, 2013, p. 4).

Value creation and the business model

Moving forward from the 2004 CIMA Enterprise Governance model, it is clear that, nine years later, CGMA (2013, p. 4) makes a new connection between value creation (mentioned in the framework of 2004), but now links it to the idea of the *business model*, noting two key themes:

> ... firstly, that business models focus upon the way in which organizations seek to create and define sustainable value, both financial and non-financial. Secondly, a business model provides a statement of the basic logic of the business: "how we do it".

However, to continue with an unchanging business model is insufficient as one of the most influential management thinkers, Charles Handy (1994, p. 49), observed that "the world keeps changing. It is one of the paradoxes of success that the things and ways which got you where you are, are seldom the things to keep you there". Identifying when it is time to re-evaluate or change a business model is critical in building long-term sustainability (in the performance dimension) and is now discussed.

Understanding what makes your business model sustainable matters even more in today's environment, where, on account of new technologies, greater and faster connectivity such as cloud technology, global economic integration, changes in

---

on the principle of "comply or explain". It sets out good practice covering issues such as board composition and effectiveness, the role of board committees, risk management, remuneration and relations with shareholders. Listed companies are required under the Listing Rules either to comply with the provisions of the Code or explain to investors in their next annual report why they have not done so. If shareholders are not satisfied, they can use their powers, including the power to appoint and remove directors, to hold the company to account (FRC, 2014).

customer attitudes, shifting supply chains, moves by competitors, etc., the models themselves must change to deliver continued success: "the *responsiveness to change* is a key element of an effective and sustainable business model" (CGMA, 2013, p. 3 [italics added]). Basically, innovation in business models, be they new pricing models, a shift to selling products as services etc., will be a more subtle way of differentiating a company from its competitors than purely on a functional basis of "product is king" (CGMA, 2013, p. 19).

Some help as to whether it is time to change a company's business model is offered by the management consultancy firm Deloitte, which offers a series of questions and advises that too many "no" answers may signal it is time to change the model (see CGMA, 2013, pp. 20–1). In the same report, accountants can take the lead by considering a series of questions concerning changes to the business model; for example, "are the outcomes of the current business model being measured appropriately?" and "how do the financial risks of pursuing the new model compare to the risks of following the status quo?" (CGMA, 2013, p. 23). The role of the finance function in prompting change in the business model is thus assured.

The six capitals and the value creation process

Basically, business models create value through the dynamic conversion of resources and capabilities (or inputs) into outputs through business activities. As part of the strategic planning process, the business model is informed by the strategy, vision and mission statements of the firm (CGMA, 2013, p. 3).

The work of the IIRC on the IR framework uses the concepts of "capitals" to illustrate the resources and capabilities used by a firm to create value. The availability and appeal of these capitals may change over time, as market conditions buffet the business model and require it to be overhauled. There are six such capitals as noted (CGMA, 2013, pp. 4–5) and the relative importance of each capital to the value creation process will vary by business. The six IR capitals are: financial; manufactured; human; intellectual; natural; and social and relationship.

Organizations, such as hotels, need to understand how the capitals interact with each other to create or potentially destroy value, as noted in Figure 6.3. The figure shows that outputs are different from outcomes. Outputs are key products or services produced by businesses to create value as well as the waste or other by-products that may either create or erode value.

By contrast, in line with the IR framework, outcomes are the internal and external consequences for the capitals as a result of an organization's business activities and outputs, including customer satisfaction, profit (loss), shareholder return and contribution to the local economy through taxes. More value is coming from people rather than physical and financial assets—with customers and employees shaping the future business agenda for organizations. CGMA (2012b, p. 5) notes the

Figure 6.3 **The performance dimension and value creation**

Source: This figure is an extract from *Enterprise Governance: Getting the Balance Right* of the Professional Accountants in Business (PAIB) published by IFAC (International Federation of Accountants) in February 2004 and is used with the permission of IFAC. Any views or opinions that may be included in this publication are solely those of the author, and do not express the views and opinions of IFAC or any independent standard setting body supported by IFAC.

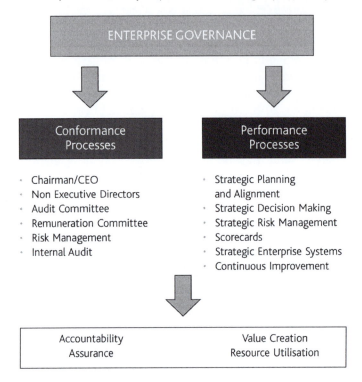

need for an emphasis by companies on how the non-financial human dimension contributes value, implying support for the IR framework already discussed. This human dimension is very vital in hotels, particularly in luxury hotels, where service is as important as physical facilities.

Pressures from shareholders and financial markets may, however, put the focus on short-term profitability and take attention away from customer relationships, knowledge and human capital, technology, strategic vision and intellectual property, which, as shown in Figure 6.4, are the crucial value drivers. The current reporting system was agreed by 76% of respondents as focusing on the financials, while 75% of those surveyed in the CGMA (2012b) report agreed on a need to put more emphasis on the non-financial, so emphasizing the long-term sustainability of the business.

ACCA (2011, p. 12) concurs, noting the intangible factors that drive value:

> increasingly the "value" of an organization is driven by broader intangible factors—the reputation of its brand, its influence in the marketplace, and of course the talents, skills and innovation of its employees. Different

Figure 6.4 **Creating value through business activity**

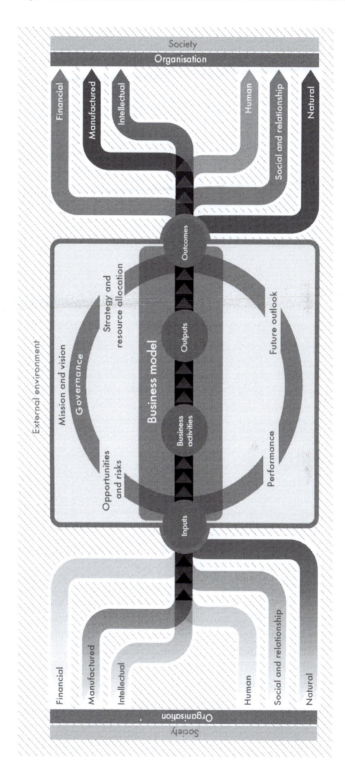

Source: This diagram is originally taken from IIRC framework (IIRC, 2013, p. 13). Copyright © December 2013 by the International Integrated Reporting Council ("the IIRC") which is also quoted in CGMA (2013), *Building Resilience: An Introduction to Business Models.* London: Chartered Institute of Management Accountants and New York: American Institute of CPAs, p. 6. Copyright permission from IIRC gratefully acknowledged.

Figure 6.5 **Financial and non-financial sources of value provided to the business**

Source: CGMA (2012b). *Rebooting Business: Valuing the Human Dimension*. London: Chartered Institute of Management Accountants and New York: American Institute of CPAs, p. 5. Copyright permission from CGMA gratefully acknowledged.

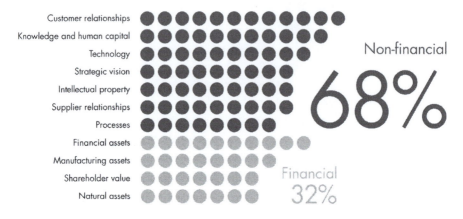

(Percentage of those who selected 8-10 on a scale of 1-10)

businesses create value in different ways. They operate in different industries, in different markets, they offer different products and services and have different customers. They have different competitive advantages and unique selling points, different cost structures and different operating margins; their value chains are different.

Communicating the value through integrated reporting

As a follow-up to the TBL reporting, and to render and guarantee consistency in social and environmental information, the GRI (Global Reporting Initiative) was established with the goal of providing guidelines to organizations reporting on sustainability. GRI is an international not-for-profit organization, with a network-based structure. Its activity involves thousands of professionals and organizations from many sectors, constituencies and regions and its mission is to make sustainability reporting standard practice (www.globalreporting.org). The GRI promotes the use of sustainability reporting as a way for organizations to become more sustainable and contribute to a sustainable global economy.

To increase transparency and accountability and to build stakeholder trust in the organization, GRI has pioneered and developed a sustainability reporting framework that is widely used around the world. The framework, including the sustainability reporting guidelines, sets out the principles and standard disclosures organizations can use to report their economic, environmental and social performance and impacts. A sustainability report presents the economic, environmental and social impacts caused by the firm's everyday activities. It also demonstrates a commitment on the part of a company to make their operations sustainable and contribute to sustainable global economy (GRI, 2013). It used to be submitted as a separate report to the financials.

IFAC is the global organization for the accountancy profession, with its members being drawn from national professional accountancy bodies, covering accountants working in public practice, industry, government and academia (see www.ifac.org/paib). More recently, IFAC has been significantly involved with the IIRC, which is developing an international framework to help organizations report how strategy, governance, performance and prospects lead to the creation of value over the short, medium and long term (IIRC, 2013). This is discussed next.

In 2010, the Prince's Accounting for Sustainability Project (A4S) and the GRI co-convened the IIRC (http://integratedreporting.org). It is a global coalition of regulators, investors, companies, standard setters, the accounting profession and NGOs. Together, this coalition shares the view that communication about value creation in the form of an IR should be the next step in the evolution of corporate reporting. Previous experimental attempts by companies self-declaring "integrated reports" date back to 2010 and this sparked an international debate. In 2013, IIRC launched the first version of an IR framework, which clearly defined what an integrated report comprises (see http://integratedreporting.org/resource/international-ir-framework).

An IR would be prepared instead of an annual financial report (or the published accounts of public companies) and a separate annual sustainability report. However, of more interest for this chapter is the focus on "business model" in the deliberations surrounding the framework.

Currently, IR is voluntary. Its aim is to describe and disclose how an organization's business model uses financial and non-financial capital in producing value. Research by GRI (2013) on companies who have pioneered these reports from 2010 to 2013 (756 reports) revealed interesting insights such as that financial services, energy utilities and mining are the leading sectors experimenting with IR (GRI, 2013, p. 28). A selection of interesting quotes from the latter research are noted below:

> The core part of an integrated report is, to me, the *business model,* as that explains how the business creates value. But for the description of the business model to accurately report value creation, it is critical that it explains how the company impacts the capitals upon which its success is based, including its impact on natural and social capital (GRI, 2013, p. 33) [italics added].
>
> For companies in certain industries, there will necessarily be a greater focus on sustainability in the environmental and social sense, as their operations may have a greater potential impact on the people they employ and/or affect through their operations. For example, the integrated

> reporting of a virtual organization that provides consulting services might be expected to focus more heavily on intellectual capital and less on environmental and social and relationship capital than a company in the extractive industries ... the key for any company is to consider all six of the capitals covered under IR and to give emphasis in their reporting to those areas which are most relevant to their ability to create and maintain value within the context in which they operate (GRI, 2013, p. 37).

This is a telling comment, which would indicate hotels need to focus on the human, social and relationship capital elements, so vital to the quality of service in luxury hotels.

Finally, the research mentions that a report is only genuinely integrated when the company's sustainability is integrated into strategic planning, risk management, innovation and forecasts. External financial analysts will therefore perceive that sustainability is more than an environmental issue or a theme confined to social causes, but "is a business variable" (GRI, 2013, p. 35). Thus, the opening comment in this chapter of the need to move beyond checkbox compliance and "eco-bling" resonates here.

Tracing the corporate social responsibility story: From philanthropy to corporate shared value

CSR is a concept that is constantly changing. Long-term sustainability will result not from movement along a smooth trajectory, but rather from continuous adaptation to changing conditions, as illustrated by Figure 6.6 (CGMA, 2012a). This definition of CSR requires the view of an organization as a system that is closely coupled with social, environmental and economic systems at different levels or scales—such as at the product or process level to the enterprise wide level to the regional or global level.

Figure 6.6 shows that many companies progress from mere compliance with externally imposed environmental, social and governance requirements to corporate philanthropy (giving support to charitable and social causes). More recently, companies have tried to consume resources more efficiently to reduce impact on the environment (environmental sustainability). Further evolution in the concept of CSR in Figure 6.6 is the idea of CSV (corporate shared value). This means that companies create economic value in a way that also creates value for society (social value) by addressing the needs and challenges of (and considering the benefits of their plans to) society and local communities:

> The idea of enhancing business competitiveness, but at the same time advancing the economic and social conditions in the communities in which the business operates, is the basis of the concept of shared value (CGMA, 2012a, p. 2).

Figure 6.6 **CSR as a evolutionary curve**

Source: CGMA (2012a). *Sustainable Business: Shared Value in Practice*. London: Chartered Institute of Management Accountants and New York: American Institute of CPAs, p. 2. Copyright permission from CGMA gratefully acknowledged.

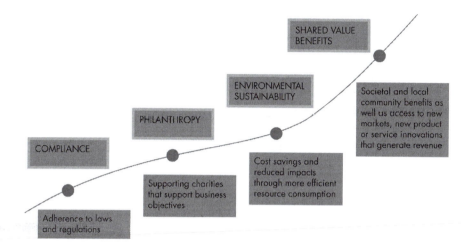

Porter & Kramer (2011, p. 65) writing in *Harvard Business Review*, describe three ways in which companies can create this CSV.

- *Re-conceiving products and markets*: There are societal needs for clean drinking water, nutrition, care for the aged, etc. So, for example, food producers concentrate more on nutrition and less on attributes that have previously driven consumption, such as taste. Energy companies now market products and services designed to reduce energy usage, helping to make the industry more sustainable.

- *Redefining productivity in the value chain*: For example, efforts to minimize pollution have been seen as increasing business costs and are mandated by regulation and taxes, but under CSV there is growing awareness of the need to consider the external costs arising through neglecting the pollution issue—such as diminishing the brand and reputation of the company.

- *Enabling local industry cluster development*: A company uses a supply chain for the products and services for its operations. Recent trends have been to source supplies from distant locations, because of short-term unit cost considerations. However, building a cluster around the local community can increase its economic vitality and improve the reliability of the supply chain. Shifting activities to even lower cost locations is not a sustainable solution to competitive challenges as they are overlooking the broader issues that contribute to success—the well-being of their customers, the depletion of natural resources vital to their businesses, the viability of key suppliers and the economic distress of local communities in which they produce and sell.

As these examples show, CSV is more than philanthropy—it is a new way to achieve economic success (Porter & Kramer, 2011).

In this chapter, some case examples from the Irish hotel industry that fit these three categories will be given in the penultimate section "Case evidence from Ireland".

Some background to Irish tourism is now presented to convey the reality of the difficulties in value creation in the light of the deep recession of 2008 and attempts made by the industry to recover from this.

Tourism in Ireland and the challenge of value creation

Tourism is Ireland's largest indigenous industry and a critical component of the export economy, accounting for €5.7 billion in spending in 2013 and represents 4% of Ireland's GNP (gross national product) (IHF, 2014). Hotel stock is currently (as at latest available information—namely 2013) listed as 835 properties and 57,362 rooms. The number of hotel rooms grew far more dramatically. The figure jumped from 26,400 rooms in 1996 to 59,000 in 2009—a 123% increase in the number of hotel rooms in just 13 years (Garvey, 2012).

Much of the new capacity since 2001 was driven not by a realistic appraisal of underlying demand or by measurement of the likely cash flows from the constructed property, but by tax incentives on offer for new hotel construction. In a 2009 report for the IHF (Irish Hotels Federation), economist Peter Bacon estimated that this expansion in hotel capacity had cost a total of €5.2 billion, of which €4.1 billion had been borrowed (Garvey, 2012). The year 2008 brought deep recession with the twin issues of low demand and bedroom stock capacity at its highest ever, as well as the debt burden.

Tim Fenn, CEO of the IHF, commented in BDO (2013, p. 14) on many hoteliers being in survival mode with uneconomical room rate prices being charged. In relation to sustainability, he says:

> … you either have to reduce your costs and restructure your debt or achieve some degree of improved usage. So while we address our cost base we must achieve sustainable levels of activity. The markets will ultimately dictate whether increases in price levels occur, but it is important that we take a long-term view in terms of our pricing, particularly if we want to see real growth in visitor numbers.

Irish hotels have had to drop prices to recover from the low occupancies of 2008–9, but the cost base has remained high, such as energy costs and very high local authority rates (at roughly €1,500 per hotel room) (BDO, 2013, p. 15). Labour costs account for 30–40% of annual turnover for most hotels, even higher for 4/5 star hotels (AIB, 2013, p. 7), with Ireland having the third highest minimum wage in Europe.

They face the inevitable challenge of seasonality and the ever-present burden of fixed costs as well as over-hanging debt associated with room stock—over 60 hotels have gone into receivership (BDO, 2013, p. 12). Discounting room rates is not sustainable in the long run, given that rates and energy costs are outside their control. Hoteliers need to effectively identify the markets which have a genuine growth opportunity and get back to basics and effectively market and sell their businesses (BDO, 2013, p. 5).

A recent survey by Allied Irish Banks (2013, p. 9) on the Irish hotel sector noted online bookings accounting for 56% of all bookings, with just over one-third of bookings made over the phone. A quarter of all bookings are through third-party websites, the main ones being booking.com and Expedia. The online booking channel has helped to grow sales, but at a price in terms of profitability on account of the commission levels.

Irish hotels are responding to shifting customer profiles (such as domestic tourists, over 55s and couples who are value-for-money hungry consumers) as well as the impact of the digital revolution. Their response is through introducing special offers as well as sourcing cheaper suppliers where feasible. Interestingly, the report noted that "hoteliers are not waiting to see what the future might bring ... in the past 12 months, half of those surveyed had undertaken training in online development" (AIB, 2013, p. 11).

Given the capital intensive and high fixed cost nature of the hotel sector and the need to refurbish the product to sustain repeat business, it was encouraging that many were intending over the next three years to invest in upgrading and refurbishing their properties, but using reinvested profits from the business rather than loans. Shaun Quinn, CEO of Fáilte Ireland (the Irish Tourist Authority), commented on the learning involved in experiencing a recession:

> Any manager in the hotel business in their early 30s, or younger, has gone through what is, probably, a once-in-a-lifetime shock. There will be a lot of learning from that when demand returns in terms of creating a lean business model that creates value.

This quote reflects the challenge of renewing the business model to ensure continued resilience in changed circumstances.

Case evidence from Ireland

This section briefly discusses the empirical work for the Fáilte Ireland study (Mattimoe, 2010) featuring the following 12 case sites (see Table 6.1). Six of these (E, F, G, H, J and L) were hotels or guesthouses, with the rest being activity centres, which drive demand for the hotels.

Table 6.1 **The case sites in the Fáilte Ireland study**

- A: Rothar—cycling company in West
- B: Equus—riding school in Midlands
- C: Sub-Aqua—diving centre
- D: Sea Spa—seaweed spa in North-West
- E: Island Retreat—guesthouse in island location
- F: Rustic lodge—guesthouse in rural Midlands location
- G: The Cedars—hotel subject to preservation order in North-West
- H: The Oaks—small indigenous hotel chain in West
- I: Orangerie—vegetarian restaurant in Dublin
- J: Fairways Country Club—golf and hotel facility—North Co. Dublin
- K: Tonnta—surf school in South-East
- L: Castle—historic castle used for accommodation in North-East

Some examples from Case H illustrate two of the three strands of CSV while an example of the third strand—local industry cluster development—is evident in the overall study.

Case H was located in a popular scenic part of the rural, maritime West of Ireland, accessible by train and hosting a thriving community of artists. It was a three-star hotel with 111 bedrooms and was part of the "Poplars" hotel group, a chain of five family-run hotels in the West of Ireland. The chain was recognized for its friendly and homely atmosphere, high standards of accommodation, cuisine and comfort. The general manager, with the help of his father-in-law (founder of the Poplars Group), bought "The Oaks Hotel" in 1995. The hotel had received EU grant aid for the construction of new bedrooms and the refurbishment of existing ones, extension of the restaurant, construction of a new lobby, kitchen and banqueting room.

Re: CSV theme (i)—Re-conceiving products and markets

We can see this theme in the area of renovation of the hotel:

> There was a big renovation done, and 33 rooms were extended and reno-
> vated at the back and 11 more were put on top. And, as part of that con-
> struction, it was designed to the highest environmental standard. In fact,
> Sustainable Energy Ireland put out a call for a competitive grant and you
> had to make your submission and apply for it. And we were one of the
> ones who were awarded the grant.

Re: CSV (ii)—Redefining productivity in the value chain

This theme is exemplified through greater efficiency through the reduced consumption of energy in Case H:

> But an end result of all of that is that, between energy efficiency, managing
> the energy a bit better, better insulation, energy-efficient lighting, we've

reduced our consumption of energy by about half a million kilowatts per annum.

The heating of the hotel, bedrooms, etc. as well as of the water in the swimming pool was achieved with a boiler run on wood pellets.

Each year, there's 1,000 tonnes fewer of CO_2 being emitted from these buildings.

Furthermore, in the area of waste management and recycling:

Yes, all waste used to go into bins, and it was dumped in landfill, and you were charged by the weight. And the total was about 250 tonnes. We put the composter in and all the food waste is put through that and that naturally breaks down into a compost. And it reduces the volume of landfill by approx. 90%. It's down to 40 tonnes now. Waste food is dead weight. It's loaded with water. So instead of having ten bags, we end up with one bag of compost, which we can put out on the grass.

And we take the ashes we've left from the boiler, because it burned down to a fine powder. We can put that on the land. It's carbon.

To show the commitment of the hotel to best practice in energy and environmental matters, the hotel appointed an environmental manager who represented the hotel as part of an environmental group called Green Hospitality:[2]

I deal with all the environmental matters and the energy matters.

So we have a green team, and we hold meetings with them every so often, and we just watch what's going on, and [as regards lights in the bedrooms] … that some sort of a sequence would be in place, so that when somebody came in and turned on the main switch in the bedroom only certain lights would come on.

Re: CSV theme (iii)—Local industry cluster development

Small firm literature identifies networks as the essential support structure in any training intervention to help entrepreneurs to learn and it would appear to positively affect the quality of this experiential learning. Networks are closely followed by business mentors, with appropriate industrial and sector expertise (Kelliher *et al.*, 2009, pp. 81–2). International studies also support these findings, so small firm network-centred learning is vital (Morrison & Teixeira, 2004).

A powerful example of these networks is taken from the overall study cohort, where eight out of the twelve case site owner-managers belonged to TLNs (Tourism

2   The Green Hospitality Programme is the only Irish-developed environmental certification standard for the hospitality sector. The Green Hospitality Eco-label and Awards are recognized both nationally and internationally as standards that allow members to achieve good environmental performance and allow visitors to choose "Greener" hospitality businesses, knowing that defined criteria are being implemented and monitored. This is a voluntary programme that aims to develop leadership and best practice within the hospitality sector. http://www.ghaward.ie/index.php?id=10.

and Learning Networks). TLNs were unanimously positively rated by those eight owner-managers (in the study) who had attended them.

Typically, participants in TLNs are owner-managers of small and micro tourism enterprises, particularly those employing less then 20 people. These networks also include "associate members" such as tourism representative bodies, county enterprise boards, county councils, LEADER groups and other interested parties. Currently, Kelliher *et al.* (2009, p. 81) report there are "35 networks throughout Ireland".

The TLNs are focused on action-based learning where participation and interaction are encouraged. Generally, they have a minimum of 25 participants on each one. The programme includes a core element, representing about 70% of the total input. The remaining 30% consists of a variable element, to meet individual networks' specific needs. The Extranet is a follow-up web community after the TLN events have finished, whereby participants can keep in touch through online discussion groups.

The TLNs she attended prompted one of the respondents (Case C) to start a very successful marketing network where local businesses would join up and prepare a brochure of activities, accommodation and restaurants in the area around a central theme, to "create a buzz" to attract the domestic market to the area. As part of her TLN, a dialogue had started about setting up a honeypot of activities for a particular area, but, owing to lack of funding for the Extranet after the TLN had ended, this dialogue stopped (Case F). This shows the potential of the TLN to prime business among the local tourism operators.

A second example of clustering is when links are created between activity centres and local hotels to create reciprocal demand and so build sustainability. It was found that vouchers to stay at local hotels were available at the activity centres used by overseas clients such as Cases A, C, D and K (the activity centres).[3] Similarly, the hotels would carry information about activities in the local area, be it surfing, riding, diving, wind-surfing, etc.

Finally, life-cycle issues were recognized as part of the sustainability problem. Some owner-managers, concerned that their businesses were not sustainable in their current form, were planning to sell on or adapt their property to other uses. Others in well-performing businesses (Case H) were developing add-on businesses, such as beach riding, but were tying this business to their own personal assets, so that this stream became an exit route for himself and his family should his hotel business fail.

By contrast, one case site (Case G) was a hotel that was based in a small town in the North-West of Ireland, a favourite destination for family holidays. The son of the owner had inherited the hotel, located in the main street of the town, and it still retained its original décor and design from the 1950s and was subject to a preservation order. Regrettably, this hotel was an example of a failure by his father (who had previously run the hotel and then bequeathed it to his son) to plan for

---

3   The riding school tended to cater for children of local families, who did not require accommodation and attended usually just for a lesson each week.

sustainability, as it needed huge re-development, which was not affordable by the current owner. It had achieved the end of its life cycle as a hotel in its current form, as many of the children of the families that used to stay in the hotel had become parents and had purchased holiday homes in the area and used these, in preference to staying at the hotel. After much soul-searching, the current owner, who was a trained chef, surmised that those holiday home owners might come to his hotel for food and beverage. A secondary opportunity to renovate the kitchen area and then run cookery lessons for adults and children alike also seemed plausible.

Conclusions

Sustainability is not just about being ethically and socially responsible—it is about smart business. As the case examples show, reducing energy costs and eliminating the cost of waste has a "bottom line" impact as well as protecting the environment. The challenge for the finance professional is to recognize and unlock the latent value from the sustainability levers relevant to the business.

The finance function must make the connections between tangible short-term shareholder profits from revenue generation and cost control, while at the same time realizing the longer term non-financial gains from good risk management and the building of trust with other stakeholders to enhance brand value and reputation. Indeed as the CGMA (2012b, p. 10) notes, "one thing we can be sure of in this uncertain world is that people—their ideas and relationships—will be more important than ever before".

References

ACCA (Association of Chartered Certified Accountants) (2011). *The Value Creation Model for Business: 2010 and Beyond.* London: Association of Chartered Certified Accountants.

AIB (Allied Irish Banks) (2013). Outlook: AIB's series of sectoral research reports—hotels, issue 2. Retrieved from http://business.aib.ie/help/hotels, accessed 19 May 2013.

BDO (2013). *Mapping the Future for the Irish Hotel Sector.* Dublin: BDO.

Brennan, N.M. & Solomon, J. (2008). Corporate governance, accountability and mechanisms of accountability: An overview. *Accounting, Auditing & Accountability Journal*, 21(7), 885–906.

Brundtland Commission (1987). Our common future. Retrieved from http://www.un-documents.net/our-common-future.pdf, accessed 1 June 2014.

CGMA (Chartered Global Management Accountant) (2012a). *Sustainable Business—Shared Value in Practice.* London: Chartered Institute of Management Accountants and New York: American Institute of CPAs.

CGMA (2012b). *Rebooting Business: Valuing the Human Dimension.* London: Chartered Institute of Management Accountants and New York: American Institute of CPAs.

CGMA (2013). *Building Resilience: An Introduction to Business Models.* London: Chartered Institute of Management Accountants and New York: American Institute of CPAs.

CIMA & IFAC (2004). *Enterprise Governance: Getting the Balance Right.* London: CIMA. Retrieved from http://www.ifac.org/publications-resources/enterprise-governance-getting-balance-right, accessed 11 August 2015.

EC (European Commission) (2001). *Promoting a European Framework for Corporate Social Responsibility.* Green Paper. Luxembourg: Office for Official Publications of the European Communities.

Eisenhardt, K. (1989). Agency theory: An assessment and review. *Academy of Management Review,* 14(1), 57–74.

Elkington, J. (1997). *Cannibals with Forks: The Triple Bottom Line of 21st Century Business.* Oxford, UK: Capstone Publishing.

FRC (Financial Reporting Council) (2014). UK corporate governance code. Retrieved from https://www.frc.org.uk/corporate/ukcgcode.cfm, accessed 10 May 2014.

Freeman, R.E. (1998). A stakeholder theory of the modern corporation. In L.B. Pincus (ed.). *Perspectives in Business Ethics.* Singapore: McGraw-Hill, pp. 171–81.

Garvey, G. (2012). "Insolvent" hotel sector is facing tough times despite rise in visitors. Retrieved from http://www.independent.ie/business/irish/insolvent-hotel-sector-is-facing-tough-times-despite-rise-in-visitors-26827220.html, accessed 1 June 2014.

GRI (Global Reporting Initiative) (2013). The sustainability content of integrated reports—A survey of pioneers. Retrieved from https://www.globalreporting.org/information/sustainability-reporting/Pages/default.aspx, accessed 1 June 2014.

Handy, C.B. (1994). *The Empty Raincoat: Making Sense of the Future.* London: Hutchinson.

IFAC (International Federation of Accountants) (2013). *Competent and Versatile: How Professional Accountants in Business drive Sustainable Organisational Success.* New York, NY: International Federation of Accountants.

IFAC (2014). Why is sustainability important? Retrieved from https://www.ifac.org/global-knowledge-gateway/sustainability?overview, accessed 1 June 2014.

IHF (Irish Hotel Federation) (2014). Retrieved from http://www.ihf.ie, accessed 1 June 2014.

IIRC (International Integrated Reporting Council) (2013). The international integrated reporting framework. Retrieved from http://www.theiirc.org/international-ir-framework, accessed 13 April 2015.

Kelliher, F., Foley, A., & Frampton, A.M. (2009). Facilitating small firm learning networks in the Irish tourism sector. *Tourism and Hospitality Research,* 9(1), 80–95.

Killian, S. (2012). *Corporate Social Responsibility, A Guide, with Irish Experiences.* Dublin: Chartered Accountants Ireland.

Mattimoe, R. (2010). *The Fragility of Smallness: Financial Management Skills in Owner-Managed Irish SME Tourism Businesses: Findings and Recommendations.* Dublin: Fáilte Ireland.

Morrison, A. & Teixeira, R. (2004). Small business performance: A UK tourism sector focus. *Journal of Small Business and Enterprise Development,* 11(2), 166–73.

Porter, M.E. & Kramer, M.R. (2011). Creating shared value. *Harvard Business Review,* January–February, 62–77.

St Paul's Institute & CIMA (2014). *Looking Beyond the Checkbox: Mitigating Risk, Maximising Performance, Summary Report.* London: CIMA and St Paul's Institute.

Tilt, C. A. (2007). Corporate responsibility accounting and accountants. In S.O. Idowu & L.F. Walter (eds). *Professionals' Perspectives of Corporate Social Responsibility.* Berlin-Heidelberg: Springer Verlag.

7

Evolving towards truly sustainable hotels through a "well-being" lens
The S-WELL sustainability grid

Z. Gulen Hashmi and Katrin Muff

Business School Lausanne, Switzerland

This chapter aims to provide hotels, academia and students with a multidimensional sustainability grid, the S-WELL (sustainability for well-being), which represents different types of hotel sustainability as phases of an evolutionary process. The S-WELL focuses on competitive sustainability strategies and sustainable hotel practices, based on a model with two axes: the vertical axis is built on the hotel's need to manage the business with an economic concern while simultaneously building a competitive advantage through external concerns that derive from sustainability challenges. The horizontal axis looks at the hotel's need to create shareholder value while also contributing to societal value creation aimed at well-being. The four quadrants that represent different types of hotel sustainability are compliance, CSR, managing for the TBL and societal well-being, respectively. The S-WELL is an analytical tool for understanding and challenging hotel sustainability strategies and practices to benefit society at large.

Introduction

In the face of troubling scientific facts and figures about the unsustainable state of our economy and environment, an increasing number of hotels have engaged in some form of activity regarding sustainability over the past few years. Whether named as CSR, green environmentalism, social justice or sustainability, corporate leaders are feeling pressure to address environmental and social concerns along with financial performance (Holliday, 2001; Livesey & Kearins, 2002). Hotels, in particular, are in a context squeezed between the push of legislation, the pull of consumer pressure groups and economic concerns related to cost savings (Goodno, 1994). The business case for cost savings is already well understood, and hotels have focused primarily on cost savings as the initial step in their multi-faceted sustainability journey (Chong & Verma, 2013). The most cited benefit of sustainable business practices is, in fact, cost reduction (Landrum & Edwards, 2009; Hitchcock & Willard, 2009; Bohdanowicz *et al.*, 2004; Hobson & Essex, 2001).

Cost savings is largely associated with "green credentials"; thus, several authors have long criticized the tourism industry, in particular the hotel industry, for its limitation to the environmental dimension to become "sustainable" (Font & Harris, 2004; Roberts & Tribe, 2008). Yet Kernel (2005) considers taking environmental initiatives as the initial step towards sustainability in tourism enterprises according to the four-step model for sustainable development; and further challenges organizations to go further to include social and ethical aspects as well as integration in the community.

Indeed, some forward-thinking hotel companies are successfully finding new opportunities in social and environmental issues to create new corporate strategies, business models and collaborative partnerships while simultaneously serving their shareholders. Their approaches vary widely from activities related to compliance to next-practice platforms in the form of collaborative partnerships.

A review of literature suggests that companies often go through stages starting with simple, easy to implement strategies and progressing towards more complex and potentially rewarding approaches (Mirvis & Googins, 2009; Hoffman & Bansal, 2012). This seems to hold true for the hospitality industry, as well. While the nature and number of stages differ, nearly all hotels first engage with sustainability by focusing on legal or voluntary compliance, with the aim of saving costs, managing economic risks and opportunities, and increasing shareholder value. Once hotels have learnt to manage risks and efficiencies through compliance, many of them further evolve to engage in CSR activities such as charity projects and community involvement that reflect deeply held values. As McGehee *et al.* (2009) assert, CSR is largely viewed as a separate area via donations of goods, services and volunteer hours. In the hotel industry, CSR projects are believed to lead to guilt-free hotel operations, enhanced corporate reputation in the eyes of eco-minded hotel guests and even attraction of new guests (Euromonitor International, 2012).

Once hotels have enjoyed the benefits of simultaneously managing internal efficiencies and being socially responsible across hotel boundaries, they tend to easily recognize the relevance and the need to respond to social and environmental concerns in addition to economic concerns. With broadened focus on stakeholders, a growing number of hotels create value not just as a side effect of their business activities, but also as a result of deliberately defined goals addressed at specific environmental and social issues, or stakeholders. Marriott International can be considered a good example of this type of business sustainability: its staff diversity, community involvement and anti-corruption policies relate to the hotel chain's social concerns; its CO_2 footprint, LEED building certification and "reduce, reuse and recycle" programme relate to its environmental concerns; and its investment for sustainable actions relates to its economic concerns.

Hotels that have advanced to this point try to innovate, produce and report measurable results in well-defined sustainability areas through organizational transformation. Although this is a big step from creating shareholder value to creating social, economic and environmental values, the business case is still the overarching driver to manage these so-called TBL concerns and values. As Deale (2013) asserts, although environmental and social sustainability matter to hoteliers, it is economic sustainability that is pivotal to their very existence.

However, in today's business context of increasing economic, social and environmental uncertainty, individually, almost every organization is unsustainable to solve societal challenges alone. Furthermore, giving corporate success an economic value does not entail that such businesses should be, or are in practice, valued by society. Judging hotel sustainability solely in economic terms misses the key fact that economic sustainability is a means to an end, not an end in itself. A strong and healthy hotel financial performance may be desirable, but it is desirable because it allows its various stakeholders to get on with doing the things that are really important—living happy, fulfilling lives. In other words, additional corporate wealth does not represent an efficient way to significantly increase the much-needed societal well-being societies seek. Moreover, the model of unending economic growth, which we have been following, is taking us beyond our environmental limits.

In this light, the case for a more meaningful purpose of business sustainability becomes compelling: to act as positive change agents of an interconnected ecosystem, starting off with societal challenges and contributing to societal well-being as an ultimate goal of corporate sustainability endeavours. To solve societal challenges, hotels would need to ask themselves, "How can we contribute to resolving pressing sustainability issues with novel products, services or business models that are impossible to achieve alone?" or "How can we enhance the positive common good by doing new things with others?"

The conceptualized framework, the S-WELL grid, aims to contribute to the literature on hotel sustainability, drawing attention to the evolving phases of hotel sustainability with regard to the type of concern and the type of value created. Hotels need to manage the business with an economic concern while simultaneously building competitive advantage through external concerns such as sustainability challenges. Furthermore, hotels need to create shareholder value while also contributing to societal value creation. A number of frameworks and models have taken shareholder value into consideration in corporate sustainability (Elkington, 1997; Orsato, 2006; Nidumolu *et al.*, 2009; Porter & Kramer, 2011). However, none of these conceptualized works has examined types of hotel sustainability in light of both shareholder value and societal value. In this respect, the S-WELL serves as an analytical tool to understand and challenge existing and emerging sustainable hotel practices and strategies with relevance to an ideology of sustainability that is much needed: societal value creation.

More importantly, the S-WELL grid, with its focus on societal well-being as the most advanced hotel sustainability phase, can be described as a radical and robust proposal to guide the direction of future hotel sustainability efforts to benefit society. Business leaders can use this sustainability grid to fundamentally re-evaluate hotel sustainability strategies that have long been established within well-defined sustainability areas, often with focus on "green" credentials.

Rethinking hotel sustainability through a holistic "well-being" lens

A holistic worldview necessitates system thinking whereby everything is related in some way and each part and each person in the business can contribute towards more sustainability (Landrum & Edwards, 2009). A key issue to become a truly sustainable company is the integration of different actions and sectors of society, economy and environment, taking a holistic view and overcoming barriers between disciplines (Hashmi & Muff, 2014). This has two justifications: our lives are embedded within the societal systems; and our lives ultimately depend on the ecological system. Given the nature of the hotel industry, it is not only hotels themselves but also an open, dynamic and complex system with various interacting components and different stakeholders that are involved (Mill & Morrison, 1997; Thanh & Bosch, 2010). And it is this complexity that makes it difficult to manage towards sustainability (Thanh & Bosch, 2010).

Thus, looking into the evolutionary process of sustainable hotels through a holistic worldview such as a "well-being" lens, a change of perspective may make perfect sense. A "well-being" lens would bring about an understanding of the various interacting components, systems and different stakeholders, the happiness of whom is the ultimate purpose of being sustainable in the hotel industry. It is this interconnectedness between the resources, human systems and the goal of human well-being that requires systems thinking.

Achieving well-being is, in many respects, the essence of human existence. In recent years, well-being has moved from the realm of philosophy to that of science, with a growing body of research into what contributes to the quality of people's experiences of their lives. This has brought about a new understanding of the factors that both influence and constitute well-being. Well-being is best thought of as a dynamic process, emerging from the way in which people interact with the world around them (Foresight Mental Capital & Well-Being Project, 2008). While "well-being" is defined as "the extent to which people experience happiness and satisfaction, and are functioning well" (NEF, 2011), academic debate continues about precisely how "well-being" should be defined. In this context, well-being is most usefully thought of as the dynamic process that gives people a sense of how their lives are going, through the interaction between their circumstances, activities and psychological resources or "mental capital" (ONS, 2011).

A successful society is one in which people have high levels of well-being that is sustained over time. This has led to the recent growing importance of well-being (Michaelson *et al.*, 2009). For instance, in 2010, the director generals of Europe's National Statistics Offices, including the UK's ONS (Office for National Statistics), signed the Sofia Memorandum, which recognizes the importance of "measuring progress, well-being and sustainable development" and mandates further work on the issue by Eurostat (DGINS ESSC, 2010). More recently in 2011, research undertaken by the UK ONS found key issues of societal well-being to be social relationships, environment, security and health (physical and mental).

The concept of "well-being" fits very well within the hotel industry, mainly because hospitality requires people involving and serving people for happiness. Hotels serve the needs of the travelling public, and the majority of people working in the industry are in contact with guests and customers. Hotels are open 365 days a year and 24 hours a day, which involve longer working hours including weekends and holidays. Hotels also depend heavily on shift work and strive for guest satisfaction, yet services are intangible (for use, not possession; and cannot be test driven). Even more interestingly, production and consumption take place at the same time with the guest present. Finally, the product, which is the guest experience itself, is of a perishable nature. All these characteristics of the hospitality industry point towards the importance of well-being, which is captured in four major aspects: education, health, social justice and overall satisfaction with life, as derived from a national report in the UK (DEFRA, 2010).

Indeed, all the afore-mentioned well-being aspects relate to hotels to a great extent. In the context of education, hotels, in particular the chain hotels, offer opportunities for advancement either in the form of employee transfers from one property to another every few years, or through in-house training, certification and apprenticeship programmes that offer invaluable learning for employees to develop themselves. In the context of health, while relatively longer working hours point to a need to balance the work/life challenge in the industry, foodservice operations and daily housekeeping draw attention to sanitation that is critically important. Regarding social justice, hotels are great places for employee diversity and in terms of job possibilities for the disadvantaged groups in communities because many of the jobs require low levels of skill and education. Hotels further help to contribute to gender equality by providing jobs for women in developing countries.

Finally, the sense of pleasure and feeling of happiness lie in the heart of any hospitality service including hotels. Thus, forward-thinking hotels that prioritize social sustainability and well-being are highly likely to contribute positively to society at large.

Through a "well-being" lens nested in a holistic worldview, the proposed business sustainability grid—the S-WELL—aims to be a practical guide for sustainable hotels that aspire to evolve into truly sustainable hotels, whereby the term "truly sustainable" indicates hotels that are the most advanced in their evolutionary sustainability journey. Yet it is not about perfection, but rather an ongoing balancing act in the real world; as Harrison (2001) noted, "Sustainability is not a destination; it is a journey."

Business sustainability grid: The S-WELL

The S-WELL grid draws on the Dyllick & Muff business sustainability typology that uses three elements of a typical business process model: the relevant concerns considered (inputs); the organizational perspectives applied (processes); and the type of value created (outputs) (Dyllick & Muff, 2013). Dyllick & Muff (2013) assert that ,while the traditional business concern is one-dimensional deriving solely from an economic imperative, the sustainability perspective typically addresses social, environmental and economic concerns. Regarding the organizational perspectives applied, the authors draw attention to an "outside-in" approach which starts with sustainability challenges that lie beyond the boundaries of a company. Finally, the authors highlight the need for businesses to contribute to positive common good such as the health of the planet or society as a whole. This would require going beyond interests of direct stakeholders to also include stakeholders that are only indirectly affected by business activities. The typology serves as a relevant framework to clarify the drivers and purpose of business sustainability (Hashmi & Muff, 2014). As business sustainability evolves from 1.0 to 2.0 and 3.0, the relevance and the contribution to resolve sustainability issues increases, with business sustainability 3.0 representing a "true business sustainability".

S-WELL further builds on the Dyllick & Muff's proposed business sustainability typology expanding on its two elements of the business process model: the concerns; and type of value created. The grid presents hotel sustainability as a multi-dimensional construct with two axes, key dimensions of which are: external versus economic concerns on one axis; and shareholder versus societal value on the other axis. The vertical axis is built on the hotel's need to manage the business with an economic concern while simultaneously building competitive advantage harnessing external concerns that derive from today's and tomorrow's sustainability challenges. The horizontal axis looks at the hotel's tension to create shareholder value while also contributing to societal value creation for the ultimate goal of high well-being. Taking into consideration the nature of the hotel industry and the current sustainable hotel practices and environmental strategies, the four quadrants of the S-WELL grid distinguish between compliance, CSR, managing for TBL and societal well-being, which represent different types of hotel sustainability relevant to the sustainability journey of a hotel (see Fig. 7.1).

While the quadrant "compliance" implies business as usual with basically some "green" add-ons, the quadrant "CSR" characterizes business sustainability that goes beyond compliance and engages in voluntary CSR projects. These lower two quadrants demonstrate a reactive approach to business sustainability. Quadrant "managing for TBL" is where the TBL of sustainability (Elkington, 1997) comes into play with three dimensional concerns (social, environmental and economic). This phase is characterized with a mix of various strategies such as eco-branding, redefining productivity in the value chain and re-conceiving environmentally or socially friendly products or markets, coupled with ongoing CSR activities. Finally, quadrant "societal well-being" is where the creation of common good would take place with truly sustainable strategies. Truly sustainable hotels pursue strategies such as next-practice platforms or local cluster development to solve specific sustainability challenges. These upper two quadrants demonstrate a proactive approach to business sustainability. The quadrants build on each other, making the process a cumulative one. In this respect, the sustainability journey can be considered a continuous evolution for hotels.

Figure 7.1 **The sustainability for well-being grid, highlighting types of hotel sustainability**

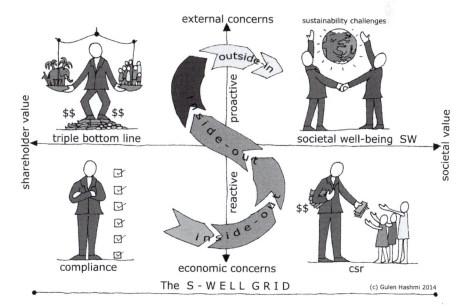

The S - W E L L   G R I D

(c) Gulen Hashmi 2014

Now let's walk through each of the four phases of hotel sustainability represented by the S-WELL grid quadrants. The quadrants challenge hotels to think about which sustainable hotel practices and strategies they should pursue with regard to type of concern and value they create for society and for themselves.

The first S-WELL quadrant: Compliance

This is the initial phase of hotel sustainability that starts with "going green" in the sustainability journey. Sustainable hotel practices in this quadrant stem from compliance with government regulations or policy, which are heavily focused on the current environment. As the cost of non-renewable energy continues to rise, regulatory pressure increases and travellers become more demanding, "green practices" justifiably become the baseline requirement for hotels. Hotels in this phase actively reduce their current environmental impacts without fundamentally changing their business model. They tend to focus on new technologies as ways to reduce impacts while maintaining business as usual. Innovations are typically incremental, addressing a single issue at a time and company-centric as the primary intent is cost reduction or profit maximization. Thus, "compliance" can be considered a reactive approach towards the business case for sustainability, which is fuelled by an economic concern aimed at increased shareholder value.

Existing environmental regulations related to the hotel sector are still largely focused on aspects of facility operations such as hazardous materials handling, environmental health and safety or storm water management (Goldstein & Primlani, 2012). Current legislation ranges from the broad and long-term cap and trade legislation regarding emissions, to the specific US Energy Independence and Security Act of 2007, which dictates phased efficiency standards to incandescent light bulbs. Such a wide range of present and future legislative activities is likely to impact hotel design, construction and operations. Some environmental policies may increase costs, which then are likely to be passed on to the customers. This could either act as a disincentive or as a way of marketing a "green" hotel. However, a previous survey of US business travellers by Watkins (1994) shows that 71% of respondents preferred to stay in environmentally friendly hotels but would not consider paying extra to fund these green policies, compared with 28% who would be willing to pay a premium ranging between $5 and $10 only.

Policymakers increasingly emphasize the importance of the business case for sustainability to companies, which can explain a hotel's economic concern and interest in the adoption of cost reduction competitiveness strategies such as eco-efficiency or cost and risk reduction. Eco-efficiency within and beyond the firm is the prevailing environmental strategy used in this quadrant. Its goal is to diminish the negative effects on the environment through reducing resource consumption, energy use, emissions and waste, landfill use and toxic releases and recycling

(McDonough & Braungart, 2000). However, the authors assert that eco-efficiency as a sustainability strategy is a misconception as simply reducing and recycling does not really stop environmental degradation and destruction; and that product redesign and radical innovation should indeed be carried out to ensure long-term sustainability.

Cost and risk reduction is another strategy in this quadrant. Achieving competitiveness through cost reduction is rooted in the resource-based view of enterprise, which argues that business will engage in sustainability actions to gain a competitive advantage that others cannot quickly imitate (Hart, 1995). Hotels with this understanding of sustainability are concerned with how sustainable practices in operations and governance reduce risks and costs (van Marrewijk, 2003). Cost and risk reduction supports eco-efficiency in the sense that reduced use of resources would potentially result in quarterly earnings growth and reduction in exposure to liabilities and other potential losses (Hart & Milstein, 2003).

However, as Bronn & Vidaver-Cohen (2009) assert, it is actually more desirable for businesses to have less regulation in order to have more freedom in decision-making to be able to meet market and social factors. Some large hotel chains have already increased awareness of the business opportunities inherent in environmental and social issues; and thus gone far enough to go beyond compliance and become socially responsible businesses. As McDonough & Braungart (2000) assert, going beyond compliance can give companies huge opportunities for out-designing the competition. Thus, the following phase of hotel sustainability "CSR" is characterized by voluntary activities, which environmentally sustainable hotels engage further in their sustainability journey.

The second S-WELL quadrant: Corporate social responsibility

The quadrant "CSR" represents the type of hotel sustainability whereby positive public relations, improved hotel image with shareholders and community, and beyond compliance leadership can be a differentiating factor, a source of competitive advantage and new market opportunities (Hitchcock & Willard, 2009; Landrum & Edwards, 2009). It is perhaps this relatively recent concept of CSR that enables an understanding of evolution implied in the meaning of sustainability from mandatory environmental add-ons to the necessity of being socially responsible (Kalisch, 2002).

By already having mastered compliance to environmental policy, hotels in this slightly advanced phase of business sustainability also seek to be acknowledged for their CSR activities in addition to their "greening" efforts. Having reached some ongoing operational efficiency in the previous "compliance" phase, hotels in this quadrant concentrate on what society wants from them and what value they can uniquely add to society through CSR activities. They start to "think more deeply" about how they give back to society and, specifically, the societal issues on which they choose to focus. Although they react positively to societal issues, they lack the focus needed for economic value creation. Thus, the approach remains reactive and non-strategic, as the underlying purpose is to seek reputational benefits and legitimization for economic concerns, yet with no focus on a related economic value creation. This is largely because being socially responsible contributes to societal value creation as a positive side effect of being environmentally friendly, rather than as a well-planned solution to societal challenges.

In this phase, hotels continue to increase efficiencies throughout the value chain with focus on separate CSR activities that are in the form of donations of goods, services and, more recently, volunteer hours (Deale, 2013). They seek societal legitimization in the eyes of stakeholders, which, once achieved, may lead to enhanced reputation and a growth of shareholder value. As the theory of legitimization extends to numerous external stakeholders in the value chain, stakeholders' interests are likely to affect or can be affected by the achievement of an organization's objectives (Hart & Milstein, 2003).

Although methods and reasons for societal legitimization will differ between small to medium hotels and large hotel chains, legitimization can still be considered a valid driver of sustainability by both large and small hotels (Font *et al.*, 2014). A previous study shows that large hotels, hotels with a classification between three and five stars and chain hotels were more likely to experience positive CSR benefits than small, two-star classified and independent hotels (Kirk, 1998). Yet, although search for competitiveness is largely rooted in the belief that there is a relationship between CSR and CFP (corporate financial performance) (Carroll & Shabana, 2010), existent research finds positive, neutral and negative associations in the relationship between CSR and CFP, making it inconclusive (Griffin & Mahon, 1997; Margolis & Walsh, 2001).

In this second quadrant, hotels start to engage in being socially responsible. They voluntarily spend resources on environmental improvements beyond what is required, through voluntary membership to third-party organizations such as certification bodies or internationally recognized sustainability reporting programmes (Orsato, 2006). Nidumolu *et al.* (2009) assert that, going beyond compliance with voluntary CSR activities and with more stringent standards before they are enforced, fosters innovation as well as a first-mover advantage. Interestingly, sustainability research shows that earning a green certification does not automatically result in a large revenue bump or a revenue fall in hotels (Chong & Verma, 2013). A hotel receives an eco-friendly designation by earning any of several dozen certifications to which the consumer as decision-maker is not exposed (Chong & Verma, 2013). Furthermore, the fact that various regions and companies prefer different certifications complicates the global green standards landscape, which accounts for the lack of a much-needed unified global standard in the industry (Ricaurte, 2011).

Yet some forward-thinking hotels see themselves integral to society and thus feel responsible "to do good by doing new things". This is often the outcome of a radical shift in mindset from doing things better to doing new things. They simply move from operational optimization and voluntary CSR activities towards a strategically focused organizational transformation phase. Such hotels are further advanced in the evolutionary sustainability journey and are positioned higher up in the S-WELL grid, as they go even further than reputation, legitimacy and beyond compliance leadership; and strive to balance economic, social and environmental concerns to create TBL value creation.

The third S-WELL quadrant: Managing for triple bottom line

In this phase of the evolutionary sustainability journey, hotels start with the three-dimensional concerns of profit, people and planet, and then try to optimize economic, social and environmental value creation for a balanced stakeholder value. According to research by Deutsche Bank, which evaluated 56 academic studies, companies with high ratings for ESG (environmental, social and governance) factors have a lower cost of debt and equity; 89% of the studies they reviewed show that companies with high ESG ratings outperform the market in the medium (three to five years) and long (five to ten years) term (Fulton *et al.*, 2012). Similarly, companies in the Carbon Disclosure Leadership Index and Carbon Performance Leadership Index, which are included based on disclosure and performance on GHG (greenhouse gas) emissions, record superior stock-market returns (Eccles *et al.*, 2011).

Hotels positioned in this upper left quadrant demonstrate a proactive approach to sustainability, contrary to the first two phases, as they purposefully develop programmes and take actions in the areas of governance, processes, products and services, instead of positive side effects resulting from actions. Rather than focusing on "doing less harm", they believe their organization can benefit financially from "doing good". They create disruptive new products and services by viewing sustainability as a market opportunity. Their focus is largely on delivering services and to a less extent on creating products. Their innovations are both technological and socio-technical—designed to improve quality of life for people inside or outside the firm. At the Red Carnation Hotel in London, for instance, guests are updated about money saved from reduced consumption of electricity, which are given to local charities and communicated to guests. Similarly, Lancaster London educates its guests by involving them in a Green Week fair, where guests are educated about the property and allowed to try out bikes provided on site (Caterer & Hotelkeeper, 2010).

In addition to participating and initiating CSR projects on issues of poverty, social equity, health and education, they actively engage in stakeholder dialogues with the purpose of contributing positively in these areas. Programmes and activities are managed, measured and reported through integration of sustainability goals into management and governance structures such as cross-functional commit-tees, policies and guidelines. Internal reporting includes differentiated TBL activi-ties and results with improved TBL value creation. However, hotels in this phase of business sustainability are still primarily internally focused in that they see their organization as an independent figure in the economy. Although they do work up and down the value chain and collaborate closely with external stakeholders, sus-tainability challenges are still not the starting point and societal value is yet to be created in a holistic way.

Hotel sustainability strategies in this phase further explore opportunities for environmental differentiation in terms of products and services, which could fur-ther provide a competitive advantage (eco-branding). As Orsato (2006) asserts on his eco-branding strategy, such environmental product differentiation would cre-ate greater environmental benefits or impose smaller environmental costs, com-pared to similar products. This is in line with assertion that "becoming sustainable" is an outcome of developing sustainable offerings or redesigning existing ones to become eco-friendly (Nidumolu *et al.*, 2009). Although raised operating costs would be an issue, such differentiation would either enable the hotel to command a price premium, or increase market share (Reinhardt, 1998) by simply satisfy-ing the green market niche willing to pay a premium for environmentally friendly products (Blanco *et al.*, 2009). Some hotels in this phase are even envisaged to go further enough to develop new business models, to create value that will change the basis of competition (Nidumolu *et al.*, 2009). This would require considering not only if a guest's hotel experience is environmentally friendly, but also if it is socially just and guilt-free throughout the stay.

The concept of TBL measures the multidimensional business contributions to sustainability (Elkington, 1997). It is a search for creating synergistic (economic, environmental and social) value through the adoption of sustainability efforts (Hart & Milstein, 2003), with focus on innovation. Although the concept may look convincing and appealing to many sustainable hotels at first sight, measuring and comparing the trade-offs between economic, social and environmental values still causes confusion. This is mainly due to the fact that, while environmental initia-tives can easily be measurable in the short-term with objective data, social ini-tiatives require a longer time span and thus are relatively harder to measure for companies due to requirement on subjective data. Social criteria and assessment are still considered scientifically uncertain and unreliable (Sasidharan *et al.*, 2002); and this ambiguity of measurements increases costs (Toth, 2002), as this requires more thorough procedures.

A more recent development of TBL is the concept of creating shared value, which rests on the principle of creating economic value in a way that also creates value for society by addressing its needs and challenges (Porter & Kramer, 2011). Although the concept of shared value creation is a much-applauded revitalizing contribution to linking corporations to society at large—and thus a progressive leap from the opposing views of shareholder value management (Rappaport 1998; Friedman 1970) and stakeholder value management (Freeman, 1984)—it is limited to those issues and concerns that emphasize "the business case for sustainability" and thus economic value for business (Dyllick & Muff, 2013). Considering the ancillary benefits of sustainability such as employee engagement, innovation culture and the broader brand (Haanaes *et al.*, 2011), there is great need for businesses to go beyond this phase and become eco-effective or socio-effective by solving sustainability issues of societies (Dyllick & Hockerts, 2002).

One way of solving sustainability issues of societies could be to contribute to sustainable societies themselves. At this point, the concept of "well-being" becomes more important, as well-being of future generations directly depends on the well-being of the present generations. Furthermore, well-being is the only ultimate purpose of human existence to which almost every and each company, including hotels, can contribute. Fortunately, hotels readily have higher potential in terms of this much-needed contribution because of the high impact area they possess.

The final quadrant in the S-WELL grid is thus "societal well-being", which represents the highest phase of hotel sustainability. Hotels in this phase are described as the pioneers of a new movement as they seek to go further and shift their focus from being "less bad" to becoming a positive contributor to the well-being of the environment and society. Because the purpose of business in this type of business sustainability reflects an unconventional economic paradigm, very few hotels or industries occupy this realm.

The fourth S-WELL quadrant: Societal well-being

"Societal well-being" represents an idealist last phase in hotels' sustainability journey, as its intention is to be in the best interest of future generations. Hotels in this quadrant are called "truly sustainable hotels" as they start with sustainability challenges relevant to their contexts and, through an "outside-in" approach, create or adapt their resources to solve sustainability challenges creating societal well-being, a novel ultimate purpose for a society. This is a radical shift from the three-dimensional concerns of sustainability that is concerned with creating well-defined TBL values deriving from the business case for sustainability. Truly sustainable hotels shift their organizational focus from organizational transformation to systems building, often through interdependent collaborations between many disparate organizations that create positive impacts on the society and the planet.

Although such an ambitious systems building approach of "doing good by doing new things with others" may look like an utopian idea, recent research findings suggest that companies can start with societal challenges, adapt to them, profit from them and improve societal well-being (Network for Business Sustainability, 2012). In a recent report for the UN Global Compact, 84% of the 1,000 global CEOs surveyed agreed that business "should lead efforts to define and deliver new goals on global priority issues". But only a third said, "that business is doing enough to address global sustainability challenges" (UN Global Compact, 2013). Hotels that demonstrate this type of advanced business sustainability recognize that a myopic obsession with growing the economy has meant that they have tended to ignore its negative impacts on well-being such as longer working hours and rising levels of indebtedness. Furthermore, they firmly believe that the economic imperative in the system has systematically squeezed out opportunities for individuals, families and communities to make choices and pursue activities, which promote positive well-being and human flourishing.

While there is now a rising worldwide demand that policy be more closely aligned with what really matters to people as they themselves characterize well-being, it makes perfect sense for hotels, in particular, to act ahead of the new policies and regulations and reorganize around these well-being issues. In the industry, Lancaster London hotel, for example, has recently adopted "happiness" as the newest of its eight hotel values in the vision statement. The hotel strives to be the happiest hotel in London by 2017–18 (Hashmi, 2014).

While some authors and organizations develop new business models in search of finding a "social purpose" for business in alignment with the wider society it operates within, a "well-being" perspective may well trigger further rethinking on a broader question: "Why does a company need to contribute to societal value creation?" One could argue that the answer is the prevailing global challenge of "Happiness", which almost every corporation as a living entity has been striving for. Research in the United States, Britain and Japan shows that, although there has been an increase in living standards and income over the past 40 years, there has not been a corresponding rise in people's happiness (Hashmi & Muff, 2014). This supports Layard's (2005) assertion that, once a certain level of income is reached, further increases are not associated with an increase in well-being.

Hotels demonstrating this type of advanced sustainability may choose to contribute to societal well-being in one or some of the four well-being aspects identified previously: education, health, social equity and quality of life. Such a choice may depend on a hotel's size, category or location. Such hotels create new products and services as a voluntary and proactive response to these well-being issues, more likely in collaboration with new partners and collaborators. Again, Lancaster London can be considered a good example of an individual luxury hotel that appears to be leading the way in this arena. The hotel, in addition to the newly formed Lancaster London Community Consortium that works on five CSR projects with volunteering hours, is leading an apprenticeship programme as well as the Lancaster Academy in partnership with the Institute of Hospitality and a few other individual hotels in London. The hotel justifiably contributes to the well-being aspects of education and social equity in a proactive way.

As Nidumolu *et al.* (2009) assert, creation of next-practice platforms in the form of synthesizing technologies, business models or regulations in different industries would require becoming a network of alliances either across the value chain or in partnership with other hotels, or in collaboration with policymakers. To be truly sustainable and solve societal challenges, businesses need to form alliances (Larson *et al.*, 2000) or, in other words, enable local cluster development, which means collaboration with all sections of the society (Porter & Kramer, 2011). Relevant societal representatives such as policymakers or NGO representatives would be integrated into the relevant decision-making processes at all levels of the organization. This would require reorganized corporate structures around the well-being issues as well as sustainability reporting with well-being metrics.

Yet the type of economic and social metrics that is meaningful to societal well-being is qualitative. Qualitative measures are a challenge for standard setting and benchmarking (Wöber, 2002). Although it is very difficult (if not impossible) to understand all environmental and social interactions in financial terms on the same valuation basis (Gray *et al.* 1996, p. 104), the outcome of using the same currency to present sustainability challenges allows companies to understand that they can make up poor performance on one issue by doing better on another one (Korhonen, 2003). As Beckett & Jonker (2002) assert, measurement with the same or at least comparable methodology for different elements of sustainability remains a challenge.

Truly sustainable hotels, however, would almost always remember the following quote as their pathway to the very purpose of societal well-being, regardless of challenges:

> The two most important days in your life are the day you are born and the day you find out why (Mark Twain).

Conclusion and implications

Green initiatives—from soap conservation to laundry reduction to waste recycling—have long been the major green focus of sustainable hotel practices, yet there's more to creating a green hotel than saving water and power by asking guests to reuse their towels. The hotel industry is increasingly expanding its sustainability focus beyond "going green" in parallel with a host of eco-labels, certifications, awards and public reporting programmes that have emerged over the past decade, the sum of which mainstream sustainability in the hotel industry. Yet the differences in the meaning of a sustainable hotel practice or operation are still varying among hoteliers, academia and students. The S-WELL grid, in this sense, aims to provide scholars, students and hospitality professionals with a multidimensional model that helps to understand and differentiate between various sustainability strategies and sustainable hotel practices.

Being an integral part to society, hotels need to link their sustainability practices and sustainability strategies to societal well-being; and solve sustainability challenges by going beyond an environmental policy, a code of ethics, human rights policy or optimizing their TBL values. Although prospective sustainable hotels are likely to be those that take a long-term TBL view of sustainability with a focus on shareholder value, true sustainability leaders will be those truly sustainable hotels that solve societal challenges prioritizing societal value over shareholder value.

The chapter highlights awareness of the ultimate purpose behind hotel sustainability practices and strategies through a "well-being" lens; and serves to guide sustainable hotels to become truly sustainable hotels that solve sustainability challenges such as public health, poverty, education, energy, social equity, water and quality of life, all of which have been channelled into the concept of well-being. The theoretical contribution, the S-WELL grid, is the first attempt to link "happiness or well-being" to a business sustainability grid to bridge the gap between the purpose of sustainable hotels and society. It is an analytical tool for sustainable hotels to position themselves in their sustainability efforts with regard to concerns and value they create for society. The four quadrants of the grid distinguish between compliance, CSR, TBL and societal well-being, which represent different types of hotel sustainability, respectively.

Although the S-WELL grid is affected, to a certain extent, by perceptions of reality that are rooted in the author's background, values and heuristics, and is only a proposed theoretical contribution that requires further empirical research to reinforce its applicability in the hotel industry, it is likely to be replicated in other segments of the hospitality industry such as restaurants, casinos, cruise ships and hospitals, which have relatively large impacts on society. The framework offers important insights, especially to hotel owners, management and brands that are committed to sustainability and that are interested in applying business principles to environmental and societal challenges while increasing the overall competitiveness of their companies. Finally, the S-WELL business sustainability framework can be considered a significant contribution to strategy formulation in an era that will only grow in importance and significance to practitioners in the hospitality industry over the next decade.

References

Beckett, R. & Jonker, J. (2002). Accountability 1000: A new social standard for building sustainability. *Managerial Auditing Journal*, 17(36), 36–42.

Blanco, E., Lozano, J., & Ray-Maquieira, J. (2009). A dynamic approach to voluntary environmental contributions in tourism. *Ecological Economics*, 69(1), 104–14.

Bohdanowicz, P., Zanki-Alujevic, V., & Martinac, I. (2004). *Attitudes Towards Environmental Responsibility among Swedish, Polish and Croatia Hoteliers*. Conference proceedings. Esbjerg, Denmark: BEST tourism think tank IV.

Bronn, P.S. & Vidaver-Cohen, D. (2009). Corporate motives for social initiative: Legitimacy, sustainability or the bottom line? *Journal of Business Ethics*, 87, 91–109.

Carroll, A.B.& Shabana, K.M. (2010). The business case for corporate social responsibility: A review of concepts, research and practice. *International Journal of Management Reviews*, 12(1), 85–105.

Caterer & Hotelkeeper (2010). 25 ways to turn your guests green. *Caterer & Hotelkeeper*, 200.4648: 34–38. Business Source Elite: EBSCO. 2014.

Chong, H.G. & Verma, R. (2013). Hotel sustainability: Financial analysis shines a cautious green light. *Cornell Hospitality Report*, 13(10), 6–13.

Deale, C.S. (2013). Sustainability education: Focusing on hospitality, tourism and travel. *Journal of Sustainability Education 2151–7452*, 4 (January), 34.

DEFRA (2010). *Measuring Progress: Sustainable Development Indicators 2010*. London: National Statistics Compendium Publication. Retrieved from http://www.apho.org.uk/resource/item.aspx?RID=94191, accessed 24 April 2013.

DGINS ESSC (2010). Sofia memorandum: Measuring progress, well-being and sustainable development. Retrieved from http://ec.europa.eu/eurostat/documents/118025/118126/Sofia+memorandum+final/989e8c0a-c762-47a5-b60a-0cbce8cbbc21, accessed 25 April 2014.

Dyllick, T. & Hockerts, K. (2002). Beyond the business case for corporate sustainability. *Business Strategy and the Environment*, 11, 130–41.

Dyllick, T. & Muff, K. (2013). Clarifying the meaning of sustainable business: Introducing a typology from business-as-usual to true business sustainability. Retrieved from http://ssrn.com/abstract=2368735, accessed 1 June 2014.

Eccles, R.G., Ioannou, I., & Serafeim, G. (2011). The impact of a corporate culture of sustainability on corporate behaviour and performance. Harvard Business School working paper, *HBS Working Knowledge*, 12–035 (November). Retrieved from www.hbs.edu, accessed 12 August 2015.

Elkington, J. (1997). *Cannibals with Forks: The Triple Bottom Line of 21st Century Business*. Oxford: Capstone.

Euromonitor International (2012). *Travel and Sustainability: Striking the Right Balance*. London: Euromonitor International.

Font, X. & Harris, C. (2004). Rethinking standards from green to sustainable. *Annals of Tourism Research*, 31(4), 986–1007.

Font, X., Garay, L., & Jones, S. (2014). Sustainability motivations and practices in small tourism enterprises. *Journal of Cleaner Production*. Retrieved from http://eprints.leedsbeckett.ac.uk/146/1/Font%20Garay%20Jones%20JCP%20pre%20publication%20version.pdf, accessed 28 April 2014.

Foresight Mental Capital & Well-Being Project (2008). *Final Project Report—Executive Summary*. London: The Government Office for Science.

Freeman, R.E. (1984). *Strategic Management: A Stakeholder Approach*. Boston, MA: Pitman.

Friedman, M. (1970). A Friedman doctrine: The social responsibility of business is to increase its profits. *New York Times Magazine*, 13, 33.

Fulton, M., Kahn, B., & Sharples, C. (2012). Sustainable investing: Establishing long-term value and performance. DB Climate Change Advisors, Deutsche Bank Group. Retrieved from www.dbadvisors.com, accessed 8 August 2014.

Goldstein, K.A. & Primlani, R.V. (2012). Current trends and opportunities in hotel sustainability. *HVS Sustainability Services* (February). Retrieved from www.hvs.com, accessed 27 April 2014.

Goodno, J.B. (1994). Eco-conference urges more care. *Hotel and Motel Management*, 209(1, 3 and 22).

Gray, R., Owen, D., & Adams, C. (1996). *Accounting and Accountability: Changes and Challenges in Corporate Social and Environmental Reporting.* Hemel Hempstead: Prentice Hall.

Griffin, J. & Mahon, J. (1997). The corporate social performance and corporate financial performance debate. *Business and Society*, 36(1), 5.

Haanaes, K., Arthur, D., Balagopal, B., Kong, M.T., Velken, I., & Hopkins, M. (2011). Sustainability: The "embracers" seize advantage. *MIT Sloan Management Review and BCG Research Report* (winter).

Harrison, D. (ed.) (2001). *Tourism and the Less Developed World: Issues and Case Studies.* New York, NY: CABI Publishing.

Hart, S.L. (1995). A natural-resource-based view of the firm. *Academy of Management Review*, 20(4), 986–1014.

Hart, S.L. & Milstein, M.B. (2003). Creating sustainable value. *Academy of Management Executive*, 17(2), 13.

Hashmi, Z.G. (2014, May 7). The Lancaster London case study survey.

Hashmi, Z.G. & Muff, K. (2014). Rethinking corporate sustainability within the "well-being" context: The "COGWHEEL" sustainability framework. *Building Sustainable Legacies*, 2, 67–96

Hitchcock, D. & Willard, M. (2009). *The Business Guide to Sustainability: Practical Strategies and Tools for Organizations* (2009 ed.). London: Earthscan.

Hobson, K. & Essex, S. (2001). Sustainable tourism: A view from accommodation businesses. *The Service Industries Journal*, 21(4), 133–46.

Hoffman, A. & Bansal, P. (2012). *Business and the Natural Environment.* Oxford, UK: Oxford University Press.

Holliday, C. (2001). Sustainable growth, the DuPont way. *Harvard Business Review*, 79(8), 129–32.

Kalisch, A. (2002). *Corporate Futures: Consultation on Good Practice: Social Responsibility in the Tourism Industry.* London: Tourism Concern.

Kernel, P. (2005). Creating and implementing a model for sustainable development in tourism enterprises. *Journal of Cleaner Production*, 13, 151–64.

Kirk, D. (1998). Attitudes to environmental management held by a group of hotel managers in Edinburgh. *Hospitality Management*, 17, 33–47.

Korhonen, J. (2003). Should we measure corporate social responsibility? *Corporate Social Responsibility and Environmental Management*, 10(25), 39.

Landrum, N.E. & Edwards, S. (2009). *Sustainable Business: An Executive's Primer.* New York, NY: Business Expert Press.

Larson, A.L., Teisberg, E.O., & Johnson, R.R. (2000). Sustainable business: Opportunity and value creation. *Interfaces*, 30(3), 1–12.

Layard, R. (2005). *Happiness: Lessons from a New Science.* London, UK: Penguin.

Livesey, S.M. & Kearins, K. (2002). Transparent and caring corporations?: A study of sustainability reports by The Body Shop and Royal Dutch/Shell. *Organization & Environment*, 15(3), 233–59.

Margolis, J.D. & Walsh, J. (2001). *People and Profits?: The Search for a Link between a Company's Social and Financial Performance.* Mahwah, NJ: Lawrence Erlbaum Associates.

McDonough, W. & Braungart, M. (2000). A world of abundance. *Interfaces*, 30(3), 55–65.

McGehee, N.G., Wattanakamoichai, S., Perdue, R.R., & Calvert, E.O. (2009). Corporate social responsibility within the US lodging industry: An exploratory study. *Journal of Hospitality & Tourism Research*, 33(3), 417–37.

Michaelson, J., Abdallah, S., Steuer, N., Thompson, S., & Marks, N. (2009). National accounts of well-Being: Bringing real wealth onto the balance sheet. Retrieved from www.nationalaccountsofwellbeing.org, accessed 26 April 2013.

Mill, R. & Morrison, A. (1997). *The Tourism System: An Introductory Text* (1997 ed.). Dubuque, IA: Kendall Hunt.

Mirvens, P. & Googins, B. (2009). *Moving to Next Generation Corporate Citizenship*. Berlin: CCCD Century for Corporate Citizenship Deutschland.

NBS (Network for Business Sustainability) (2012). Innovating for sustainability: A guide for executives. Retrieved from www.nbs.net, accessed 6 May 2014.

NEF (2011). Measuring our progress. Retrieved from www.neweconomics.org/publications/measuring-our-progress, accessed 24 April 2013.

Nidumolu, R., Prahalad, C., & Rangaswami, M. (2009). Why sustainability is now the key driver of innovation. *Harvard Business Review* (September), 57–64.

ONS (Office for National Statistics) (2011). *Measuring What Matters: National Statistician's Reflection's on the National Debate on Measuring National Well-Being*. London: The National Archives. Retrieved from www.ons.gov.uk/ons/rel/wellbeing/measuring-national-well-being/discussion-paper-on-domains-and-measures/measuring-national-well-being---discussion-paper-on-domains-and-measures.html, accessed 25 April 2013.

Orsato, R.J. (2006). What does it pay to be green? *California Management Review*, 48(2), 127–43.

Porter, M. & Kramer, M. (2011). Creating shared value: How to reinvent capitalism and unleash a wave of innovation and growth. *Harvard Business Review*, January–February, 62–77.

Rappaport, A. (1998). *Creating Shareholder Value* (1998 ed.). New York: Free Press.

Reinhardt, F. (1998). Environmental product differentiation: Implications for corporate strategy. *California Management Review*, 4(4), 43–73.

Ricaurte, E. (2011). Developing a sustainability measurement framework for hotels toward an industry-wide reporting structure. *Cornell Hospitality Report, Center for Hospitality Research*, 11(13).

Roberts, S. & Tribe, J. (2008). Sustainability indicators for small tourism enterprises: An exploratory perspective. *Journal of Sustainable Tourism*, 16(5), 575–94.

Sasidharan, V., Sirakaya, E., & Kerstetter, D. (2002). Developing countries and tourism eco-labels. *Tourism Management*, 23, 161–74

Thanh, V.M. & Bosch, O.J.H. (2010). Systems thinking approach as a unique tool for sustainable tourism development: A case study in the Cat Ba biosphere reserve of Vietnam. *International Society for Systems Sciences*, Wilfrid Laurier University, Waterloo, ON, Canada, 18–23.

Toth, R. (2002). Exploring the concepts underlying certification. In M. Honey (ed.), *Ecotourism and Certification: Setting Standards in Practice*. Washington DC: Island Press, 73–102.

UN Global Compact (2013). Accenture CEO study on sustainability 2013: Architects of a better world. Accenture and United Nations Global Compact. Retrieved from www.unglobalcompact.org, accessed 12 August 2015.

Van Marrewijk, M. (2003). Concepts and definitions of CSR and corporate sustainability: Between agency and communion. *Journal of Business Ethics*, May, 95–105.

Watkins, E. (1994). Do guests want green hotels? *Lodging Hospitality*, 21(4), 70–2.

Wöber, K. (2002). *Benchmarking in Tourism and Hospitality Industries: The Selection of Benchmarking Partners*. Wallingford, UK: CABI

8

The Swiss ibex sustainability scheme

A comprehensive sustainability orientation for hotels

Arthur Braunschweig

E2 Management Consulting AG, Switzerland

Domenico Saladino

Saladino Umweltprojekte, Switzerland

The "ibex fairstay" is a label for hotels denoting the hotels' level of sustainability performance and management. In a comparative study, the ibex fairstay was seen as one of the best sustainability labels in tourism. Some 55 hotels and hostels are certified against the "ibex" method, a dozen of which with the highest "platinum" level. The methodology allows a hotel to assess—and ultimately to improve—its sustainability level in five dimensions: management, economic, environmental, societal and regional/cultural. The ibex fairstay is built similarly to the ISO management standards (9001 and 14001), but focuses on actual content compared to management system. A full management system according to the Swiss Tourism Quality Programme can be built up with the ibex fairstay as well, leading to the highest (QQQ) level. The ibex fairstay improves the quality of management as much as it spurs improvements towards more sustainable performance of hotels. The chapter describes the ibex fairstay structure, as well as some detailed analyses of hotels' performance in selected environmental and societal issues, such as energy, waste and staff-related management. In addition, the chapter presents learnings from participating hotels and across all ibex certified houses.

Introduction

To bring broad sustainability orientation into the hotel business—a key industry of Switzerland—and use its innovation potential, the local NGO "ö-plus" in 2001 asked the authors of this chapter to develop a full sustainability assessment for hotels: the "ibex fairstay" scheme and label.[1] Today, some 50 hotels use the ibex for the assessment, improvement and labelling of their environmental, social, cultural, financial and management performance. In 2010, a broad comparative study by Lucerne University on sustainability schemes for hotels and tourism[2] identified the ibex fairstay as one of four top sustainability labels globally.

Figure 8.1 **The ibex fairstay logo**

Sustainability in the Swiss hotel sector

Sustainability is a widely discussed topic in Switzerland, supported by societal convictions, a generally high quality of life and adherence to the legal framework. The Swiss hotel and tourism organizations have, to some extent, supported sustainability orientation for many years, mainly with an environmental focus. Formal uptake among hotels was limited, though, with some ten EU-flower labels, 50 ibex labels and some self-declared environmental hotels. In this combination, the ibex is the only broad sustainability assessment.

The major quality scheme in Swiss tourism, "Q"[3], which exists in three levels (Q to QQQ), covers sustainability issues to a limited extent. While hotel chains often use the ISO management standards (ISO 9001 for quality management, ISO 14001 for environmental management), the Swiss Q label has supported the entry of smaller organizations such as individual hotels, cable cars, local bus lines, etc. into the quality management world.

1   Braunschweig, A. & Saladino, D. (2006/2009/2012). *Steinbock-Label. Schweizer Nachhaltigkeits-Label für Hotels. Fragebogen zur Zertifizierung für Steinbock-Label, Qualitäts-Gütesiegel Stufe III, EU-Umwelt-Zeichen* (unpublished). For some background information see: www.steinbock-label.ch. Note that, until 2012, the ibex scheme was named in its various language versions, i.e. 'Steinbock' in German and 'Bouquetin' in French.

2   Barth, M. & Weber, F. (2010). *Nachhaltigkeitslabels in Tourismus und Hotellerie, Schlussbericht.* Luzern: Institut für Tourismuswirtschaft, Hochschule Luzern.

3   See Fédération Suisse du tourisme STV-FST, www.swisstourfed.ch, search term 'programme qualité', or direct link to (French version) http://www.swisstourfed.ch/index.cfm?parents_id=939, accessed 24 June 2014).

To encourage uptake of the ibex, its methodology was enlarged over time and today can include certification against the EU-flower label and/or the Swiss QQQ at the same time. In addition, various other sustainability-oriented programmes and labels can be found among Swiss hotels and tour operators' signage of hotels. Examples range from the general industry standards on environment (ISO 14001), food safety (ISO 22000) and organizational health and safety (OHSAS 18001),[4] to the international sector label "Green Globe", against which 11 Swiss hotels are currently certified,[5] the European Eco-label for hotels,[6] to local or even individual sustainability charters.[7]

The structure of the ibex: Ecology, society, culture, finance, management

The ibex fairstay scheme[8] consists of:

- A systematic assessment in five dimensions: environmental; social; cultural and regional; financial; and management quality

- The assessment of performance in all these dimensions

- A certification system, with triannual external audit and independent certification board

The ibex assesses a hotel based on criteria and on activities, in all five dimensions mentioned above. With better performance and more activities, a hotel gets a higher ranking, from bronze (= entry level) to platinum ibex. Roughly a dozen out of some 55 hotels and hostels currently carry a platinum ibex.

Examples of performance assessment and of activity assessment are given in Table 8.1.

---

4   See e.g. http://www.swissotel.com/news/green/swissotel-sustainability-report, accessed 28 August 2014.
5   See http://greenglobe.travel/category/switzerland, accessed 28 August 2014.
6   See http://www.ecolabel-tourism.eu or http://www.bafu.admin.ch/recht/00245/12705/index.html?lang=en&msg-id=7644, for its application in Swiss tourism.
7   See e.g. with the new Andermatt resort, which includes the "Chedi" Hotel (http://www.andermatt-swissalps.ch/en/about-us/sustainability.html, accessed 28 August 2014), or the Davos InterContinental Hotel, which is part of the IHG hotel group and its "green engage" programme (http://www.ihg.com/intercontinental/hotels/gb/en/davos-dorf./zdvda/hoteldetail/about-the-hotel/green-engage, accessed 28 August 2014), to name just a few.
8   See http://ibexfairstay.ch, accessed 20 June 2014. Information on the certification can be found under "ibex fairstay".

Table 8.1 **Examples of criteria used for the ibex fairstay assessment**

	Performance Assessment, e.g.	Activity Assessment, e.g.
Management quality	Targets and goals on multiple sustainability areas Quality improvement groups	Strategy Quality management Fostering of (various) staff capabilities Mystery checks
Environmental quality	Energy cons. per guest night Water cons. per guest night Soil use per bed Share of organic F&B (food and beverage)	Share of freshly cooked food Waste management Rain water use TVs etc. are off (not on stand by) Daylight/shadowing of rooms Quality of building materials Teaching energy issues to kitchen staff Ecological quality of chemicals used
Regional quality	Share of regionally produced F&B Share of guest arrivals with public transportation	Regional food specialties Staff command of local languages Offering bikes, electric cars, etc. to guests Cooperation with local cultural groups/ regional cultural programmes for guests
Social quality	Disabled access Number of apprentices Positions offered to disabled staff Staff training	Fair trade labelled F&B Vegetarian dishes offered regularly Radiation sensitivity (phones, LAN) Minimal space of living quarters for staff Fruit and vegetables offered to staff Safety training for staff
Economic quality	Turnover per staff FTE Cash flow	Share of returning guests Budgeting, investments planning Insurance management

The inclusion of ecological and social aspects in a sustainability scheme would seem obvious in the current understanding of sustainability. The ibex, however, includes all sustainability areas and also assesses the economic performance of the hotel. Based on a theoretical sustainability concept for companies,[9] economic performance considers service quality as well as financial results (i.e. market and financial performance). This feature—assessing economic performance as part of sustainability—has a very different meaning for different types of hotels: while hotel chains usually have a more or less centralized management system, which obviously will cover financial performance aspects, individual hotels in many cases lack (financial) management know-how and structures. In Switzerland, this can clearly be seen by the fact that numerous individually owned hotels are actually not profitable enough to ensure mid-term financial stability. As "sustainable" means the capacity to survive, it seemed absolutely necessary to include the financial health

9   Schmid-Schönbein, O., Rufer, D. & Braunschweig, A. (2004). Nachhaltigkeitsmanagement: Von den Zinsen statt vom Kapital leben; English translation of the article: Living off interest, not capital. *iO new management*, 05, 16–23; http://www.e2mc.ch/images/stories/e2_bilder/downloads/artikel_io_e.pdf

in the ibex assessment scheme: It is neither advisable to excel ecologically and go broke, nor to excel financially while polluting the environment. Therefore, the ibex label includes performance in all sustainability areas—including economic.

The ibex fairstay also contains a check of the environmental legal compliance of the hotel; this is an element taken over from the ISO 14001 environmental management standard and adapted for the hotel industry (currently for Switzerland).

A first small introductory self-test on all sustainability dimensions of a hotel can be accessed online.[10] For the hotelier, this list of performance criteria and activities serves as a checklist, and at the same time contains numerous ideas for continuous improvement. But a hotel also needs data and other information to assess performance. Therefore, many hoteliers show strong feelings about the ibex—either because they see it as a great improvement opportunity, or because they feel put off by the work demanded.

Comparison of the ibex with other standards

A comparison of the ibex fairstay scheme with other approaches relevant on the Swiss market can be seen in Table 8.2 (for a more detailed analysis see Barth & Weber, 2010).

The ibex is performance oriented—which differentiates it from the usual system and process orientation of e.g. ISO 14001 or the European EMAS (Eco-Management

Table 8.2 **The ibex fairstay compared with other sustainability labels and management standards—Scopes**

Assessment Areas	Ibex Fairstay	EU Eco-label[1]	Green Globe[2]	ISO 14001	Swiss Tourism Q Labels
Management	+++	-	+++	++	+++
Ecology	+++	+++	+++	++	-
Society	+++	-	+++	-	+
Regional culture	++	-	+++	-	-
Finance	+++	-	+	-	++
Service quality	+	-	-	-	+++
Hospitality sectors	+ (hotels, hostels, clinics)	++ (hotels, hostels, camping, etc.)	+++ (12 standards)	+++ (all sectors)	+++ (all tourism sectors)

10 http://ibexfairstay.ch > "FR(ench)" > ibex fairstay > Test succinct (French) or > Zertifizierung > Kurztest Nachhaltigkeit (German), accessed 20 June 2014.

and Audit Scheme).[11] And the ibex is very broad—as compared to e.g. the environmental Eco-label of the EU, the EU-flower or organic (food) labelling schemes. But the ibex is no simple marketing scheme. A high ibex level proves high sustainability performance, yet a guest may miss a specific element, as the ibex demands broad orientation but very few "must-haves".

Table 8.3 shows and compares a few sample specifics of a few selected standards and labels.

On a more general level, the GSTC (Global Sustainable Tourism Criteria) aim at setting a common level for sustainability labels and schemes. In its "hotel and tour operators" version,[12] the ibex is not yet among the so-called GSTC-recognized standards. But it would seem that the ibex fulfils the GSTC, as the ibex permits certification against the Austrian Eco-label, which in turn is already GSTC-recognized. If international tour operators will increase their demand for hotels' sustainability orientation, voluntary GSTC recognition certainly become an agenda item.

What hoteliers say about the ibex

Three types of hotels can be seen participating:

- Top-level, five- and four-star hotels striving for top management quality
- Hotel chains aiming for a broad management focus
- Sustainability oriented, intrinsically motivated hoteliers

Some 80 Swiss hotels have passed certification, 55 of which currently participate in the scheme.[13] Feedback regularly shows the ibex's wide array of improvement possibilities—in top-level five-star hotels as well as in more simple ones. A recent survey among a few participating hoteliers yielded similar results:

- *A neutral sustainability challenge*: Across hotels—be it in the large top-class hotel "Schweizerhof" (Lenzerheide), the Swiss Youth Hostels or the small cooperative "Salecina" (Maloja)—the ibex is considered a valuable, broad, external and neutral assessment basis. It helps where hotel management is actively interested in what nowadays is called CSR. The wide array of specific measures (proposals) helps to continuously improve performance over time

---

11 The EMAS of the EU is similar to the ISO 14001 scheme, as it contains the ISO 14001 provisions and adds some others, such as a public environmental statement. As Switzerland is not a EU member state, EMAS is not relevant for Swiss hotels.

12 See http://www.gstcouncil.org/en/gstc-criteria/criteria-for-hotels-and-tour-operators.html, accessed 7 November 2015.

13 See http://ibexfairstay.ch, accessed 23 June 2014.

Table 8.3 **The ibex fairstay compared with other labels and standards—Assessment approaches and examples**

Examples of Specifics	Ibex Fairstay	EU Eco-label	Green Globe	ISO 14001
Scope	· Broad sustainability orientation	· Environment	· Broad sustainability orientation	· Environmental management
How improvement gets evaluated	· Improved key figures (c.30) on numerous sustainability issues · More measures implemented	· Reach resource use and emission limits · Implement measures	· Implement policies and programmes in predefined sustainability areas · Assess performance	· Implement policies and programmes · Assess performance
Freedom for the hotel to choose on how to implement the scheme	· Issues are predefined · Policies and measures are developed by the hotel · For Swiss Q-scheme, quality policies are mandatory	· Measures are all predefined (and partly mandatory)	· Issues are predefined · Policies and measures are developed by the hotel	· All individual: the hotel sets scope, goals and measures
What is mandatory?	· Legal compliance · ibex ranking only possible with measures in all sustainability area	· Many specific ecological measures	· Legal compliance · Policies in all sustainability areas	· Legal compliance · Environmental management system (policy, targets, controlling, etc.)
Example: Energy consumption and efficiency	· Electricity use: key figure is assessed · Fossil energy use: key figure is assessed · Various measures (e.g. type of lamps; stand-by management in guest rooms; own renewable energy production; etc.) are assessed	· Mandatory measures include e.g. electricity production mix; type of lamps used; types of electric appliances bought	· Energy management is mandatory · Measurement is mandatory · Energy efficiency measures (self-defined) must be shown · Renewable energy sourcing is encouraged	· (Not mandatory) Energy is usually a key element of the environmental management system · Measurement is mandatory
Example: Integration of and into local culture	· Incorporation of local culture (architecture, food, ownership, cultural activities, etc.) is assessed	--	· Incorporation of local culture (architecture, food, staff, trade, etc.) is assessed	--
Example: Sustainable construction and design	· Legal compliance (mandatory) · Various measures are assessed (environmental construction; biodiversity/greening of plots; use of "sustainable" materials; etc.)	· Legal compliance (mandatory) · Various measures (climate oriented building; greened roofs; etc.) are assessed	· Legal compliance (mandatory) · Various aspects are asked for (sustainable design and construction; protection of historic sites; etc.)	· Legal compliance (mandatory)

Example: Economic and social effects	· Various aspects are assessed (gender issues, e.g. salary; integration issues, e.g. re disabilities; education, e.g. apprenticeships; local sourcing; fair trade; etc.)	--	· Various aspects are assessed (protection of employees, children, etc.; local sourcing; fair trade; etc.)	--
Example: Economic performance of the hotel	· Financial state (e.g. cash flow, interest on capital)	--	--	--

- *Quite a challenge …*: Again both in larger as well as in smaller hotels, the ibex fairstay certification process creates some workload for which time has to be found. Even though over time it becomes easier to gather the information, it remains a challenge, especially when the responsible personnel change

- *Management quality*: The comparison between hotels and over time improves quality of management. For the Swiss Youth Hostel chain, this is a key advantage of the ibex. (On the other hand, the smaller "Sunstar" chain considers the benefits not large enough and ended participation after their first certification period)

- *Label bundling*: The ibex contains modules for two additional labels—the Swiss QQQ programme award and the European Eco-label—which can be certified in the same process. In addition to a few hotels, most Youth Hostels also chose to use this feature

Sustainability performance of ibex hotels

Ecology

For a scientific analysis of the sustainability level of hotels certified with the ibex compared to hotels not carrying the ibex label, similar data from certified hotels as well as from average non-ibex-certified hotels need to be compared. Such an analysis does not yet exist, basically because of a lack of access to non-ibex hotel data.

However, this first ever analysis of ibex hotels' performance[14] enables us to draw some conclusions. Overall, we can see that in a number of important issues, hotels

---

14 All results described in this chapter are based on the data of some 60 certifications of 40 hotels. For each issue, the respective available data was used, the number of available

carrying the ibex label show a performance that increases with an increasing ibex level, as the following analyses and comparisons indicate.

Energy consumption and energy cost vary widely among ibex hotels: cost of energy ranges between CHF 1 and almost CHF 6 per SU (service unit), a measure that includes both guest nights and warm dishes served.[15] Energy obviously is no core cost driver but, as it is a core environmental "footprint" driver, it is usually environmentally relevant regarding the hotel's own processes.[16] Regarding energy use (in kWh), we analysed the consumption per m^2 heated floor surface—in Switzerland called "energy reference area". The analysis on one hand related to climatic situation (expressed by the height over sea level; see Fig. 8.2) while on the other hand it related to service level (expressed by hotel stars; see Fig. 8.3):

As the climatic effects can to some extent be neutralized by a normalization according to height over sea level, no clear trend can be seen in Figure 8.2. On the other hand, a higher service level clearly indicates higher energy consumption (Fig. 8.3). Both the climatic effects (mainly from height above sea level) and the service

Figure 8.2 **Total energy use, relative to height above sea level**

Source: authors' own calculations

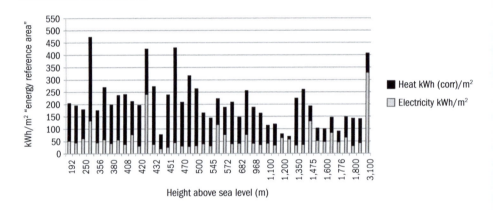

data points indicated with "n = xxx"). Certifications from 2007 and earlier were considered only where indicated specifically.

15 SUs are a measure developed to encompass GN (guest nights) as well as hot meals sold (1 GN = 1 SU; 3 hot meals = 1 SU).

16 There are no wide overall "ecobalances" (LCA for organizations) of hotels on a well-defined and comparable level available to date. However, comparing hotel environmental data with the results of other organizations' ecobalances (e.g. of financial institutions) leads us to the statement above. Analysis of the carbon footprint of hotels also supports this statement (see e.g. the greenhouse gas emission statement of the Sunstar Hotels, http://www.sunstar.ch/sustainability/overview, accessed 17 June 2014). Outside the hotel's core processes, F&B supply chains are the largest greenhouse gas emissions driver, and probably also the largest overall environmental impact driver, of the hospitality business.

Figure 8.3 **Total energy use/hotel stars**

Source: authors' own calculations

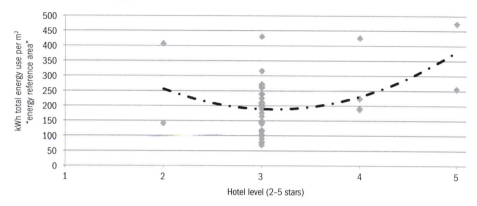

levels (expressed as hotel stars) can be seen in the regression lines of Figures 8.2 and 8.3.

Interestingly, total energy consumption does not seem to be mainly driven by climatic factors (Fig. 8.2), as these values are corrected for altitude. On the contrary: hotels lying on similar altitudes vary strongly in energy consumption per m², with values between <100 to >400 kWh/m² at similar altitudes.

The second analysis (Fig. 8.3), however, shows a direct relation between hotels' service levels (expressed by the two to five stars) and the total energy use (per m²). (The non-intuitive step from two to three stars is not significant, as data was available from only two two-star hotels.) On average, the energy use of four- to five-star hotels is about double compared to three-star hotels when counted per m². Yet energy-efficient four- and five-star hotels fare much better than non-energy-efficient three-star hotels!

On a side note it may be noted that energy expenditure increases with service levels, too: the average energy cost for three-star hotels is about CHF1.80 per guest night, a value that rises to about CHF4 for five-star hotels (not shown in Fig. 8.3).

As higher service levels mean more space per guest, the spread of "energy consumption per night" becomes even larger (Fig. 8.4), with averages of 20 kWh/guest night in three-star hotels compared to 60 kWh/guest night in four- and five-star hotels. Yet, even in this view, we find an energy-efficient four-star hotel (a city hotel in this case) consuming 20 kWh/guest night as well, and we find three-star hotels with energy uses of >40 kWh/guest night.

"Sustainable" F&B can be introduced independently of hotel size. Figure 8.4 shows that shares of regionally produced and/or organic ("bio") F&B vary across the board, almost independently of the size of the hotels (expressed with the annual F&B spend of a hotel). It is interesting to note that in 5 of the 41 hotels shown here, organic F&B (regional and not) accounts for more than 10% of all F&B. In nine hotels, its share is above 5%.

Figure 8.4 **Hotels' total specific energy use per guest night**

Source: authors' own calculations

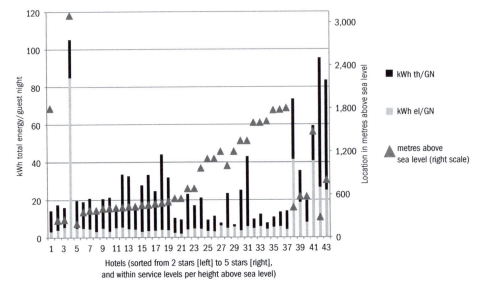

Figure 8.5 **Organic and regionally sourced food and beverage (F&B) relative to total F&B spent**

Source: authors' own calculations

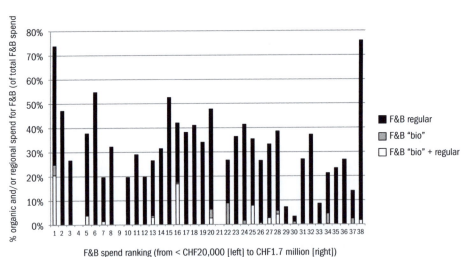

Societal aspects

Activities oriented towards staff and general society encompass, for example: improving access for disabled people/guests; training staff; and integrating staff with physical or mental disabilities. For 16 hotels, it has become possible to analyse the development of such activities over the period ranging from 2007/8 to 2010/11.

According to the analysis in Figure 8.6, two hotels showed substantial changes over the last certification period. One house ("St2") increased both accessibility for disabled people and job integration, while another house ("Sch1") has reduced its number of integrated jobs. Overall, the score of the 16 houses increased on all issues. Six houses increased their overall score in these areas, and four show a lower score. Five houses showed no change in these areas. (Numbers are rounded.)

Better than others?

Does the ibex level indicate better sustainability performance? For a first quantitative analysis, we looked at the cases of waste and water—and they show diverging results. In Figures 8.7 and 8.8, hotel data from certification years 2009–2012 is shown in the order of the hotels' ibex ranking, from silver on the left to platinum on the right.

Waste management improves with better ibex ranking (Fig. 8.7), as the falling trend line indicates: from 0.6 kg of residual waste per guest night to some 0.35 kg on the right (platinum) side of the graph. This is equal to almost 50% reduction of waste! At the same time, values vary very much, between 0.1 kg and >1 kg per guest night. These highest values indicate possible improvements, and the next recertification will show whether any improvement were realized.

Figure 8.6 **Changes in socially oriented activities (access; training; integration)**

Source: authors' own calculations

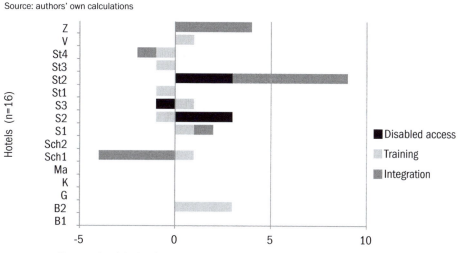

Change of activity levels over last certification period (c. 2007/8–2010/11; total changes: Access +5, Training +3; Integration +6)

Figure 8.7 **Waste production per guest night (kg)**

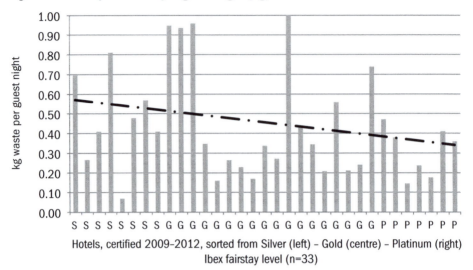

Hotels, certified 2009–2012, sorted from Silver (left) – Gold (centre) – Platinum (right)
Ibex fairstay level (n=33)

Water use per guest night (Fig. 8.8), however, does not seem to be connected with the ibex ranking. Most hotels show a consumption of around 120 litres per guest night. But ten hotels range(d) between 250 and >500 litres per guest night. This can be due to wellness areas with pool, sauna, etc., but it can also indicate technical problems.

If we now turn to the overall sustainability performance, expressed in overall ibex points, we can clearly see how the total values increase with rising ibex rankings (Fig. 8.9). This figure shows the numbers of ibex points of 38 ibex audits based on the 2009 or the 2012 methodology, respectively, sorted according to ibex ranking. Hotels with a silver ibex level (left side on Fig. 8.9) have a lower score than hotels with a platinum score (right side on Fig. 8.9). The top three results are about one-third better than the lowest three. Even bearing in mind that all hotels that participate in such a scheme have a certain interest in sustainability, the analysis indicates that higher ibex rankings are connected with a more intensive sustainability orientation.

An important detail of the ibex method can be recognized in Figure 8.9 as well. For each ibex level, a hotel must show performance in all sustainability areas. It cannot compensate weak performance in one of the five areas (see legend of Fig. 8.9) by superb performance in another area. If minimum levels per area are not reached, the ibex rank will be reduced. This explains why some hotels have a high overall score but are still positioned further to the left. The most obvious case is hotel No. 11, which shows a high overall score, but which has not enough ecological and regional scores to qualify for a "gold" rank. This rule implements to a certain extent the concept of "strong sustainability", where each area has to be cared for separately (as opposed to "weak sustainability", which allows for compensation between sustainability areas).

Figure 8.8 **Water use per guest night (litres)**

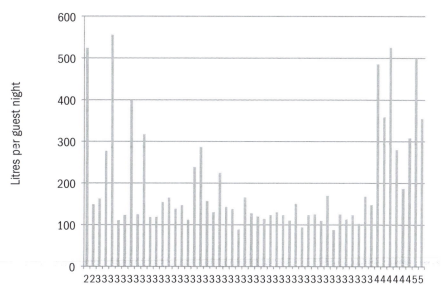

Hotels, sorted by hotel stars (from 2 at left to 5 at right, and by ibex fairstay level) (n=54)

When the ibex was developed in the late 1990s, it was the only tourism label assessing not only environmental but also all sustainability areas (as shown by the analyses of VISIT tourism eco-label project[17] in 2003ff.). Since then, other international sustainability schemes, such as the Green Globe or the GSTC, have also

Figure 8.9 **Overall performance across sustainability areas relative to ibex ranking**

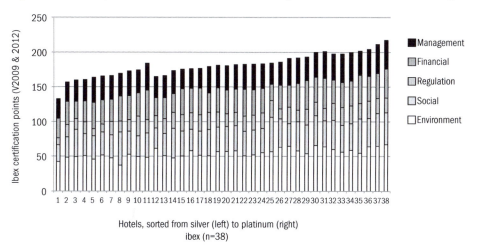

Hotels, sorted from silver (left) to platinum (right)
ibex (n=38)

17 See http://www.visit21.net, accessed 28 August 2014.

moved from pure eco-labelling to a broad orientation. The ibex still excels because it assesses real performance. Its application is therefore still relevant, certainly for hoteliers who want to go beyond using such a label for marketing and management purposes and who also want continuous real improvements on the ground.

Marketing or management tool?

A sustainability orientation often runs on two tracks. On the one hand, the hotel wants to attract guests. To the extent guests care for sustainable development and behaviour also in their holiday or business stay, a sustainability orientation may directly be used in marketing. Regular research indicates growing sustainability interest of tourists, but, as in most other markets, sustainability in the hotel will often not be a core criterion but rather an additional aspect for the selection of a hotel—after, for example, type of hotel, location and activity style. In line with this, the ibex label can be seen as a supportive, additional quality aspect, but it will attract guests only where sustainability performance is a core selection criterion. This is the case where the organizer of an event already has a sustainability orientation. Few of the ibex certified hotels have invested and innovated in this direction. A possibility would seem to present an ibex hotel, for example, as a sustainable seminar hotel. A recent example is the Hotel FerienArt in Saas-Fee. For a sweepstake in its *Naturstrom-Magazin*, the Zürich electricity utility offered a weekend in this top ibex five-star hotel as winner's prize.[18]

On the other hand, many other management approaches are not directly used in marketing either (starting with the accounting system, which is rarely used as specific accomplishment in marketing …), but rather is used to pave the way for better services, which then will be marketed. The ibex works perfectly in this way.

Improvement and innovation effects

The ibex fairstay aims to support improvement and innovation in the broadest sense—oriented towards all sustainability areas. Experience from hotels shows the following improvement and innovation drivers:

- Upon deciding to participate, the hotel's management often starts to analyse the system (the criteria and point distribution) and to look for improvement possibilities, in order to boost the initial ranking result

18 EKZ Elektrizitätswerk des Kantons Zürich (2014, June). *Naturstrom-Magazin*, 1(14), 19.

- Sometimes, a hotel gets a result close to a limit for a higher ibex rank. In this situation, the management will more often than not look for additional improvements, in order to overcome the rank limit

- In the assessment of sustainability-oriented measures, a hotel can add up to six additional measures not yet included in the ibex methodology, which can amount to 10% of the measures' total. Many hotels include such entries. On the one hand, after thorough auditor checks, this adds to the hotel's ibex result. On the other hand, such entries add knowledge to the methodology and over time get formally included (see Table 8.4)

It would be interesting to compare the improvement and innovation effects of the ibex to those of other labels. Due to the lack of such data across various labels, this is a task still to be accomplished.

A system for individual hotels or for hotel chains?

Both individual hotels as well as hotels from three chains have been certified to date. Is the ibex system easier or does it have a greater impact in either one of these hotel types? Discussions with various hoteliers and the various audit experiences have resulted in the following impressions.

The workload per hotel is smaller for chain hotels, as some information will always be managed centrally for all houses. This, in turn, also allows a chain to realize improvements and therefore potentially increase the ibex certification level on these very areas—the ones managed centrally—across all its members.

On the other hand, there are specific areas for which a decentralized management yields higher marks within the ibex scheme, especially regarding regional aspects (such as the regional sourcing of F&B or the regional part of invested capital), which will benefit—or at least put in a better starting position—an individual hotel.

Table 8.4 **Sustainability-oriented measures, developed by ibex certified hotels and mentioned as "additional measures" in the ibex certification process**

Examples of "additional measures" developed by hotels
· We periodically do internal audits of key processes
· We periodically analyse staff satisfaction and communicate results to our staff
· We regularly instruct/inform our kitchen staff about energy saving possibilities
· The hotel is actively engaged in a sustainability or environmental sector initiative, and the hotel or the hotelier represent sustainability issues in the public
· We actively inform our guests on how to reach the hotel and move locally with public transportation (e.g. timetables, free transport by hotel taxis, etc.)
· We have a neutral contact point for cases of conflict (e.g. between staff and superiors)
· We buy fair-trade labelled products

We also remarked that an individual hotel, whose management understands sustainability issues and which is committed towards a sustainability orientation, will more easily implement measures and therefore more easily reaches a higher ibex ranking. In a chain hotel, reaching the platinum level is possible as well, if local management is firmly committed to do so.

International application?

The ibex fairstay can currently be certified for Swiss hotels. It could easily be expanded for hotels in countries with similar characteristics, especially regarding climate and the legal system. For example, hotels in Germany, Austria, France and northern Italy, and also in Benelux, Poland and the Baltic states, could use the ibex methodology as it is, except for the legal compliance check.

For use in countries that differ considerably from central Europe, the methodology would have to be adapted more thoroughly, as, for example, the environmental aspects—energy consumption, water use, waste and recycling treatment—would warrant a detailed review to ensure reasonable results.

Institutional uptake in Switzerland

The Swiss hotel association, one of the central tourism organizations in Switzerland, has recently included the ibex fairstay scheme as one way of proving environmental and/or sustainability orientation.[19] The association defined two types: "green living", which should represent a mostly environmental orientation of the hotel; and "sustainable living", which stands for an broad approach. Of the 46 hotels identified as having "sustainable living" in mid-June 2014, all but four carry the ibex fairstay label. Of the more easily attainable "green living" category, about half of the hotels entered via the ibex label.

In addition, the ibex today is an accepted method to obtain the highest-quality management label ("QQQ") of the Swiss Tourism Association.[20] While it certainly

---

19 See http://www.swisshotels.com/?l=en > "Specialisation": "Sustainable living" as well as "Specialisation: Green Living"; details can best be found in the respective application form http://www.hotelleriesuisse.ch/files/docl/Antragsformular_Green_Living-Hotel_1.doc, accessed 24 June 2014.

20 See Fédération Suisse du tourisme STV-FST, www.swisstourfed.ch (e.g. direct link to http://www.swisstourfed.ch/index.cfm?fuseaction=sprachewechseln&sprache=fr&parents_id=1060), accessed 24 June 2014.

took a long time to have the ibex included into the traditional hotel assessment schemes, this was finally reached in 2012.[21]

As in many highly developed countries, the Swiss market recognizes numerous eco-labels across all markets and goods, a situation that in turn provoked numerous label-comparing studies and websites. The most well-known local assessment of sustainability labels, Labelinfo.ch, reached a moderate quality conclusion,[22] while the German Verbraucher-Initiative called it "recommended".[23]

Hotel or destination sustainability?

The ibex fairstay certifies the sustainability level of a hotel. From a guest's point of view, the sustainability of the hotel is very much bound up with the sustainability of the region in which it is situated. A sustainable hotel in the midst of coal mines or fossil or nuclear power stations seems difficult to imagine … Yet one hotel usually cannot influence development of the whole destination, and to delay development of more sustainable tourism until a whole destination buys in is equally unhelpful. The ibex cannot solve this problem, but contains a number of criteria and measures that are directed towards enlarging the sustainability orientation of a whole destination. If a hotel finds partners for sustainability, it will allow them to jointly improve their own ibex ranking, thereby improving the destination's overall sustainability. Examples could be the development of recycling facilities, of local and regional public transport or other transport alternatives, the sourcing of F&B, the development of local/regional cultural activities, etc.

So while the ibex clearly measures the hotel, it opens and strengthens sustainability potentials for the destination.

The future

In order to allow for a simplified entry into the ibex system, the ibex office prepares a simplified system, the "ibex basic" (as compared to the full "ibex fairstay"), focusing on core elements, without external audit. This should reduce the hotel's

---

21 See Fédération Suisse du tourisme, STV-FST: *Anerkennung eines Qualitätsmanagement-Systems—Voraussetzungen und Hinweise*, Bern, not dated. http://www.swisstourfed.ch/Files/q_programme/qqq/reglement_qqq_anforderungen_de.pdf, accessed 24 June 2014).

22 http://labelinfo.ch/de/labels?&compare=124,123,60,35,72,165,147,136, accessed 28 August 2014.

23 http://www.reisekompass-online.de/reisecheck.php/cat/8/aid/8/title/Durchblick_bei_Labeln, accessed 24 June 2014.

initial workload, while retaining the broad performance assessment. Experience will show if this will encourage uptake of the ibex, or if it dilutes the approach by weaker interpretation of the rules.

Should the ibex be seen as a tool to oversee multiple important management areas? Or should the ibex allow direct marketing towards guests and tour operators? These are the two main expectations for the market. While the ibex is perfectly designed for the former, the latter needs the hotel's own and specific creativity.

Various ideas were raised to adapt the methodology to other markets, be they hotels in other markets, other tourism sectors (cable cars, tour operators, tourism destinations), or other sectors altogether. Such projects need a combination of sector know-how, assessment know-how and funding.

Interesting research would be to analyse the sustainability performance levels of ibex versus non-ibex hotels. This obvious question is, however, not easy to answer, as non-ibex hotels will be less inclined to collect their data.

For sustainability improvement, performance assessment is important, yet it is not widely developed across sectors. Outside the hotel sector, the ibex can serve as a role model for such assessments. Within the hotel sector, the ibex can help hotels to become sustainability flagships, as with Fredi Gmür from the Swiss Youth Hostels and Andreas Züllig from the "Schweizerhof" in Lenzerheide.

Figure 8.10 **Four ibexes, carved in ice**

Source: Hotel FerienArt, Resort & Spa, Saas-Fee

References

Barth, M. & Weber, F. (2010). *Nachhaltigkeitslabels in Tourismus und Hotellerie, Schlussbericht.* Luzern: Institut für Tourismuswirtschaft, Hochschule. (Note: The study and a presentation of the results can be retrieved from http://www.hotelleriesuisse.ch/files/pdf1/label_teil1.pdf, http://www.hotelleriesuisse.ch/files/pdf1/label_teil2.pdf, http://www.hotelleriesuisse.ch/files/pdf1/Durchblick_im_Label_Dschungel.pdf, all accessed 24 June 2013.

Braunschweig, A. & Saladino, D. (2006/2009/2012). Steinbock-Label. Schweizer Nachhaltigkeits-Label für Hotels. Fragebogen zur Zertifizierung für Steinbock-Label, Qualitäts-Gütesiegel Stufe III, EU-Umwelt-Zeichen (unpublished). For some background information see http://ibexfairstay.ch, accessed 18 November 2015; "Zertifizierung", "Zertifizierung ibex fairstay".

EKZ (Elektrizitätswerk des Kantons) (2014). *Naturstrom-Magazin,* 1(14). Retrieved from http://www.ekz.ch/naturstrom-magazin, accessed 24 June 2014.

EU Commission Green Store (2014). The EU Eco-label for tourist accommodations. Retrieved from http://ec.europa.eu/environment/ecolabel/documents/hotels.pdf and http://www.ecolabel-tourism.eu, both accessed 28 August 2014.

Fédération Suisse du tourisme STV-FST, see below: Swiss Tourism Federation.

Greenglobe Travel, http://greenglobe.travel/category/switzerland, accessed 28 August 2014.

GSTC (Global Sustainable Tourism Council) (2014). Criteria for hotels and tour operators. Retrieved from http://www.gstcouncil.org/en/gstc-criteria/criteria-for-hotels-and-tour-operators.html, accessed 15 November 2015

Ibex fairstay, http://ibexfairstay.ch, accessed 23 June 2014.

ISO (International Organization for Standardization) (2004). *ISO 14001:2004: Environmental Management Systems—Requirements With Guidance For Use.* Geneva: International Organization for Standardization.

Labelinfo.ch, http://labelinfo.ch/de/labels?&compare=124,123,60,35,72,165,147,136, accessed 28 August 2014

Reisekompass-online.de, http://www.reisekompass-online.de/reisecheck.php/cat/8/aid/8/title/Durchblick_bei_Labeln, accessed 15 August 2015.

Swiss Hotel Association, http://www.swisshotels.com/?l=en > "Specialisation": "Sustainable living", accessed 24 June 2014.

Swiss Tourism Federation (n.d.). Anerkennung eines Qualitätsmanagement-Systems—Voraussetzungen und Hinweise, Bern, http://www.swisstourfed.ch/Files/q_programme/qqq/reglement_qqq_anforderungen_de.pdf, accessed 24 June 2014.

Voluntary Initiatives for Sustainability in Tourism (Visit), http://www.visit21.net, accessed 28 August 2014.

Hotel and hotel chain websites

Andermatt resort, http://www.andermatt-swissalps.ch/en/about-us/sustainability.html, accessed 28 August 2014.

IHG hotel corporation, http://www.ihg.com/intercontinental/hotels/gb/en/davos-dorf./zdvda/hoteldetail/about-the-hotel/green-engage, accessed 28 August 2014.

Sunstar Hotels, http://www.sunstar.ch/sustainability/overview, accessed 23 June 2014.

Swissotel, http://www.swissotel.com/news/green/swissotel-sustainability-report, accessed 28 August 2014.

9

Can hotels educate consumers about sustainability?

John Hirst

Durham University Business School, UK; Higher Education Academy, UK

This chapter presents, as a case study, the International Enterprise Project (IEP) at Durham University Business School, delivered as an MBA elective combining problem-based learning with action research, focusing on *The Quest for Sustainable Business* (Visser, 2012). Participants undertake fieldwork in Sri Lanka where their host company for the last three years has been ASHH (Aitken-Spence Hotel Holdings) which operates a range of eco-hotels, including the five-star Heritance Kandalama. This has given participants deep insights into the challenge of operating eco-hotels, particularly concerning sustainability marketing and reporting, customer perceived value and service excellence, staff training/development and community involvement. Instead of a product-oriented view of sustainability and quality performance, they gain a more holistic and interconnected worldview, encompassing economic, cultural and political issues and a belief in the interconnectedness of mind, body and spirit. This chapter addresses the question of how eco-hotels can leverage customer attitudes and behaviour in the same way and whether they should seek to do so. If this is part of their purpose, then understanding how to motivate their customers relies on an understanding of the differences between people and how they perceive and respond to the sustainability agenda. We conclude that service in sustainability hotels needs to be understood as a relational process in which consumers and hotel operators co-create memorable transformative experiences, which may require hotels to have the courage to confront the "attitude-behaviour" gap and customers to step outside their "comfort zone". While environmental and social performance contribute to the brand-equity of sustainability hotels, their success depends on the bond they construct with customers, based on mutual respect and trust, and how they integrate this into their product offerings and sustainability marketing approaches.

Introduction to education for sustainable development

This chapter seeks to link theory to practice in a way that can make a distinctive contribution to the quest for sustainability (HEA, 2013, p. 2). Guidance for providers of ESD (Education for Sustainable Development) defines ESD as "enabling learners to develop the knowledge and understanding, skills and attributes needed to work and live in a way that safeguards environmental, social and economic well-being, both in the present and for future generations". This guidance recommends "experiential and interactive approaches", which encourage learners to develop and reflect on their own values, beliefs and norms, and can lead to "transformational" or "epistemic" learning. ESD encourages students to:

- Consider the concept of global citizenship and what this might mean in the context of their own discipline

- Consider the concept of environmental stewardship and what this might mean in the context of their own discipline

- Think about issues of social justice and equity, and how these relate to ecological and economic factors

- Develop a future-facing outlook, learning to think about consequences of actions, and how systems and societies can be adapted to ensure sustainable futures.

At Durham University Business School, we have been incredibly fortunate in developing a partnership with a company in Sri Lanka that operates a range of sustainability hotels. A team of MBA students taking a course in International Enterprise visits this company each year to carry out a one-week mini action-research project, developed in conjunction with, and supported by, the hotel company's management team. Their studies have sought to holistically explore linkages between sustainable business practices and product/service delivery dimensions of the customer experience as viewed by management and customers. In the process, our students become hotel customers themselves, but their experience goes way beyond that of most tourists, because they are privileged to "see the world behind the product". Their input to co-creating their own "customer experience" thus constitutes a highly "experiential and interactive approach" (HEA, 2013, p. 11).

Further details about this course can be found in the *UN PRME Inspirational Guide* (PRME, 2014). The course includes a range of teaching and learning methods that are considered to be particularly effective in terms of preparing learners for their experience and then engaging them in it. They are intrinsically motivated by their interest in learning more about sustainable enterprise in a country that most of them have never visited before, and they are extrinsically motivated by the desire to do well in their assessment. The course includes various methods recommended by the HEA (Higher Education Academy), as shown in Table 9.1.

Table 9.1 **Implementation of teaching and learning methods identified as particularly effective for ESD**

Pre-course reading	*The Quest for Sustainable Business* (Visser, 2012)
Lectures	Themed around the "five managerial mindsets" (Mintzberg & Gosling, 2003), "design-thinking" (Martin, 2009) and "Buddhist economics" (Schumacher, 1993, pp. 38–46)
Case studies	Case studies of the hotel company in Sri Lanka
Stimulus activities	Videos, stories, poetry, team-building exercises
Simulation	Application of theoretical models to practical situations (using a Ketso Toolkit)
Experiential project work	Development of an action-research project in conjunction with the hotel company with the intention of making it a "lived experience"
Place-based learning	Visiting the hotel company's head office and some of its hotels (in Sri Lanka) to conduct research in a context that stimulates "experienced reflection" (Mintzberg, 2009)

The course is constructively aligned to achieve the learning outcomes identified in the HEA/QAA's (Quality Assurance Agency) *ESD Guidance* (HEA, 2013, p. 9), that is, development of the learners':

- Capacity for independent, evidence-based integrated thinking as the foundation for developing their personal code of ethics

- Awareness of their own values and how they influence their interpretation of and approach to addressing sustainability problems

- Ability to clarify their own views on ways that sustainability can be achieved in different local and global communities and circumstances and communicate them to a variety of audiences

- Ability to reflect upon and analyse their own values, decisions and behaviours

- Ability to evaluate the consequences of their own actions, and of collective actions, and be able to use this information strategically to develop new social norms where appropriate

- Willingness to take responsibility for their own actions, reflect on them and make transformational changes

- Ability to adopt a proactive approach and a belief in their ability to take action

- Ability to engage listeners, convey complex concepts clearly and generate buy-in from audiences

- Capacity to be flexible and adapt their problem-solving mindset to fit changing or unforeseen circumstances

- Vision, motivation and resourcefulness, enabling them to contribute towards developing a more sustainable society, both locally and globally

- Commitment to lifelong advancement in their ESD

For our learners, the experience has certainly been memorable, and in some cases life-changing, as indicated by the following quotations from two students' reflective papers:

> It has been an experience I shall never forget. I feel that a lasting legacy has started that has penetrated right into my heart. I know this will make my life forever fruitful.

> The IEP [International Enterprise Project] module gave me a chance to experience a totally different culture with its own socio-political context that has revealed an approach to business that appeals to me. The blend of caring and sustainability suggests a more balanced approach which puts an equal emphasis on the means as well as the ends, which I shall take forward with me.

Relevance to hotels

There are greater similarities between the educational experience and the tourist experience in regard to sustainability than perhaps we realize. In fact, some authors positively recommended hotel managers to "invest in educating consumers about sustainability" (Kovaljova & Chawla, 2013, p. 1). "Achieving sustainability will depend ultimately on changes in behaviour and lifestyles, changes which will need to be motivated by a shift in values and rooted in the cultural and moral precepts upon which behaviour is predicated" (UNESCO-EPD, 1997, p. 34). Kovaljova & Chawla (2013, p. 8) conclude that customer ESD provided by hotels can indeed play a significant role in helping customers to "remodel their values and find true value in sustainability". However, they warn that this "can only result in successful outcomes if it is sincere and embedded in all aspects of the organization's operations and management". They urge hotels to "rethink strategic policies and practices" by creating "strategic partnerships" with their customers to co-create experiences that will inform and help each other to "achieve genuine sustainability".

The idea that hotels can also be "providers of Education for Sustainable Development" may seem rather far-fetched. However, on reflection, the objectives of both tourism and education share a similar focus on the provision of experiences that create memories which become who we are (Kahneman, 2011). Our sense of identity is based almost entirely on how we relate to our existential context and on our memories, which together shape our values, beliefs and norms (Stern, 2000) and translate into how we think, feel and perceive, and, in turn, condition our cognitions, attitudes and behaviours (Ajzen, 1991). Both HEIs (higher education institutions) and, increasingly, hotels focus on influencing their SVPs (stakeholder value perceptions) by engaging with the cognitive, emotional and material drivers of their behaviour. Making and developing these connections is a profoundly educational process, closely resembling the aims of "psychographic marketing", which also recognizes the significance of the mental processes that drive consumer behaviour.

Customer service value creation

For both educational establishments and hotels, the emphasis is now on long-term relations and on addressing the various dimensions of stakeholder value. CSV (customer service value) is significantly affected by intangibility and perishability, so enduring value is primarily vested in memory of the experience (reinforced by photographs and other memorabilia) and lifestyle value impact. The "lived experience" that both hotels and (particularly residential) universities provide is their key product offer. CSV can be classified as shown in Table 9.2.

Theories of customer value creation and co-creation (Prahalad & Ramaswamy, 2004; Gentile *et al.*, 2007) suggest a complex interrelationship between the company and the stakeholder, whereby the stakeholder becomes part of the service/product through engagement with it. In other words, the stakeholder experience emanates from the interaction between the stakeholder and the product/service provider from which associated values are derived (Addis & Holbrook, 2001).

A life-time value approach has always been acknowledged by educational establishments, which segment their stakeholders according to various categories of membership relating to progression within the institution: freshers and under-graduates (junior common room members); post-graduates (middle common room members); graduates (alumni association members); honorary graduates and teaching masters/doctors (senior common room members), etc. Each of these constituencies is laden with both symbolic and emotional value, serving to create a lasting bond between students and their "alma mater", which institutions can leverage to their advantage (e.g. by soliciting philanthropic donations) through relationship marketing. At the time of writing, the UK government is also exploring ways of extending this to repayment of student loans. While hotels also seek to enrol guests into various clubs and loyalty schemes, these tend to be more overtly instrumental (materialist/hedonistic value) and focus on attracting repeat business. In terms of the MCV (multi-faceted customer value) model (see Table 9.3), the long-term interest of hotel establishments tends to focus on "self-oriented value", whereas the long-term interest of educational establishments is more likely to focus on "other-oriented value", which the government is now opportunistically seeking to exploit.

Operationalizing sustainability and ESD: The dilemma of troublesome knowledge

Both HEIs and hotels are clearly interested in putting sustainability into effect, and there are many similarities, particularly between hotels and residential universities: for example, they can both subscribe to the UK's Green Tourism Accreditation Scheme and the Hospitality Assured Standard. Hotels can also participate in the Green Globe Award, while the HEI equivalent is the Green Gown Award. There are a wide range of practical initiatives relating to UK HEIs, ranging from the regulatory Higher Education Funding Council's Strategy for Sustainable Development (to which the author contributed at the consultation stage), to the developing partnership between the EAUC (Environmental Association of Universities & Colleges), which initiated the LiFE index, and the NUS (National Union of Students), which initiated the Green Impact Model. The latest initiative is the "sustainability literacy test", which is intended to provide an internationally recognized standard for

Table 9.2 **CSV classification**

CSV classification	Service/product characteristics
Materialistic	A service/product that provides functionality and good value for money compared to other competitor's offerings, often determined in the selection stage
Hedon(ist)ic	A service/product that provides pleasurable experiences e.g. by sight, hearing, touch, taste or smell, thereby stimulating delight, enjoyment: e.g. first impressions of a hotel
Affective	A service/product that provides an emotional experience (happiness, excitement, satisfaction) that creates an affect memory (particularly peak-end experiences): e.g. the feel-good factor that a hotel inculcates
Cognitive	A service/product that engages customers' conscious thinking processes: e.g. what they think about the quality of the hotel service/product itself or the local surroundings
Pragmatic	A service/product that engages customers in the practical act of doing something, e.g. the usability of the service/product itself, or participation in hotel leisure activities: e.g. tours, lectures, classes
Lifestyle	A service/product that synchronizes with the customers' system values, beliefs and norm:, e.g. through identity, lifestyle behaviour and well-being
Symbolic	A service/product that emphasizes the customers' dignity/esteem through relationships, either with staff or other customers: e.g. by promoting a sense of belonging through connectedness or membership that transcends a purely instrumental relationship

Table 9.3 **The multi-faceted customer value model**

Source: Peloza & Shang, 2011, p. 3.

Multi-faceted customer value	Intrinsic value	Extrinsic value
Self-oriented value	Quadrant 1 Utility/hedonism (materialistic) The experience satisfied my wants for vfm, functionality and pleasure	Quadrant 3 Status/esteem (symbolic) The experience enabled me to demonstrate my concern for the well-being of others/nature
Other-oriented value	Quadrant 2 Virtues/aesthetics (affective) The authenticity and awe of the experience impressed and inspired me	Quadrant 4 Philanthropy/spirituality (transformative) The experience enabled me to make a contribution to a better/more sustainable world

assessing the learning outcomes of ESD, as well as evidencing the embeddedness of ESD within institutions themselves (an increasingly important aspect of educational accreditation schemes: for example, EQUIS (Excellence in Management Development Quality Improvement Scheme) and AACSB (Association to Advance Collegiate Schools of Business). While the tourism industry lacks the coherence of the UK Higher Education system, many sustainability initiatives—for example, the Green Hotels & Responsible Tourism Initiative—are clearly being developed and implemented in parallel. The international sustainability literacy test is an initiative that has the potential to become an internationally recognized assurance standard spanning ESD providers in both education and tourism.

Research to date suggests that sustainability value per se is not yet a primary driver of choice, although sustainability marketing is increasingly creating opportunities that will make it so in the future. In another sector, the Sustainability Apparel Coalition has established a ground-breaking scheme based on sustainability value-chain indices, a process that is helping to inform stakeholders of the "world behind the product". Its Higg Index provides an internationally recognized tool for benchmarking against industry standards, continuous improvement, organizational learning, customer lifestyle value enhancement, impact assessment, due diligence, etc. An educational board game has also been developed to introduce learners (university students and industry employees) to the methods by which the Higg Index contributes to sustainable value-chain management and hence sustainable consumption. The UK's Green Tourism scheme seeks to serve a similar purpose but has no direct ESD component, whereas Green Globe has established its own Academy providing training courses to support its members in achieving compliance with the following training requirement of its certification standard:

> All personnel receive periodic training regarding their role in the management of environmental, sociocultural, health and safety practices. The success of the business' sustainability management system depends on the effective integration and internalization of the system by employees at all levels (Green Globe Academy).

The dilemma for ESD, irrespective of who provides it, is how to handle "troublesome knowledge"—knowledge that is discordant, disturbing and discomforting, that requires us to step outside our "comfort zones" and not only acknowledge that we are part of the problem which needs to change, but also then to do something about it. The Durham University module referred to above is constructively aligned with Mintzberg's framework for management education (Mintzberg, 2009), based on five manager mindsets:

- Reflective mindset—questioning the way we think

- Global mindset—questioning how our contexts influence us

- Analytical mindset—questioning how our systems and structures shape us

- Collaborative mindset—questioning the quality and purpose of our relationships

- Action mindset—questioning how we initiate/respond to challenges and change

This framework recognizes that we shape our environment at the same time as our environment shapes us. This phenomenon is captured by the biological term "autopoiesis", which Luhmann (1990) holds can be extended to the social domain. Acknowledging this also helps us to address concerns that we over-internalize or individualize the problems that our context imposes on us (Smail, 1997). Smail blames Freud for opportunistically exploiting this by converting victims into patients (and fee-paying clients), thus disempowering them still further, rather than challenging the existentialist problems themselves. Although we are all part of the unsustainability problem, neither burying our heads in the sand nor psychotherapy provide any solution—there is no option but to encounter "troublesome knowledge" (Meyer & Land, 2003), particularly that which is required to enable nine billion people to achieve sustainable livelihoods while at the same time not compromising the ability of future generations to do the same. ESD is therefore inherently "troublesome" and the educational institutions in which it is taught become critical lenses through which its complexity is illuminated. They become a disruptive threshold across which learners must pass from one state of awareness—for example, "that God's in his heaven and all's well with the world" (Yevtuschenko, 2008, p. 52)—to another—for example, that in truth we're like "the sleepwalker whistling a happy tune as he ambles towards the abyss" (McGilchrist, 2010, p. 237).

Comprehending the abyss of unsustainability

Critically contrasting the "abyss" of unsustainability, associated with Enlightenment rationality, with the optimism of natural human care and understanding prior to their corruption and distortion by greed and self-aggrandizement, can be traced as far back as William Blake's 18th-century *Songs of Innocence and Experience*. The poet stands beyond innocence and experience, taking an objective stance from which to identify and address the illusions of both perspectives. While he deplores tyrannical domination systems that derive power from injustice and inequality (and deepen the abyss of unsustainability), he also protests about the silent majority's unwillingness to confront them; his poetry provides insights relevant to sustainability about the way in which separate modes of social control combine to create a co-dependency that is profoundly destructive of our ability to sustain humanity, that is, to "build Jerusalem" on "green and pleasant land", in his verse.

McGilchrist (2010) explains how these separate but co-dependent modes of social control mirror the operation of the hemispheres of the human brain itself. The brain is an autopoieic organism that both shapes, and is simultaneously shaped by, its context, to which McGilchrist relates the history of the Western world. In particular, he argues that increasing left hemisphere dominance manifests itself in the efficiency cult, which progressively reduces everything to its utilitarian or functional value, institutionalized by social control and domination systems, exactly as poetically portrayed in Blake's *Songs of Innocence and Experience*. The consequence of this, McGilchrist (2010) concludes in much the same way as Blake, is that higher order values (also associated with sustainable development), for example, of social and environmental justice, compassion, virtues, aesthetics, love and anything conceived of as "sacred", are either commodified or otherwise dismissed and denigrated as useless, pointless or counterproductive. While Blake blames the state of innocence for its weakness in colluding with this state of affairs, a theme that Nietzsche (1889) carries to extremes in "Also sprach Zarathustra", McGilchrist attributes it to the dysfunctionality caused by the suppression of right hemisphere neural processing. He contends that the modern (particularly Western) world is the result of "the attempt by the left hemisphere to take control of everything" (McGilchrist, 2010, p. 402) in the interests of utility and efficiency, in which people "are simply interchangeable parts of a mechanistic system" (McGilchrist, 2010, p. 431). Two years after publication of Norbert Wiener's prophetic treatise on "The human use of human beings", novelist Kurt Vonnegut predicted that which McGilchrist now observes: "Machines and organization and pursuit of efficiency have robbed ... people of liberty and the pursuit of happiness" (Vonnegut, 1992, p. 292).

McGilchrist concludes that the "return to the right hemisphere is of ultimate importance" (McGilchrist, 2010, p. 437) for any hope of "saving paradise" (Brock & Parker, 2012), personified as "Gaia" (Lovelock, 2000)), which is dependent on higher order (right hemisphere) values being served, not ruled, by lower order (left hemisphere) values, personified by "Mammon" (in the Bible). The novel *The Business* captures the global market's all-consuming demand for allegiance, "There is a strict rule in *The Business* that all executives — anybody above Level Six — must renounce all religious affiliations, the better to devote themselves to pursuing a life dedicated to Mammon" (Banks, 1999). As Capra explains:

> The global market is really a network of machines—an automaton that imposes its logic on all human participants. However, in order to function smoothly, this automaton has to be programmed by human actors and institutions. The programmes that give rise to the new economy consist of two essential components—values and operational rules. The global financial networks process signals that assign a specific financial value to every asset in every economy ... However, underlying all evaluations is the basic principle of unfettered capitalism: that moneymaking should always be valued higher than democracy, human rights, environmental protection or any other value. Changing the game means, first and foremost, changing the basic principle (Capra, 2003, p. 185).

McGilchrist (2010) contends that the goods of the Western world (i.e. what we value) have been predicated on left hemisphere dominance, which has itself been predicated on the practices of the Western world (i.e. what we do). This is also consistent with the philosophical concept of how "goods internal to practices" are developed (MacIntyre, 2000). McGilchrist (2010) argues that many eastern societies have preserved better balanced hemispherical strategies, reflected in more symbiotic relationships between economic, social and environmental responsibility (e.g. "Buddhist Economics"), but that these are now being destabilized by Western capitalism's reductionist influence (particularly short-term profiteering) through globalization, resulting in widespread social and environmental disruption and destruction. McGilchrist therefore calls for a rebalancing of our hemispherical processing strategies, which corresponds to demands from management disciplines for a better balance of analytical and intuitive thinking in management education (Martin, 2009), and from scientific disciplines for a better balance between assertive and integrative values and cognitions (Capra, 2003). In customer value perception terms, this translates into the need for a better balance between self-oriented (egoistic) values and other-oriented (altruistic) values.

Capra (2003) emphasizes that:

> The current form of global capitalism is ecologically and socially unsustainable, and hence politically unviable in the long run. More stringent environmental regulations, better business practices and more efficient technologies are all necessary, but they are not enough. We need deeper systemic change (Capra, 2003, p. 184).

Vonnegut, however, captured the essence of why "epistemic" change is so problematic:

> For generations they've been built up to worship competition, and the market, productivity and economic usefulness, and the envy of their fellow men—and boom! It's all yanked out from under them ... Their whole culture's been shot to hell ... [they need to regain] the feeling of participation, the feeling of being needed on earth—hell, *dignity*" (Vonnegut, 1992, pp. 90, 92).

As Capra concludes:

> The values of human dignity and ecological sustainability ... form the ethical basis of reshaping globalization ... .globalization has no future unless it is designed to be inclusive, ecologically sustainable and respectful of human rights and values (Capra, 203, p. 188).

Traversing the abyss of unsustainability: A Sri Lankan case study

The foregoing discussion is intended to frame the contrast between instrumental Western (left hemisphere) approaches to sustainable business and those that Durham University students experience in Sri Lanka, which reflects a predominantly right hemisphere approach and which effectively "blows" their (largely Western) minds(ets). As critically objective observers, these post-graduates encounter a business phenomenon that is entirely new to them. It transforms the theory from their pre-course reading in *The Quest for Sustainable Business* (Visser, 2012) into a practical realization of this quest—a model of authentically sustainable hotel management that also provides them with a practical vision of how the "abyss of unsustainability" might be crossed. While many Western businesses respond to sustainability concerns by simply bolting on some social and environmental objectives in a rather reactive approach to getting on the sustainability bandwagon, these MBAs come face to face with a holistic integrated approach, embedded in deeply held beliefs, values and norms. In stark contrast to Bank's (1999) portrayal of Western business thinking that encourages leaders to "amoralize" their operations and offerings, they find that the beliefs and values of senior executives actually set the ethical tone of the organization. They observe that emotional discourse about moral conscience, social responsibility and ecological protection are positively encouraged rather than evaded. They are even more astonished by the revelation that, given the degree of long-term effort and commitment to sustainability embedded in a whole range of sustainability practices, the hotels make very little use of this instrumentally in their publicity or marketing strategies.

They discover a business model based on Capra's concept of sustainability, which postulates:

> That sustainability—in ecosystems as well as human society—is not an individual property, but a property of an entire web of relationships: it involves a whole community. A sustainable community ... What is sustained in a sustainable community is not economic growth or development, but the entire web of life on which our long-term survival depends. It is designed so that its ways of life, businesses, economy, physical structures and technologies do not interfere with nature's inherent ability to sustain life" (Capra, 2003, pp. 187–8)

A strong sustainability-consciousness and a long-term focused sustainability strategy have been the Sri Lankan company's hallmarks since long before the global paradigm shift towards sustainable development. Throughout its history, of over 150 years, the company has always sought ways of making a meaningful and relevant contribution to all of its key stakeholders, thereby generating sustainable value and enduring relationships. By mid-2009, it began implementing a group-wide integrated sustainability policy, which enabled the formal and structured integration of sustainability into its business model. The policy encompasses 19 clauses on compliance, ethical conduct, environment, community outreach, sustainable processes, governance, stakeholder engagement, quality, customer service, talent management, innovation, health and safety, human rights, information security, continuous improvement and credible reporting. The policy framework is implemented on a tiered basis, to ensure that basic requirements in all key areas are met. From a patchwork of sustainability initiatives tackled in different manners, the integrated policy now serves to blanket all areas identified as important for the sustainable growth of the organization, and ensures its implementation across

Figure 9.1 **The company's sustainability management structure**

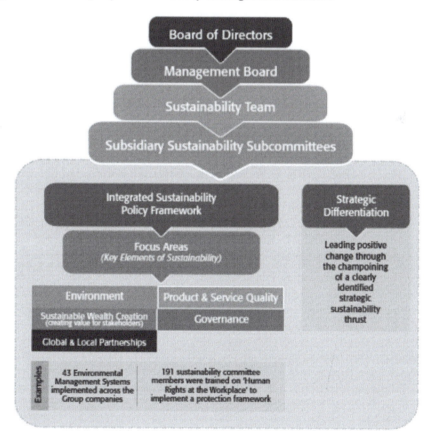

essential activities in all areas across the group. Simultaneously, subsidiary companies are required to pay closer attention to key areas specific to their operation, as per the impacts, risks and opportunities identified. The company has developed a rating scheme to assess the sustainability implementation standards of its various subsidiaries. This is presented to the sustainability team and the management board by way of a performance scorecard every six month:.

> Sustainable development requires an organization to look closely at its three pillars: economic, social and environmental performance: by first identifying the impact it has on each. The integrated policy was drafted looking at all areas of our operations where we can potentially impact the economic performance, natural environment and social sustainability. Using the integrated policy as a guideline we have or are in the process of implementing management systems to focus on mitigating any adverse impacts and strengthening the positive impacts in each of these spheres. We are currently looking at how we can improve this process by improving our stakeholder engagement practices and also by comparing our practices with the ISO 26000 guidelines (company's sustainability policy).

Tables 9.4 and 9.5 summarize the company's sustainability goals and priorities.

The strategic direction for this hotel company, over the short to medium term, involves consolidating and growing the traditional European market through product differentiation and competitive pricing, as that market continues to hold the strongest potential for Sri Lanka. However, it is also focusing on emerging markets, identified as having high potential while also concentrating on new specialized segments "such as nature, wildlife, wellness and medical tourism". The company recognizes that world tourism is shifting towards "an experiential model", with more travellers avoiding group travel and making greater use of online and technology platforms to "garner themselves better deals and more exciting tour options".

The company has provided leadership in environmental and social sustainability and has consistently benchmarked itself against international standards and best practices, winning numerous accolades and awards for its sustainability practices and achieving a range of related ISO certifications. It has become the yardstick for the entire region in environmental and social sustainability through its various management systems, policies, procedures and general practices by which it identifies and manages the environmental and social aspects of its operations. Central to this is organizational governance which, in line with ISO 26000 and the new CSR Pyramid (see Fig. 9.2), is regarded as both a core process itself as well as being the prime enabler of other core processes. The company's sustainability enablers include: an integrated sustainability policy framework; a sustainable procurement framework; integration of 7R principles throughout the company; food safety, energy and water saving policies; stakeholder engagement; community outreach; and integrated sustainability reporting. The company also invests in the continuous sustainability education (i.e. ESD) of its hotel employees to achieve the behavioural changes required to meet its sustainability targets and add value to its clients. It prides itself on the fact that its sustainability activities are conceptualized, directed

Table 9.4 Aitken-Spence's sustainability goals (2012–13)

Key elements	Environment	Sustainable wealth creation	Product/service delivery	Governance	Local and global partnerships
Goals	• Mitigate adverse environmental impacts from the operations using a scientific approach • Protect ecosystems impacted by the operations of our company • Increase energy efficiency and usage of energy from renewable and cleaner energy sources • Improve waste resource management • Develop adaptation strategies to tackle climate change effects on our business interests • Develop and implement good environmental programmes and policies	• Maintain strong economic performance • Establish and maintain a strong and competitive, skilled human resource • Community upliftment through employment creation, local purchasing, child and elder care programmes • Infrastructure development • Review and revise the channels for all key stakeholders to provide feedback • Extend opportunities for skills development and lifelong learning for the employees and communities	• Ensure product/service responsibility and safety • Ensure the health and safety of all key stakeholders including employees, guests and clients • Engage with suppliers, contractors and other service providers to ensure all links within the supply chain network are aware of the group's values and commitments • Establish quality management systems aligned with internationally accepted standards	• Establish required governance structures • Review and revise group-wide code of ethics, policies, practices and procedures as per the risks, challenges and opportunities identified • Establish a workplace human rights protection framework • Maintain occupational health and safety systems within all group companies	• Internalize the ten principles of the UN Global Compact • Internalize the seven UN Women's Empowerment Principles • Maintain a GHG emission inventory and meet the requirements of the Caring for Climate initiative • Fulfil the commitment to the Global Compact Local Network • Increase awareness of global issues on a local platform • Develop a network of stakeholders with similar interests for knowledge sharing and to work on long-term strategy development

Table 9.5 Aitken-Spence's sustainability priorities (2012–13)

Key elements	Environment	Sustainable wealth creation	Product/service delivery	Governance	Local and global partnerships
Priorities for 12/13	• Reducing overall energy cost • Increasing resource efficiency • Zero waste dumping • Increase awareness of environmental sustainability among employees and other key stakeholders • Reduce withdrawal of freshwater by increasing efficiency of usage	• Increase engagement with key stakeholders to identify impacts and risks to plan adaptation and risk management strategies • Increase hours committed for skills development and lifelong learning of the employees • Engage in required skills development and improving the employability of target groups	• Carry out a customer perception study • Implement brand awareness and brand qualities within the employees • Strengthen the OHS risk management procedures of the strategic business units	• Implement the Human Rights protection framework • Internalize the seven Women's Empowerment Principles • Continue to review the established policies, procedures and general practices against ISO 26000 guidelines and improve areas vulnerable to potential risk	• Engage more effectively with entities within the Global Compact network • Increase awareness of the UN Global Compact principles, the Women's Empowerment Principles • Establish a carbon emission inventory and disclose data on emission reductions as per the Caring for Climate initiative

and managed entirely through internal expertise, driven by its own sustainability team, supported by subsidiary-level sustainability subcommittees.

Durham MBAs have evidenced the outcome of the company's sustainable development activities first-hand, wearing two hats as both customers and researchers. Although well prepared for their experience in advance, it always exceeds their expectations. Co-creating their itinerary with the company in an "experiential learning mode", they include visits to local schools, where they witness the educational support provided by the company, and observe its eco-park and recycling facilities, including a fertilizer plant, a paper factory and even a process for converting waste toothpaste into cleaning products! Reflecting on this interactive experience genuinely contributes to their ESD, particularly enhancing their understanding of ways of operationalizing industrial ecosystem theory (C2C). They are particularly impressed when they discover that the hotel's CSR manager moved to live in

Figure 9.2 **The new corporate social responsibility pyramid**

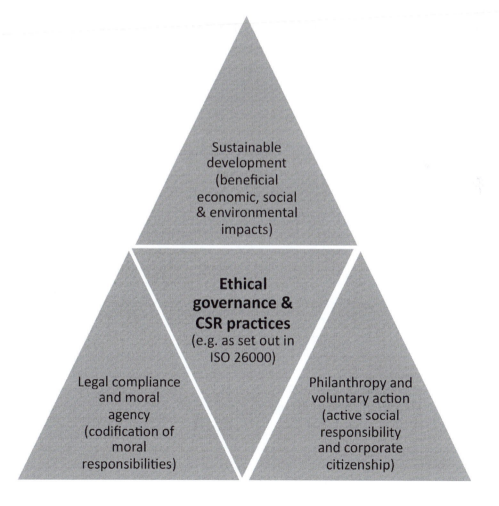

the local community, committing a great deal of time to working with community leaders, developing relationships of trust and open honest communication, to allay their fears about the impact of the hotel. This has provided a sound basis for future practice by ensuring effective engagement with community stakeholders, who now view the hotel as a positive enabler of sustainable livelihoods.

Implications for hotels

Our students also found some evidence that the company acts on Kovaljova & Chawla's (2013) recommendation that hotels should "invest in educating consumers about sustainability". It displays its environmental policy and the green philosophy behind its sustainability management approach in hotel rooms and social media sites "to educate guests". However, although there are some opportunities for customers to "see the world behind the product" as an "experiential learning" option, our students particularly recommend training staff to represent their learning about ESD to customers as a "win–win" opportunity. Research consistently shows that high employee engagement is correlated with customer satisfaction, customer retention and corporate performance (Deloitte's, 2010, p. 37).

> Brands are not built around the product but around the employees who deliver the service and (ideally) create a memorable experience ... The relationship between employees and customers is at the heart of the brand experience ... when the unity of interest is intuitive, with employees and consumers sharing the same passions, it is particularly powerful (Clegg *et al.* 2011, pp. 171, 174).

Other organizations have successfully unlocked the potential value of their staff as channels of communication: for example, the Austrian Forestry Corporation trained its 180 staff to communicate the company's sustainability vision to their 520,000 direct customer contacts and obtain feedback about how to improve their sustainability performance. Our students conclude that capitalizing on this approach would create better value for customers, the staff themselves and the hotels, thus effectively populating all quadrants of the MCV model (see Table 9.3).

While sustainability is becoming a key component of the tourism sector marketing mix, the conflict between left hemisphere (utility) values and right hemisphere (sustainability) values creates a cognitive dilemma. This translates into a pervasive distrust by consumers of marketing hype, which fails to convince them that green product offerings do anything to contribute to a better environment and, more damagingly, often exacerbates their perception that business makes a mockery of their social and environmental concerns by "greenwashing", resulting in a "value-action gap". For companies that have a genuine commitment to sustainability, this customer value-action gap is a significant deterrent to sustainability marketing, due to the fear that it may, counter-productively, arouse customer scepticism about the company's sustainability efforts.

Hotel managements are, therefore, often inclined to rely instead on the "lived experience" of their customers, and their reviews, to represent their efforts and commitment to sustainability. Fellow travellers perceive such reviews as more trustworthy and credible because their peers have nothing to lose from being honest about whether or not a hotel has fulfilled their expectations of service, amenities and sustainability, in contrast to a hotel's own marketing activities (Sparks *et al.*, 2013). Comments from social media sites influence 87% of visitors' choice of hotel (TripAdvisor, 2012). However, our students' analysis of online comments by customers from the hotels they visited in Sri Lanka revealed that the majority of consumers' comments focused on the hotel's friendly staff, beautiful surroundings and food quality, that is, on the product itself rather than on the "world behind the product". This suggests that the company's commitment to sustainability remains largely hidden from view, and yet research demonstrates that this is directly proportional to positive customer attitudes towards hotel sustainability initiatives.

The dilemma for sustainability hotels is, therefore, how to convince customers of the authenticity of their efforts and commitment without attracting the cynicism attributed to "green" rhetoric found in promotional materials (Frandsen & Johansen, 2001). The hotel sector could take a leaf out of the Sustainability Apparel Coalition's book by taking steps to develop ways of providing customers with a "behind the scene" perspective as well as putting more effort into preparing customers for "experiential learning" by "setting the scene" in advance. "Getting the consumer involved in the creation and delivery of sustainable value is one important way of harnessing consumer behaviour for sustainability" (Belz & Peattie, 2012, p. 103). Hotels employ engagement strategies to further their sustainability practices in both subtle and obvious ways, including positioning cards and brochures in hotel rooms as well as providing information on menus or brochures (Frandsen & Johansen, 2001), but this is customarily pitched at the level of "informating" associated with the MCV model's (see Table 9.3) quadrant 1. More recent research (Goldstein *et al.*, 2008) concludes that hotels can effectively engage more consumers in their sustainability practices by appealing to social identity effects, which correspond to the MCV model's (see Table 9.3) "extrinsic" social value quadrants 3 and 4.

Consumer identity is becoming particularly important in the positioning of sustainability oriented services in the marketplace (Belz & Peattie, 2012). Hotel companies, therefore, need to "drive environmentally responsible purchase behaviour" (Barber *et al.*, 2012, p. 282) by focusing on the "management of meaning", to create "a platform or arena in which negotiations about identity can take place" whereby the brand becomes "the interface between identity and image" (Clegg *et al.*, 2011, pp. 172–3). Barber *et al.* (2012, p. 297) found a "direct link between environmental consequences, their [customers'] concern for society as a whole, and the self-image that consuming environmentally friendly products would project, linking their strong values and beliefs to their self-image" which further confirms the validity of the MCV model (see Table 9.3).

By changing the message from "informating" to "transformating", and linking it to social value norms, customers can also be engaged through the medium of "social capital" (Putnam, 2000). Social capital is the medium for "collaborative consumption", which is one of the "ten ideas that will change the world" (Time, 2011). Social capital connects ("bridging social capital") and unites ("bonding social capital") customers in ways that can empower them to establish such norms and, at the same time, develop related affective and symbolic value (see Table 9.2) bonds which coalesce into a "unity of interest" or sense of common purpose and then solidify into social solidarity and accountability. This underlies the concept of "mindful consumption" (Sheth *et al.*, 2011), premised on challenging people's mindsets (thinking and behaviour) in the light of the personal, social and environmental consequences of unsustainable consumption, which takes us right back to the aims of ESD outlined at the beginning of this chapter.

Social networking technology now provides the means to leverage the transformational power of social capital to achieve social innovation through the relationship-building process. By giving consumers a voice, they can create their own "transformating" messages and contribute to developing the image of brands with which they identify. Social norms are also a significant motivator for customer support of sustainability initiatives, which cause-related marketing can help to strengthen. The hotel industry thus has the means to promote social and sustainability norms, contributing to many of the same aspirational learning outcomes as ESD, that is, a mindset which understands that more sustainable consumption is in the collective long-term interests of everyone. However, they should heed the research which demonstrates that, while learners (and customers) respond positively to a sense of participation and collective effort, they react badly to any attempt to induce guilt. The best responses were found to be achieved by empathic messages that connect with their own values rather than impersonal quasi-technical terminology: for example, by describing recycling in terms of "giving resources a second chance" (Belz & Peattie, 2012).

Much academic research focuses on the "business case for sustainability", that is, identifying to what extent guests are willing to pay a premium to enjoy a "green" hotel (Campanelli & Rizzo, 2009; Hann *et al.*, 2009; Han & Kim, 2010; Kang *et al.*, 2012). Peloza & Shang (2011) conclude that companies can gain competitive advantage by linking their CSR activities to increased customer value, or by developing new sources of customer value. Some of this research evidences a degree of customer circumspection, on the grounds that hotels are perceived to be making savings from, for example, less frequent changing of towels. Savvy customers quickly recognize "greenwashing" when they see it (e.g. one customer confessed to sticking post-it notes on his towels to verify the authenticity of espoused replenishment practice). Clegg *et al.* (2011, p. 400) attribute such scepticism to the wider distrust of business practices, "institutionalized in a legacy of exploitative organizational behaviour and misbehaviour" from which "past traditions loom nightmarishly large on their present actions, even when they are well intentioned".

The most commonly cited barrier to more sustainable consumption is customers' perceptions that their efforts are not worthwhile without commensurate effort and commitment being demonstrated by companies (and governments), and of false sustainability claims made by companies about their services (Belz & Peattie, 2012). Our students' research corroborates the importance of the way in which hotel managements incorporate and integrate "green" management practices into their policies and day-to-day operations in ways that are perceived as authentic from both internal and external perspectives of their customers' experience (James *et al.*, 2011). This strategy of embedding "a 360-degree view of sustainability within the business model" (Deloitte's, 2010, p. 42) builds the "green" image and reputation as integral to the overall customer experience. This resonates with the hotel philosophy of taking care of guests and the environment (Frandsen & Johansen, 2001) and is consistent with Sheth *et al.*'s (2011) notion of "mindful consumption". Research shows that once a guest has experienced a hotel that offers an exceptional experience, including a sustainability offering, they are more likely to expect the same thing from all hotels and are more likely to factor this normatively into their choices, either by selecting hotels that practise sustainability or by returning to ones that they have previously experienced, depending on their destination (Graci & Kuehnel, 2012; Chen & Peng, 2012). By educating their customers in sustainability, hotels both "foster the development of green tourism and promote its benefits to guests" and demonstrate their genuine commitment to sustainability, resulting in increased loyalty (Graci & Kuehnel, 2012), so maintaining the trust and credibility on which this relationship is founded is of the utmost importance.

Conclusion

This case study of a Sri Lankan hotel company demonstrates not only that sustainable hotels can deliver excellent standards of customer service, but also that they can contribute meaningfully to ESD (in this case for a group of critical-thinking Durham MBA students). It exemplifies the concept of "CSR 2.0 performance" (Visser, 2011) by embedding and integrating sustainability into its core operations in a way that positively impacts on all four quadrants of the MCV model (see Table 9.3). As Visser points out, CSR 2.0 necessitates developing an understanding of the "macro-level system (society and ecosystems)" in a way that changes attitudes and behaviours to optimize its chances of long-term survival. From this, we can conclude that hotels need to foster the notion that they and their representatives can act as change agents themselves and engage in collaborative efforts to advance sustainable development. They can leverage this through the paradigm change taking place from the "old plan and push economy to the new engage and co-create economy" (Tapscott & Williams, 2006, p. 31). Hotels are also particularly well placed to extend their offerings from "experiential" to "experiential learning" modes, based on the belief that "people interactive" institutions, which include both hotels and universities, can and do shape the world around them—Durham University's motto, which the author was instrumental in crafting, is "shaped by the past, creating the future". Like Ray Anderson's Interface, these organizations can motivate their stakeholders to begin climbing "Mount Sustainability" to create a sustainable future.

The transition from the established left hemisphere dominated world that subordinates the welfare of other species, future generations and the corporately excluded to the individual needs, rights and self-interested aspirations of affluent consumers will not be an easy ascent. Affluent lifestyles enjoyed at the expense of sustainable livelihoods are unsustainable. Stimulating right hemisphere strategies to better balance the way we think and perceive the world would be a step in the right direction towards realizing the vision of a sustainable planet economy consistent with the "Buddhist Economics" (Schumacher, 1993) that has a spiritual home in Sri Lanka. Durham post-graduates have witnessed this as a "lived experience" and, with it, the combination of VEGS (value creation, environmental integrity, good governance and societal contribution), which demonstrates "the qualitative and quantitative difference between other models of sustainable business and the CSR 2.0 DNA model" (Visser, 2012, p. 231). As Visser concludes, "the quest for a sustainable future is like a wheelbarrow. The only way we will make progress is if we pick it up and push forward" (Visser, 2012, p. 238). Hotels, as well as HEIs, must develop their own unique contribution to achieving this quest, and this chapter has sought to show that it can be done.

References

Addis, M., & Holbrook, M. (2001). On the conceptual link between mass customisation and experiential consumption: An explosion of subjectivity. *Journal of Consumer Behaviour,* 1(1), 50–6.

Ajzen, I. (1991). The theory of planned behaviour. *Organizational Behavior and Human Decision Processes,* 50, 179–211.

Banks, I. (1999). *The Business.* London: Little Brown.

Barber, N., Kuo, P.-J., Bishop, M., & Goodman, R. (2012). Measuring psychographics to assess purchase intention & WTP. *Journal of Consumer Marketing,* 29(4), 280–92.

Belz, F.-M., & Peattie, K. (2012). *Sustainability Marketing* (2nd ed.). Chichester: Wiley.

Brock, R., & Parker, R. (2012). *Saving Paradise.* Norwich: Canterbury Press.

Campanelli, A., & Rizzo, C. (2009). *Risks and Rewards for Building Sustainability Hotels.* London: Deloitte.

Capra, F. (2003). *The Hidden Connections.* London: Flamingo.

Chen, A., & Peng, N. (2012). Green hotel knowledge and tourists' staying behaviour. *Annals of Tourism Research,* 39(4), 2211–16.

Clegg, S., Carter, C., Kornberger, M., & Schweitzer, J. (2011). *Strategy: Theory and Practice.* London: Sage.

Deloitte (2010). *Hospitality 2015: Game Changers or Spectators?* London: Deloitte LLP.

Frandsen, F., & Johansen, W. (2001). The rhetoric of "green" hotels. *Journal of Linguistics,* 27(7), 55–83.

Gentile, C., Spiller, N., & Noci, G. (2007). How to sustain the customer experience: An overview of experience components that co-create value with the customer. *European Management Journal,* 25(5), 395–410.

Goldstein, N., Cialdini, R., & Griskevicius, V. (2008). A room with a viewpoint: Using social norms to motivate environmental conservation in hotels. *Journal of Consumer Research,* 35(3), 472–82.

Graci, S., & Kuehnel, J. (2012). How to increase your bottom-line by going green. Green Hotels & Responsible Tourism Initiative. Retrieved from http://green.hotelscombined.com/Pages/MainGreen/Downloads/green-hotel-whitepaper.pdf, accessed 9 November 2015.

Han, H., & Kim, Y. (2010). An investigation of "green" hotel customers' decision formation: Developing an extended model of the theory of planned behaviour. *International Journal of Hospitality Management,* 29, 659–68.

Hann, H., Hsu, L.-T., & Lee, J.-S. (2009). Empirical investigation of the roles and attitudes towards "green" behaviours in hotel customers' eco-friendly decision-making process. *International Journal of Hospitality Management,* 28, 519–28.

HEA (Higher Education Academy) (2013). *Education for Sustainable Development: Guidance (draft) For UK HE Providers.* York: HEA/QAA.

James, M., Miles, A., Nelson, M., Sledge, S., & Colakoglu, S. (2011). Going 'Green'! Exploring Customer Preference in the Hotel Industry. *International Journal of Strategic Management , 3* (2), 93-108.

Kahneman, D. (2011). *Thinking Fast and Slow.* London: Penguin.

Kang, K., Stein, L., Heo, C., & Lee, S. (2012). Consumers' willingness to pay for "green" initiatives in the hotel industry. *International Journal of Hospitality Management,* 31, 564–72.

Kovaljova, P., & Chawla, G. (2013). *Can Sustainability Really Add Customer Value? The Case of Hotel Ermiage, Evian-Les-Bains, France.* Proceedings from the International Conference on Hospitality and Leisure Applied Research. Lausanne: ICHLAR.

Lovelock, J. (2000). *Gaia: A New Look at Life on Earth* (Reissue ed.). Oxford: Oxford University Press.

Luhmann, N. (1990). *Essays on Self-Reference.* New York: Columbia University Press.

MacIntyre, A. (2000). *After Virtue* (2 ed.). London: Duckworth.

Martin, R. (2009). *The Design of Business.* Boston (Mass.): Harvard Business Press.

McGilchrist, I. (2010). *The Master and His Emissary: The Divided Brain and the Making of the Western World.* New Haven: Yale University Press.

Meyer, J., & Land, R. (2003). *Threshold Concepts and Troublesome Knowledge: Linkages to Ways of Thinking and Practising within the Disciplines.* Edinburgh: University of Edinburgh.

Mintzberg, H. (2009). *Managers Not MBAs: A Hard Look at the Soft Practice of Managing and Management Development.* San Francisco: Berrett-Koehler.

Mintzberg, H., & Gosling, J. (2003, November). The five minds of a manager. *Harvard Business Review,* 54–63.

Peloza, J., & Shang, J. (2011). Investing in CSR to enhance customer value. *Director Notes,* 3(3), 1–10.

Prahalad, C., & Ramaswamy, V. (2004). Co-creating unique value with customers. *Strategy and Leadership,* 32 (3), 4–9.

PRME. (2014). *UN PRME (UK & Ireland Chapter) Inspirational Guide .* Sheffield: Greenleaf Publishing.

Putnam, R. (2000). *Bowling Alone: The Collapse and Revival of American Community.* New York: Simon & Schuster.

Schumacher, E. (1993). *Small Is Beautiful: A Study of Economics as if People Mattered.* London: Vintage.

Sheth, J., Sethia, N., & Srinivas, S. (2011). Mindful consumption: A customer-centric approach to sustainability. *Journal of Academic Marketing Science*, 39, 21–39.

Smail, D. (1997). *Illusion and Reality: The Meaning of Anxiety.* London: Constable.

Sparks, B., Perkins, H., & Buckley, R. (2013). Online travel reviews as persuasive communication. *Tourism Management*, 39, 1–9.

Stern, P. (2000). Toward a coherent theory of environmentally significant behaviour. *Journal of Social Issues*, 56(3), 407–24.

Tapscott, D., & Williams, A. (2006). *Wikinomics: How Mass Collaboration Changes Everything.* New York: Portfolio.

Time. (2011, March 17). 10 ideas that will change the world: Today's smart choice. *Time Magazine*.

TripAdvisor (2012).

UNESCO-EPD (1997). *Educating for a Sustainable Future: A Vision for Concerted Action.* Thessaloniki: UNESCO.

Visser, W. (2011). *The Age of Responsibility: CSR2.0 and the New DNA of Business.* Chichester: Wiley.

Visser, W. (2012). *The Quest for Sustainable Business.* Sheffield: Greenleaf Publishing.

Vonnegut, K. (1992). *Player Piano.* London: Flamingo.

Wiener, N. (1954). *The Human Use of Human Beings: Cybernetics and Society* (Republication ed.). Boston (Mass.): Da Capo.

Yevtuschenko, Y. (2008). *Selected Poems.* London: Penguin Classics.

Part II
Case studies

10

A resort for generations— maintaining, protecting, renewing, improving

Tigh-Na-Mara Seaside Spa, Resort & Conference Centre, Parksville, British Columbia, Canada

Alison L. Dempsey, PhD

Vancouver, Canada

This case study examines how a small resort property set in a place of natural beauty is taking steps towards a sustainable future. The study focuses on three key themes: stewardship of the property and its environs; commitment to community; and continuity amid change. It provides insight into how smaller enterprises can have a positive impact while managing the challenges of cost, scale and profitability in a highly competitive sector.

Introduction

The case study

A sustainable economy and by extension a sustainable business is one that operates within a framework that incorporates economic growth, social equity and well-being, and environmental sustainability. Realizing the goal of a sustainable future depends on actions to reduce negative impacts and increase positive contributions on all three of these bases being taken by businesses and organizations, individually and collectively, and governments at the local, national and international levels. Examining how individual enterprises work towards more sustainable operations in practice can yield insight and learning key to sustainable business practice.

All businesses have unique attributes leading to case-specific approaches as well as issues and responses common within and across sectors. This case study is intended to exemplify how a single resort property is taking steps to maintain, increase and protect a commitment to a sustainable future through environmentally responsible activities that reduce the negative impact of operations and community-focused initiatives that make a positive social contribution while recognizing the inherent limitations and challenges of scale and cost for a smaller enterprise.

The study's focus is on three key themes that distinguish this property's commitment and approach to the challenges and opportunities presented by the ongoing cycle of "maintaining—renewing—protecting and improving", amid environmental, social and technological change, economic constraints and the pressures to ensure profitability in a highly competitive sector. These themes are:

- Stewardship of the property and its environs

- Commitment to community

- Continuity amid change

The property

Tigh-Na-Mara Seaside Spa, Resort and Conference Centre at Parksville, British Columbia is set within 22 acres of arbutus and fir forest adjacent to two miles of sandy beach on the natural shores of Vancouver Island on the Canadian west coast.

Over its nearly 70-year history, the property has grown and evolved with the changing times. From a property that in the middle of the last century comprised 11 acres and just 12 vacation cottages, Tigh-Na-Mara has expanded to its current 192 accommodation units constructed with natural tree logs, a restaurant, a lounge, conference space and one of the largest full-service spas in Canada.

In the resort's early days, amenities now considered as basic (e.g. telephones and televisions) were uncommon in visitors' own homes and would never have been expected at the resort. In fact, until the 1980s guests who wished to have a telephone or a television in their unit had to request one from the front office. Microwave ovens and dishwashers were installed only in the self-catering units during renovations in the 1990s, in response to visitor demand. Now, in keeping with the times and changing consumer demands, all units are equipped to meet telecommunication needs. Internet service is in every unit and common space for guests' often multiple wired and wireless technological devices in response to survey feed-back that placed internet access and wireless connectivity high on the list of visitor priorities.

Yet, despite such cultural and technological shifts, the values and legacy that have shaped this property are ever present, as is a consciousness of the responsibility for preserving the resort's natural setting and role in protecting the area's unique forest and coastal environment for generations of visitors to come.

Stewardship of the property and its environs

On this property, the trees comprise much more than its unique setting. With its acres of forest, tree preservation and management are critical and ongoing priorities at Tigh-Na-Mara. As the resort developed and expanded over time, the trees that had to be cleared for construction furnished the materials for the characteristic natural log buildings and accommodation. The remaining extensive forest canopy serves as a carbon offset, helping to reduce the burden of human development on the environment while the ground beneath and the branches of the firs and arbutus trees are home to indigenous wildlife.

The trees also provide natural shade for guests and visitors in the hotter summer months that, along with the cooling ocean breeze and the energy-efficient fans included in every unit, have helped to keep the guest accommodation free of artificial air conditioning and the attendant and substantial energy costs. While the issue of air conditioning is one that arises frequently on guest feedback surveys and questionnaires, management have looked for alternative solutions to ensure guest comfort, such as installing retractable blinds to reduce the heat transmitted through skylights in upper floor units.

The Tigh-Na-Mara team engages in a range of other activities aimed at reducing or minimizing the resort's environmental impact. A volunteer group of management and employee representatives from all departments—the GREEN TEAM—educate, empower and explore new opportunities for continued improvement in the resort and spa's environmental performance. This has already resulted in waste reduction, an extensive recycling programme, a comprehensive food and landscape composting programme, energy conservation and pollution reduction and prevention initiatives. Some of these initiatives, like the voluntary linen reuse and recycling programme, directly engage resort guests in the efforts to reduce water, energy consumption and waste.

Management is committed to ensuring all construction plans, community action plans and purchasing considerations have environmental sustainability as part of the decision process. In this latter regard, green and eco-friendly products and practices are used in applications across the resort from lawn maintenance to spa treatments. As well, biodegradable cleaning products are used in all areas of the resort, including laundry.

Efforts to reduce energy consumption at Tigh-Na-Mara include the replacement of older unit appliances and commercial equipment with energy-efficient models throughout the resort and a switch to energy-efficient light bulbs. Other energy conscious measures include using a fleet of electric vehicles to service the resort's 22 acres. All 18 of the resort's housekeeping and maintenance vehicles are battery-operated golf carts.

Many of these activities also benefit the financial bottom line, which is a critical consideration for resorts that, like any other business, must seek to ensure profitability alongside sustainability. For example, without the switch to energy-efficient light bulbs, electricity costs would have been significantly higher in 2013 on account of increased electrical rates; meanwhile, the more energy-efficient lighting will continue to help mitigate the impact of expected future utility rate increases.

In 2010, the resort was recognized for its green efforts with the 2010 Going Green Award at the tenth Annual Vancouver Island Business Excellence Awards, hosted by *Business Examiner Vancouver Island*.

Also in 2010, the combination of efforts towards greener and more sustainable business practices earned the resort a "4 Green Key" designation from the Hotel Association of Canada Green Key Eco-Rating programme. The Canadian programme, which is part of the Green Key Global Eco-Rating programme, employs a five-point rating scale that is designed to recognize and encourage hotels, motels and resorts in Canada that are demonstrating commitment to improving their operations' environmental and fiscal performance. The rating is based on the results of a comprehensive environmental self-assessment across the five main operational aspects of a property: corporate environmental management; housekeeping; food and beverage operations; conference and meeting facilities; and engineering. The assessment addresses nine areas of sustainable practice:

- Energy conservation
- Water conservation
- Solid waste management
- Hazardous waste management
- Indoor air quality
- Community outreach
- Building infrastructure
- Land use
- Environmental management

Following a review of the self-assessment, participating properties are awarded a Green Key rating on a scale of one to five (with five being the highest rating) along with guidance on finding and acting on further opportunities to reduce their environmental impacts and operating costs via lower energy and other natural resource consumption, employee training in sustainable best practice, sustainable SCM, supplier and customer engagement and community involvement.

As of May 2014, of the 2,381 properties active in the programme in North America, 781 properties have achieved a "4 Green Key" rating and 55 have gained the 5 Green rating. For Tigh-Na-Mara to achieve a "4 Green Key" designation for the first time in 2010 and to maintain that rating as a property that pre-dates advances in green building design and construction is quite remarkable. In fact, as an older property, the chances of Tigh-Na-Mara moving up from a "4 Green Key" rating to a 5 are virtually impossible since doing so would involve large-scale reconstruction to meet new green building standards such as those established by the LEED[1] (Leadership in Energy and Environmental Design) ratings system. Not only would the financial cost of such a reconstruction be prohibitive for the business, it would also result in significant, unnecessary and premature waste of existing materials and structures.

---

4 Green Keys

A hotel that has shown national industry leadership and commitment to protecting the environment through wide-ranging policies and practices. Hotel has mature programmes in place that involve management, employees, guests and the public, and which have shown substantial and measurable results (Hotel Association of Canada, Green Key Eco-Rating programme, http://www. hotelassociation.ca/site/programs/GreenKey.asp).

Commitment to community

Community is important to the team at Tigh-Na-Mara. In both the good and the more challenging times, the positive connections that are forged between a business and the communities it touches signify far more than mutual economic benefit.[2]

Tigh-Na-Mara's community outreach, contributions to and activity in support of the health of the Parksville and area community are extensive, both financially and through hundreds of volunteer hours contributed by the team members and leadership.

---

1 LEED is a set of rating systems developed by the United States Green Building Council for the design, construction, operation and maintenance of buildings, homes and neighbourhoods to operate in an environmentally responsible and resource efficient manner.
2 A considerable body of literature exists on the rationale for and the business, economic as well as social benefits of corporate investment of time and resources in community. See, for example: Carroll & Shebana, 2010; Kurucz *et al.*, 2008; Lee, 2008; Vogel, 2005.

With a particular focus on the needs of the local community, Tigh-Na-Mara supports three specific charities: SOS (Society of Organized Services) assists those who are in need in the Parksville area; Variety is a provincial children's charity; and the Invasive Plants Society of British Columbia coordinates efforts to preserve and restore communities' natural environments.

In 2009, Tigh-Na-Mara recognized that the negative impacts on its business of the recession precipitated by the global financial crisis—tourism being one of the industries most affected by economic downturns—would be felt throughout the local community in which tourism is a major part of the economy and, in particular, by the children. This led to the inaugural Tigh-Na-Mara Toy Drive for Kids breakfast to provide support through SOS to families in need at Christmas time. At the event in December 2014, its fifth year, the Tigh-Na-Mara team of volunteers served breakfast to over 1,800 people in exchange for the donation of a new, unwrapped gift or cash amount to be distributed through SOS. As in previous years, 100% of the toys, gift cards and cash donations were given to the SOS to help families in the local area.

Since April 2010, on Earth Day, the Resort Green team and other resort team members volunteer for a property, beach and highway clean-up and provide guest education on the initiative. The proceeds from a concurrent baking and barbecue lunch event are donated in equal parts to two of the resort's charities: Variety and the Invasive Plants Society of BC. Another annual event is at Christmas time when, each year, Tigh-Na-Mara employee volunteers purchase, cook and prepare a traditional Christmas dinner at the local Salvation Army Hall for people in need. In recent years, they have served dinners to upwards of 150 to 200 grateful recipients who attend the annual event.

Additionally, Tigh-Na-Mara reviews the over 700 requests for donations or assistance that it receives annually to identify and respond to those that are felt to align with its commitment to community. Together in 2012, donations exceeded $80,000 in kind, and similarly in 2013.

In February 2014, the property received the Hotel Association of Canada's Humanitarian Award of Excellence in recognition of its "long history and dedication as a generous supporter of many charitable campaigns and initiatives".[3]

The connection between a caring employer and a dedicated team is evident in the level of volunteerism and in the fact that team members remain with the resort despite local and regional job market competition. In an industry that traditionally has high turnover, Tigh-Na-Mara enjoys impressive employee continuity and longevity. Thirty-nine per cent of the team have five or more years of service with Tigh-Na-Mara, 57% of the team have two or more years of service and nearly 20 team members have been with the resort for ten years or more. Long service awards are given out annually to team members who reach employment milestones in

---

3   Hotel Association of Canada (HAC) Awards of Excellence—2013 Humanitarian Award
   Announcement, http://www.hotelassociation.ca/site/news/AwardsWinners.asp,
   accessed 10 August 2015.

recognition of their loyalty and commitment. This employee loyalty and commitment also benefits the resort's bottom line since employee turnover, recruitment and training can add substantially to employment costs, especially for a small resort such as Tigh-Na-Mara.

Continuity amid change

The tourism sector is constantly challenged to be current, competitive and accommodating to their customers' needs and expectations. Research has found that travellers are influenced by a broad range of considerations in their destination choices beyond location and cost. Everything from political upheaval, economic uncertainty, health risks and personal security issues can be factors in decisions on how, where and indeed whether to travel.

With increasing recognition and understanding of the need for a more sustainable future, the sector is also challenged to pay attention to the impact of their operations and how to manage their social and environmental footprint. Awareness of the sustainability dimension of travel is evident in recent research data compiled by the Center for Responsible Tourism (CREST) in its April 2014 *Trends and Statistics Fact Sheet* (CREST, 2014). This summary of the results of a variety of market surveys conducted in recent years included the following:

- 79% of travellers globally "think that it's important that accommodation providers have eco-friendly practices" ("Trip Barometer by Trip Advisor", 2013)

- 95% of business travellers surveyed believe the hotel industry should be undertaking "green" initiatives and that sustainability will become the defining issues for the hospitality industry in 2015 (Deloitte, 2010)

- 72% of meeting planners that responded to a 2013 survey by *Successful Meetings* have "green" policies in place for at least some of their meetings and a further 19% have such policies in place for all meetings. Some 73% responded that sustainable policies and procedures have some or a great deal of influence on choice of hotel (Jakobsen, 2013)

For Tigh-Na-Mara, these findings align with what they know motivates many of their guests to visit the resort. Based on the CTC (Canadian Tourism Commission) proprietary EQ® (Explorer Quotient)—which identifies travellers' preferences according to their personal beliefs, social values and view of the world as well as conventional demographic attributes—visitors to the Parksville and Qualicum region of British Columbia specifically seek out the natural experience offered by the region's coastal setting.[4]

---

4   http://en-corporate.canada.travel/resources-industry/explorer-quotient, accessed 10 August 2015

As a single property, Tigh-Na-Mara does not have the economies of scale available to larger resort groups and hotel chains so making large-scale and significant changes to structures and operations that require upfront investment is a challenge, particularly where the potential returns are likely to be realized only in the longer term, if at all. For example, advances in the alternative energy field and developments in alternative "green" energy infrastructure and power supply are making the transition to greener energy sources a reality in many parts of the world. Supportive policy environments in regions such as Europe and, more recently, in emerging economies that face critical energy choices have helped to make measurable shifts to cleaner energy sources an attainable goal. In North America, particularly in energy challenged regions such as California, a combination of private and public sector efforts are enabling businesses and increasingly individual property owners to manage the cost and process of converting to alternative energy solutions.[5] However, under current conditions and for a small business like Tigh-Na-Mara situated where it is, alternative energy solutions such as the installation of solar panels to serve some of the resort's energy needs—while potentially beneficial environmentally and financially in the medium to long term—encounter barriers of cost and logistics that preclude consideration of this kind of change in the immediate future.

Despite these economic and practical realities, resort management and owners are finding ways to manage change that minimize, mitigate and in some cases reduce the resort's negative impacts and that increase its contribution to a positive and more sustainable future. For example, on Earth Day 2015 the resort officially announced the installation of three electric vehicle charging stations available to guests of the resort who have made the switch to lower emissions vehicles.

Conclusion

From its first owners nearly 70 years ago to the present-day owners, management, partners, visitors and guests, this property has a special significance. Tigh-Na-Mara, meaning "house by the sea" in Gaelic, is a place that people return to—for generations. Protecting and continuing this legacy depends on the kind of respect and responsibility for and awareness of the impacts of development and change on the precious natural environment and the social fabric of its community—near and far—that characterize 21st-century sustainable business practice.

The team at Tigh-Na-Mara is guided by the express commitment to continually enhance guest services in a respectful, supportive and natural environment. With international recognition as a destination of choice and as a business that cares,

---

5   See, for example, the CSI (California Solar Initiative), www.gosolarcalifornia.ca.gov, accessed 10 August 2015

having recently won the 2013 Humanitarian Award from the Hotel Association of Canada, the staff are successfully achieving this balance.

There is no straightforward or "one-size-fits all" set of solutions to these challenges. This case study shows how one business, Tigh-Na-Mara, is exploring and implementing practical ways to meet guests' changing demands and expectations, while at the same time managing operations so as to make sound business decisions that take account of the need to protect and preserve the environment and natural beauty embedded in the legacy, the present and the future of the resort.

References

Carroll, A.B., & Shabana, K.M. (2010). The business case for corporate social responsibility: A review of concepts, research and practice. *International Journal of Management Reviews*, 12, 85–105.

CREST (2014). The case for responsible travel: Trends and statistics (2014 ed.). Center for Responsible Tourism. Retrieved from http://www.responsibletravel.org/projects/documents/2014_Trends_&_Statistics_Final.pdf, accessed 10 August 2015

Deloitte (2010). Hospitality 2015: Game changers or spectators. Retrieved from http://www.fairtrade.travel/uploads/files/Hospitality_2015_Deloitte_report.pdf, accessed 9 November 2015.

Jakobsen, Leo (2013, May 1). Research: Sustainable meetings survey. *Successful Meetings*. Retrieved from http://www.successfulmeetings.com/Event-Planning/conference-management/Articles/research-Sustainable-Meetings-Survey, accessed 10 October 2015.

Kurucz, Elizabeth, Colbert, Barry, & Wheeler, David (2008). The business case for corporate social responsibility. In A. Crane, A. McWilliams, D. Matten, J. Moon, & D. Siegel. *The Oxford Handbook of Corporate Social Responsibility*. Oxford, Oxford University Press, pp. 83–112.

Lee, M.P. (2008). A review of the theories of corporate social responsibility: Its evolutionary path and the road ahead. *International Journal of Management Reviews*, 10, 53–73.

Trip Advisor (2013). Trip barometer. Retrieved from http://www.tripadvisor.com/TripAdvisorInsights/n627/tripbarometer-reveals-travel-green-and-mobile-trends-infographic, accessed 9 November 2015.

Vogel, D.J. (2005). Is there a market for virtue? The business case for social responsibility. *California Management Review*, 24, 19–45.

11

Optimizing performance in a remote African hotel
Using the One Planet Living framework to maximize the sustainability performance of Singita Grumeti in Tanzania

Benjamin H. Gill
BioRegional, UK

Beverly K. Burden
Singita Grumeti, Tanzania

Singita Grumeti is private game reserve integral to the Serengeti National Park ecosystem. The luxury of the lodges and the symbiotic relationship between tourism, conservation and community development make the property unique. One Planet Living, created by BioRegional, demonstrates a world where everyone can enjoy a high quality of life within the productive capacity of the planet. Singita Grumeti used the ten sustainability principles, with targets linked to the environmental limits of the planet, to form an adaptive management plan. Implementation started with staff training, monitoring and energy efficiency upgrades. Successes include: putting the carbon footprint on a downward trajectory; 10% reduction in water consumption; and widespread staff engagement. The One Planet framework has provided clear understandable visions and targets, which can be easily communicated to staff and guests. By embracing One Planet Living, Singita Grumeti is setting a new standard, creating a positive future for local people, wildlife and guests.

Introduction to Singita Grumeti

The Serengeti is one of the most complex and least disturbed ecosystems in the world, forming an integral role in the protection and continuation of the Great Wildebeest Migration and a vast array of fauna and flora. Singita Grumeti is composed of several protected areas on the border of the Serengeti National Park (Grumeti Game Reserve, Ikorongo Game Reserve, Ikona Wildlife Area and Sasakwa Title Deed). This area forms what is known as the Western Corridor, where the plains pinch up against Lake Victoria, creating a microclimate that consistently brings richer rains and grazing—a suitable climate for the Great Migration, 70% of which has historically passed through on an annual basis.

At the turn of the century, illegal poaching and uncontrolled legal hunting had significantly reduced the biodiversity of the area. The growing demand for "bushmeat", animal skins and ivory, combined with a local population with limited access to urban markets, formed a destructive sub-economy.

In 2002, Paul Tudor Jones acquired the tender for Grumeti Game Reserve, Ikorongo Game Reserve and the Ikona Wildlife Area, consolidating the 347,000 acres of the Western Corridor into what is referred to as Singita Grumeti. But as the local economy had become dependent on poaching to supplement subsistence farming, an alternative economic model was required to ensure the conservation effort was sustainable.

In 2003, the Grumeti Fund was formed with the vision of stabilizing the area, implementing and supporting wildlife/habitat management, researching and monitoring and community outreach. Working alongside the Tanzanian wildlife division, the fund began to turn poachers into game scouts and stewards of the land. Within a decade, the Grumeti Fund arrested more than 4,500 poachers, converting a number into game scouts and thereby significantly reducing poaching in the reserves. The barren plains of ten years ago have now been restored to full wildlife-carrying capacity, with some spectacular population recoveries ranging as high as 600% (Goodman, 2014). An additional result of the re-stabilized ecosystem is the return of the wildebeest migration to the area on an annual basis (Goodman, 2014).

Today, the Grumeti Fund reaches far beyond wildlife protection, with a community support and outreach programme covering a vast array of activities, including:

- Environmental education teaching more than 1,500 youths the importance of the environment to their long-term livelihoods

- Small business support providing seed capital, construction support and management training to businesses that supply 40% of produce to the tourism operations at Grumeti

- Infrastructure schemes e.g. digging wells for clean potable water, building dams and water harvesting tanks

Such a large operation requires consistent revenue generation to sustain these long-term social and environmental programmes. Thus, in 2006 the Grumeti Fund partnered with Singita, a world leader in the ecotourism industry. The operation provides sustainable employment for approximately 700 local Tanzanians. The influence of the operation also impacts positively upon the 50,000 people that live in the 22 neighbouring villages, whose livelihoods are connected to the natural environment and the business Singita Grumeti generates.

Acknowledging that local conservation requires addressing global issues such as climate change, Singita Grumeti searched for a framework that could holistically encompass the conservation work done to date and chart a new path for sustainability in all areas of operations. BioRegional's One Planet framework was chosen as the methodology for doing this.

Singita Grumeti comprises:

- Three permanent Lodges: Sasakwa Lodge, Faru Faru and Serengeti House

- One year-round permanent tented camp: Sabora Tented Camp

- One seasonal tented camp at a permanent location: Mara River Tented Camp

- Three mobile tented camps: Explore Camps

The support infrastructure is provided in a centralized area called Makundusi supplying the project with storage and warehouses, a workshop, waste separation areas, etc.

Sasakwa Lodge, Serengeti House and Makundusi are connected to the electricity grid. The remaining locations are off grid, requiring stationary power sources. Mara River Tented Camp is the only camp which lies outside the game reserves, in the adjacent Serengeti National Park. All of the camps/lodges have been established in varying terrain (i.e. river, open plans, hills, thickets, etc.).

Figure 11.1 **Map of Singita Grumeti**

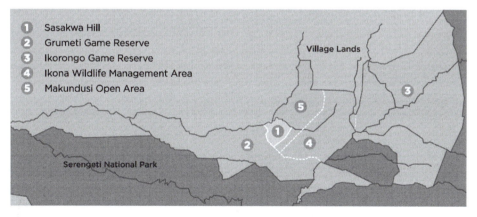

1 Sasakwa Hill
2 Grumeti Game Reserve
3 Ikorongo Game Reserve
4 Ikona Wildlife Management Area
5 Makundusi Open Area

Village Lands

Serengeti National Park

One Planet Living

One Planet Living is a vision of a sustainable world, in which people everywhere can enjoy a high quality of life within the productive capacity of the planet while leaving space for wilderness and wildlife (BioRegional, 2014). It uses ten principles of sustainability as a framework with a target for each principle that is linked to the environmental limits of the planet (see Table 11.1).

Ecological footprint

Ecological footprint analysis is at the heart of One Planet Living as the overarching indicator of what constitutes a sustainable level of consumption. The ecological footprint tracks humanity's demands on the biosphere by comparing humanity's total consumption against the capacity of the Earth to regenerate resources itself. This is done by calculating the area required to produce the resources consumed by the global population, area occupied by infrastructure, and also the area of forest required for sequestering CO_2 that is not absorbed by the ocean (see Galli *et al.* 2012; Kitzes *et al.*, 2009).

The 2012 Living Planet Report shows that, in 2008, the Earth's total biocapacity was 1.8 gha per person, while humanity's ecological footprint was 2.7 gha per person. This overshoot means it takes 1.5 years for the Earth to fully regenerate the renewable resources used in one year. If our demands on the planet continue at the same rate, by 2030 the equivalent of two planets' worth of resources will be needed to maintain our lifestyles (Living Planet Report, 2012).

An individual's ecological footprint varies significantly around the world. If all of humanity lived like an average Western European, three planet Earths would be required to regenerate humanity's annual demand on nature, and if we all lived like an average resident of the USA four planet Earths would be needed. If all of humanity lived like an average resident of Tanzania, only two-thirds of the planet's biocapacity would be used; whereas even the demand of an average South African exceeds the planet's ability to regenerate by 25% while disguising considerable variations within the country (Living Planet Report, 2012).

Carbon footprint

The One Planet initiative uses "consumption-based" carbon footprinting to inform a holistic picture of what causes our greenhouse gas emissions and the most appropriate strategies for reducing them. Consumption-based emissions are those that arise all the way through the supply chain. These include not just "direct emissions" caused by fuel and electricity consumption, but also embodied emissions in goods and services purchased including food, manufactured items and construction materials.

The latest report by the Intergovernmental Panel on Climate Change (IPCC, 2014) highlights the gravity of the threat of climate change. Current greenhouse gas concentrations in the atmosphere are 430 ppm (CO_2 equivalent). To make it likely that global average temperatures do not rise above 2 degrees centigrade concentrations must not exceed 450 ppm CO_2eq at the end of the century. This requires a drop in global CO_2eq emissions of 41–72% by 2050, so global carbon emissions that were 49 gigatonnes in 2010 (and rising) may need to average 15.75 gigatonnes a year from now until 2050. It is worth noting that there are many prominent scientists advocating much larger cuts in carbon emissions: for example, Hansen *et al.* (2008) propose an atmospheric concentration target of 350 ppm CO_2 (approximately 380 ppm CO_2eq).

In line with this, the One Planet initiative adopts the principles of contraction and convergence. This means that countries with high per capita emissions will have to reduce their emissions much more rapidly than countries that currently have low per capita emissions, whose emissions may continue to increase before also reducing down to a one tonne per capita level. The end result would be that per capita emissions from each country converge at a more equitable level and the global total of emissions would contract.

One Planet principles

One Planet Living uses ten simple principles to act as a framework for developing and managing sustainability strategies for communities and organizations (see Table 11.1). Against each principle, there are CITs (Common International Targets) based on the environmental limits of the planet, and where possible linked to the emerging work on planetary boundaries and thresholds (Rockström *et al*, 2009). The CITs are further underpinned by three "overarching targets" (see Table 11.2).

For a project to become an endorsed One Planet Community, the following requirements have to be met:

- The project must develop a publically available action plan to demonstrate how they intend to meet all the CITs by 2020

- The project must commit to delivering the action plan and reporting on progress every year in a publically available annual review

The action plan is reviewed by BioRegional and the programme's expert panel (highly experienced independent experts), and if they are satisfied that it is deliverable and will enable the project to meet the CITs, then the project becomes endorsed.

There are now hundreds of communities or companies globally that are using the One Planet principles. However, in publicly adopting all the targets for One Planet Living (One Planet Communities, 2013), Singita Grumeti becomes a world leader as the seventh endorsed One Planet Community globally.

Table 11.1 **One Planet Principles and the associated Common International Targets**

Source: One Planet Communities, 2011

One Planet Principle	Summary	2020 Common International Target
Zero carbon	Enabling access to energy, making buildings more energy efficient and delivering all energy with renewable technologies	All buildings to be "net zero carbon" in use through energy efficiency and on- and off-site renewable energy
Zero waste	Reducing waste, reusing where possible, creating products and employment through recycling and, ultimately, sending zero waste to landfill	Reduction in all waste generation including recyclables, and approaching zero waste (2%) to landfill by 2020
Sustainable transport	Encouraging low-carbon modes of transport and public transport, reducing the need to travel, ensuring a good range of local facilities within walking and cycling distance	Contract and converge rapidly to personal transport emissions that are consistent with the overarching GHG target
Sustainable materials	Using sustainable and healthy products, such as those with low embodied energy, sourced locally, made from renewable or waste resources	One Planet Communities strive to reduce the impacts of all goods and materials used in the construction, maintenance and occupation of the community, to a degree that is consistent with the overarching GHG and ecological footprint target
Local and sustainable food	Sustainable and humane agriculture and farming, access to nutritious low impact, local, seasonal and organic diets and reducing food waste	Contract and converge on personal food footprints that are consistent with the overarching targets through encouraging local, fresh unprocessed produce, organic produce, reduced waste and lower animal protein diets
Sustainable water	Access to safe drinking water and sanitation. Using water more efficiently in farming, buildings and in the products we buy. Designing to avoid local flooding and watercourse pollution	One Planet Communities adopt locally specific best practice in water conservation, water efficiency and recycling and surface-water management, making a net positive contribution to the local natural water system
Land use and wildlife	Protecting and restoring existing biodiversity and natural habitats through appropriate land use and integration into the built environment	One Planet Communities make a net positive contribution to local native biodiversity. They showcase at least one project to regenerate degraded local natural resource stocks (soils, trees, fisheries, etc.) and aim to facilitate the establishment or enhancement of valuable wild space consistent with the global need for 20–30% of biologically productive land

Culture and community	Respecting and reviving local identity, wisdom and culture. Access to education for all. Valuing and encouraging the involvement of the community in shaping their community and their lives	Create a thriving sense of place and a sense of community through enhancing and reviving valuable aspects of local culture and heritage
Equity and local economy	Creating strong, diverse local economies that meet people's needs and support fair employment and international fair trade	Helping towards a thriving, equitable future for all through inclusiveness, participation, fair employment and affordability
Health and happiness	Promote good health and well-being through access to healthcare. Encourage active, sociable, meaningful lives to promote good health and well-being	One Planet Communities strive for best practice in promoting the health and happiness of their residents and workers, through neighbourhood design, construction phase, community governance and lifestyles

Table 11.2 **Common International Targets for the One Planet Communities programme**

Source: One Planet Communities, 2011

Principle	Overarching Targets
Greenhouse gases	Contract and converge rapidly, aiming for 0.8 tonnes per person by 2050. One Planet Communities will strive to show consistency with the most up-to-date climate science and the GHG reductions necessary to avoid dangerous climate change
Ecological footprint	One Planet Communities will enable residents to achieve ecological footprints of 1.7 gha as soon as possible and 1.25 gha by 2050. One Planet Communities will strive to show consistency with the concept of living within our fair share of the Earth's renewable and replenishable resources
Clean activities	One Planet Communities will avoid any damaging pollution to air, land or water as a result of their activities at construction or occupation stage. Suppliers of goods and services with strong environmental track records and low pollution impacts will be favoured over more polluting alternatives

Singita's One Planet journey

As one of the leading luxury hotel brands in the world, located in a remote location in East Africa, Singita Grumeti's particular challenge is in reducing the impact on the environment while simultaneously meeting guests' expectations. As the concession is visited by some of the world's most influential people, Singita and its staff have the unique opportunity to raise awareness about the impact of humanity's consumption on the natural environment. The One Planet Living framework enables these issues to be tackled together—giving a coherent framework for developing strategies for reducing the impact of the operations, while also providing an engaging and convincing narrative for guest communication, and staff training.

Developing the sustainability strategy

Becoming a One Planet Community is about making a long-term commitment to constant improvement to bring the impact of the operations down to a sustainable level by 2020. Having decided to use the One Planet Living process, Singita Grumeti undertook a "gap analysis" to gain a high-level understanding of what would be required to become a One Planet Community. This was then followed by a workshop facilitated by BioRegional with key directors and technical staff at Singita Grumeti to agree to project specific targets and the strategies required to meet them.

After the workshop, the technical team developed a complete One Planet action plan covering all of the actions required to meet these targets and the likely costs and savings. This was presented to and signed off by the board in January 2013, and a partnership agreement signed in February 2013. The headline targets and main strategies for meeting them are shown in Table 11.3.

Because the Grumeti Fund already supports and implements a large portion of the One Planet programme, a unique relationship has been formed whereby the One Planet framework supports and enhances already productive and sustainable programmes that are carried out by the Grumeti Fund. Thus, through this process, the tourism and support services component of Singita Grumeti also become tied more directly to the framework and targets developed at the workshop.

Scope of this chapter

Table 11.4 and Figure 11.2 show the carbon footprint of the main activities of Singita Grumeti from 2011 to 2013 based on the Greenhouse Gas Protocol methodology (Ranganathan *et al.*, 2004). There is a steady increase in the use of electricity as the operations have expanded and the grid connections improved. There is also a spike in the footprint in 2012 due to increased generator fuel use—this is thought to be due to works on the electricity mains that year which increased the reliance on backup generators.

Excluding refrigerant gases, which were not counted in 2011, there has been a 1% increase from 2011 to 2013. However, the number of guest bed nights increased significantly over that period and the overall carbon footprint per guest bed night fell by 35% from 2011 to 2013 (see Fig. 11.3). Given that a large amount of the operations are related to conservation and not tourism, it is also useful to track carbon emissions by total bed night (guests and staff); here there has been a 12% drop in the same period. It is expected that the total emissions will begin to fall from 2013 as infrastructure and operational changes are made.

Figure 11.2 **Carbon footprint of Singita Grumeti 2011–2013 (tonnes of CO$_2$eq)**
Source: One Planet Communities, 2014

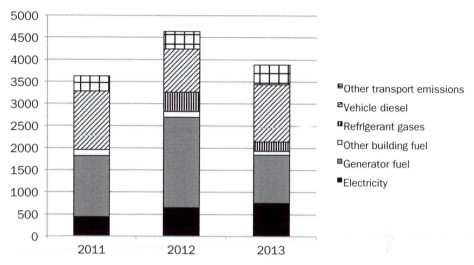

Figure 11.3 **Carbon intensity of Singita Grumeti operations 2011–2013 (tonnes of CO$_2$eq/bed night)**
Source: One Planet Communities, 2014

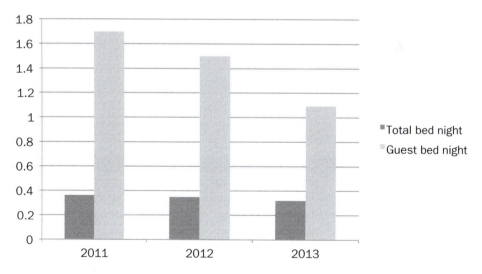

Table 11.3 **Headline targets and main sustainability strategies being implemented at Singita Grumeti**

One Planet Principle	Key 2020 target	Main strategies for Singita Grumeti
Zero carbon	30% reduction in energy use	Solar thermal: centralized and individual units
		Energy monitoring, efficiency upgrades and education
		Uninterrupted power supply for grid connected areas
	100% renewable electricity	PV/battery bank to replace generators at remote camps
		Large-scale on- or off-site renewable energy, including 200kWp on-site for the new lodges
Zero waste	90% reduction in use of plastic	Avoidance of plastic packaging (e.g. water bottles)
	10% reduction of other waste	Education and sourcing initiatives
	90–95% recycling rate	Anaerobic digestion of food waste
		Recycling of all other waste
Sustainable transport	50% reduction in land transport emissions	Fleet management: logistics, driver training
		Creation of a new slower guest experience
	50% increase in efficiency of wildlife management activities	Appropriate vehicle use and logistics management
Sustainable materials	Imports reduced	Review of all purchases for lower impact options
	Rehabilitation	Rehabilitation of quarry and murram pits
	Low impact new construction	Targeting of LEED credits for reducing waste and responsible sourcing
Local and sustainable food	60% of staff food local	New initiatives to supply key produce (e.g. poultry)
	100% sustainable fish	Review of purchasing procedures
	Healthier eating	Progressive shift to a healthier diet
Sustainable water	Less than 5% leakage losses	Metering and automated tanks shut-off
	>50% reduction in borehole extraction	Training and education for staff
		Education for guests
		Rainwater harvesting and wastewater recycling
Land use and wildlife	World Commission on Protected Areas >75%	Improved management and planning
		Tourism protocol: ensure new developments, support conservation goals

	Culture of sustainability	One Planet Centre and education
Culture and community	80% of guests going on a "cultural" tour	Increased focus on cultural, environmental and anthropological tourism
Equity and local economy	50% of salary expenditure on local staff	Joint Venture Agreement incorporating the One Planet targets and activities
	100 new jobs, >60% local	Scholarship education and training programme
Health and happiness	Improvement in key local health and education statistics	Education to include healthy living
		Support for local sporting initiatives

Table 11.4 **Carbon footprint of Singita Grumeti 2011–2013 (tonnes of CO_2eq)**

Source: One Planet Communities, 2014

	2011	2012	2013	Change 2011–2013
Scope 1	Tonnes CO_2eq			%
Generator fuel	1,382.9	2,045.3	1,094.8	-20.8%
LP gas (cooking)	107.2	107.3	67.6	-36.9%
Kerosene (lanterns)	33.8	19.2	20.5	-39.3%
Refrigerant gases (air conditioning and fire extinguishers)	n/a	440.1	207.4	
Vehicle diesel	1,325.4	977.7	1,294.8	-2.3%
Other transport fuel	226.7	226.4	282.4	24.5%
TOTAL Scope 1	3,075.9	3,816.0	2,967.5	-3.5%
Scope 2	Tonnes CO_2eq			%
Grid electricity	437.5	650.7	753.0	72.1%
TOTAL Scope 2	437.5	650.7	753.0	72.1%
Scope 3	Tonnes CO_2eq			%
Business flights			32.5	
Staff leave flights			136.3	
TOTAL Scope 3	113.3	168.9	168.9	49.0%
TOTAL	3,626.7	4,635.5	3,889.4	7.2%

Figure 11.4 **Breakdown of carbon footprint into "tourism" and "other activities"**

Source: One Planet Communities, 2014

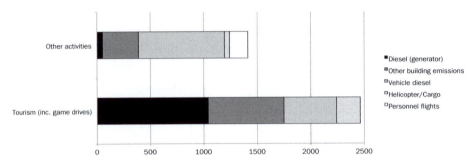

The figures relate largely to the tourism and support service component of Singita Grumeti, as the Grumeti Fund activities contribute minimally to the overall footprint. As can be seen from Figure 11.4, the tourism activities account for close to two-thirds of Singita Grumeti's carbon footprint, including approximately two-thirds of the electricity demand and 95% of the stationary fuel demand. The majority of the remaining 37% is due to the conservation activities.

Implementing the action plan

Work began in earnest in delivering the action plan in mid-2013, and the first annual review has been undertaken (One Planet Communities, 2014). The first year of the One Planet action plan has seen some significant successes, as well as a greater understanding of the challenges and benefits of implementing such an ambitious plan in the middle of the African bush.

The One Planet action plan laid out a vision for how Singita Grumeti would become a One Planet community—setting targets to define that vision and outlining key strategies. The first year of implementation focused on:

- Training to increase staff understanding of the programme; over 80% of the 750 person staff have been trained in One Planet Living

- Putting in place basic efficiency measures and establishing a programme of staff activities to demonstrate both the financial gains and the benefits to the staff

- Ensuring all new projects are compliant with the One Planet action plan

- Integrating the One Planet action plan into the operational structure, e.g. job descriptions, performance targets and staff appraisals

- Developing detailed strategies for implementing key aspects of the vision

The outcome has been to make the highly ambitious vision seem achievable, and to clearly highlight the well-being benefits to the staff, such as health benefits through more exercise and healthier eating and greater social interaction through the engagement programme. The process has also brought to light difficulties, including the low education levels of much of the staff, the remote location and high prices for equipment and installation thereof and the long lead in times as the majority of equipment is imported.

Training and staff engagement

In order to be able to reach as many of the 750 staff as possible, a training programme was established. Training sessions were run with the lodge managers, who rolled out the training to give all staff a general understanding of One Planet Living and how it could specifically be integrated into their job. Some examples of this included:

- The safari guides undergoing a half-day training, including role-play exercises to gain a better understanding of the uniqueness of their position in being able to explain to guests some of the environmental changes that they were witnessing. This has been supported by the development of a 60-page manual, knowledge of which is incorporated into their performance appraisals and tests

- Housekeeping staff being trained in new "turn-down" procedures to reduce energy use—e.g. leaving on fewer lights and not having on all the air-conditioning units

As part of the staff engagement programme, "principle of the month" activities have been established including a health-and-happiness run and a wildlife photography competition, as well as One Planet themed events—such as the Sustainable Fancy Dress Halloween Party. These events have been carefully developed to ensure they are accessible to staff of all grades and also actively encourage interaction between all staff.

Integrating One Planet Living into the social fabric of Singita Grumeti has been crucial in ensuring that it is understood by all staff. It was quite clear from BioRegional's annual review visit in March that everyone, from housekeeping and chefs to safari guides and senior managers, has embraced One Planet Living and started to incorporate its philosophy into their daily operations. Changing behaviour is a slow and ongoing process; but One Planet Living provides a framework that all the staff can relate to. Staff training and information sessions are ongoing and available to all.

Simple infrastructure upgrades

When launching a sustainability programme, it is imperative that the training and communication is matched by visible changes, to show that the company is serious about its sustainability goals and that it is more than simply rhetoric. So in 2013 a range of simple upgrades have been made. For example:

- Changing all back-of- house lighting to energy-efficient bulbs
- Energy and water meters installed, providing more accurate and timely data for staff
- Installation of solar thermal geysers in staff accommodation and in lodges (Faru Faru)
- Installation of all new inverter AC (alternating current) units in Faru Faru and Serengeti House
- Water filtration and bottling plant installed in Sasakwa Lodge, eliminating plastic bottles
- Recognition of already established sustainable operations and lodges, such as the completely solar run Mara River Tented Camp and Explore Camps

These changes have served to show that Singita Grumeti is committed to the One Planet Principles and is investing in it. Likewise, these initiatives have helped demonstrate to the finance team that One Planet Living can have long-term savings, and to the staff that it is linked to their well-being (more hot water!).

New projects

Mara River Camp was completed before the formal adoption of the One Planet action plan, but it incorporated the concepts of One Planet Living into its design and operations. For example:

- While meeting all the standards of a Singita camp, it is entirely powered by photovoltaics and solar thermal
- All lights are LED or solar operated
- Toiletry products are organic
- Gym with electrical equipment has been replaced with non-electric options

In the Singita Grumeti protected area, potential new projects include:

- Construction of up to seven new LEED accredited private lodges being built as individual homes for high net worth conservation partners
- Construction of new sites for the Explore Camps
- Renovation and limited extension to some lodges (e.g. Serengeti House)

The first lodge for a conservation partner is under construction and will become the first LEED for home accredited building in Tanzania. LEED is a US-based green building certification programme that recognizes best-in-class building strategies and practices.

The Explore Camps are the real sustainability flagship at Singita Grumeti, as they are entirely solar powered and the only permanent infrastructure is the thin mur-ram pad (clay layer used for siting the tents on) and sewage pipes.

Going forward all new projects will be planned in line with meeting the One Planet action plan.

Integration

An on-site "sustainability integrator" was trained to have overall responsibility for delivering the action plan, but delivery of the more than 100 actions requires effective delegation. In 2013, concerted "integration processes" were undertaken whereby the targets and strategies in the action plan were incorporated into the job descriptions of the key staff. Key aspects of this were:

- Developing specific action plans for each lodge
- Identifying the key roles to be played by each department, such as:
    - HR leading on integration of the targets into job descriptions
    - Maintenance leading on the infrastructure upgrades
- Identifying a One Planet champion in each department to act as the contact point for company One Planet related activities, such as the principle of the month activities

Summary

The focus of activities in the first year has been on bringing all the staff on board the programme through training and integrating it into the day-to-day operations. This has been supported by simple and easy to install infrastructure upgrades, which have also highlighted some of the challenges of operating in such a remote location, such as the increased cost and time-lag of purchasing, importing and installing the necessary equipment. Nonetheless, there have been some immedi-ate benefits in terms of environmental performance and financial saving, as shown in the analysis of 2013.

Results from 2013

The carbon footprint of the tourism operation at Singita Grumeti was 2,463 tonnes in 2013, stationary power accounted for 42%, electricity 20% and vehicle diesel 20%

Figure 11.5 **Tourism carbon footprint in 2013**

Source: One Plant Communities, 2014

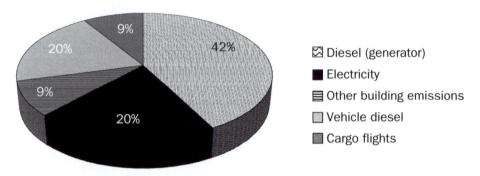

(see Fig. 11.5). Some 60% of the vehicle diesel is used in logistics of managing the camps and 40% for safari game drives.

Energy

Due to the significant impact of stationary power, this is a key focus area. In 2013, the main activity was:

- Training and education of all staff and changes to the operation of the guest rooms to reduce energy demand

- Back-of-house activities: installation of solar geysers and changing all 1,600 light bulbs

- Planning major upgrades for 2014

Water use

Water meters were installed across the property in 2013 to track both borehole water extraction and also end-of-pipe water use. There were technical difficulties with the end-of-pipe water use readings showing either water use exceeding the water extracted, or almost no water use at all. The one location where the readings were accurate showed a 6.7% water loss during the six months that the meters were installed. Figure 11.6 shows the raw water consumption for the three main lodges for the months that meters were installed. After the first One Planet training session in June, the Sasakwa Lodge manager decided to change the irrigation regime for the lodge. Although the short data period compromises accurate analysis, these changes have reduced water consumption at the lodge by an average of 10% and total water consumption for tourism uses by approximately 14%.

Figure 11.6 **Water consumption at Singita Grumeti in cubic metres**

Source: One Planet Communities, 2014

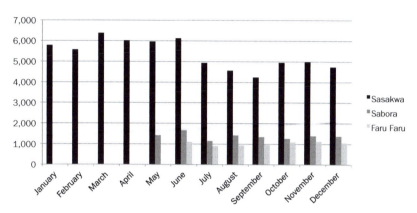

Waste

Solid waste has always been separated at Singita Grumeti but the management system has been significantly improved in 2013 with the storage cages made more secure, weighing infrastructure introduced and a kiln built for incineration of hazardous waste (medical and veterinary waste). Reuse and recycling solutions have been found for key materials previously not recycled. For example:

- Shanga recycle the glass into tableware, some of which has been purchased by Faru Faru

- The plastic water bottles are sent for recycling into mosquito nets by Olyset Mosquito Net Factory

- All cardboard boxes that are in good condition are returned to the suppliers for reuse

Kilima Lodge

Construction has started on the first new, LEED-certificated lodge for a conservation partner. LEED has been developed in the US and there are many challenges in using it in Tanzania; practices and materials that are commonplace in the US are frequently not available in a remote location in East Africa.

The LEED process has been incorporated into the overarching One Planet action plan, with the ten principles being used for on-site communication to ensure consistency across all of Singita Grumeti. However, the LEED requirements for site operations are used to guide the specifics of the site set-up (e.g. the management of recycling and rainwater harvesting). This approach highlights how the One Planet framework can be interfaced with other sustainability tools and standards.

Grumeti Construction has enthusiastically embraced LEED and One Planet Living and intends to roll out the new site and construction procedures across all their projects. Some of the improved processes include:

- All staff trained in One Planet Living and LEED
- All excavated material used in landscaping and all trees on site retained and protected
- A lighter membrane reduces roof weight by 30%—reducing the mass of the structure required
- Canteen built on site serving healthy local food every day
- 12,000-litre tanks for capturing and reusing rainwater

Achieving LEED accreditation in such a remote location of Tanzania is challenging, but demonstrates Singita Grumeti's commitment to being best in class in all areas.

Activities under way in 2014

Energy upgrade at Faru Faru

The proposed approach to energy is to upgrade a lodge or camp each year. Faru Faru has the highest stationary fuel running costs and the oldest generators. The upgrades currently under way include:

- Replacement of all air-conditioning units with new units using inverter technology that is approximately 30% more efficient
- Replacement of electric geysers with solar thermal geysers
- Complete replacement of all lights with LEDs (as part of a property-wide programme)

These upgrades are expected to reduce fuel use by approximately 20–25%, and replacement of the two 100 kva generators with five dynamically synchronized 30 kva units should cut fuel use by a further 50%.

Guest experience

Potentially one of the largest impacts that Singita Grumeti can have is through sharing its sustainability commitment with guests in an interactive and subtle way. The aim is to be able to communicate the passion and importance behind the sustainability programme without preaching to the guests so as to translate the message of sustainability to them in a way that inspires them to take it home. The guest communication programme has started with the provision of basic information in rooms and vehicles.

Furthermore, as part of the programme of giving guests a deeper experience of the African bush, the walking and cycling safaris are being promoted and expanded through exercise walks and game viewing hides. The safari guides are also using their bespoke training to reinforce the sustainability message.

Waste reduction

In 2014, the use of plastic bottles will be all but eliminated at Singita Grumeti through the installation of three water purification units across Sasakwa Lodge, Serengeti House, Faru Faru and Sabora Camp, thereby reducing plastic waste by approximately 0.5 tonnes per month. A machine composter unit will also be installed so all of the food waste need no longer go to landfill; this change will also mean that the home-made compost can be used on the in-house gardens and vegetable patches.

Conclusions

The hotels at Singita Grumeti are continually recognized as some of the best, most luxurious hotels in the world. By becoming a One Planet community, Singita Grumeti is also pledging to "operate within global environmental limits" and committing to this principle as fundamental to the way in which the company conducts its business. By aiming to deliver the ultimate in luxury tourism in a truly sustainable fashion, and in a challenging and remote location, Singita Grumeti is setting a new standard in conservation and sustainable tourism, which can influence the wider area and tourism globally.

The progress made in the first year has been impressive, and the plans and projects under way will ensure that the pace of improvement accelerates. The One Planet Principles have been instrumental in supporting the speed of change by providing a coherent framework for developing the sustainability strategy and an engaging story and vision for staff and visitors alike.

References

BioRegional (2014), http://www.bioregional.com/one-planet-living-our-unique-framework/individuals, accessed 11 August 2015.

Galli, A., Wiedmann, T., Ercin, E., Knoblauch, D., Ewing, B., & Giljum, S. (2012). Integrating ecological, carbon, and water footprint into a "footprint family" of indicators: definition and role in tracking human pressure on the planet. *Ecological Indicators,* 16, 100–12

Goodman, P.S. (2014). Personal communication.

Hansen J., Sato M., Kharecha P., Beerling D., Berner R., Masson-Delmotte V., Pagani M., Raymo M., Royer D., & Zachos J. (2008). Target atmospheric CO_2: Where should humanity aim? *Open Atmospheric Science Journal,* 2, 217–31.

IPCC (Edenhofer, O., Pichs-Madruga R., Sokona Y., Farahani E., Kadner S., Seyboth K., Adler A., Baum I., Brunner S., Eickemeier P., Kriemann B., Savolainen J., Schlömer S., von Stechow C., Zwickel T., & Minx J.C.) (2014). *Summary for Policymakers: Climate Change 2014, Mitigation of Climate Change. Contribution of Working Group III to the Fifth Assessment Report of the Intergovernmental Panel on Climate Change.* Cambridge, UK and New York, NY: Cambridge University Press.

Kitzes, J., Galli, A., Bagliani, M., Barrett, J., Dige, G., Ede, S., Erb, K., Giljum, S., Haberl, H., Hails, C., Jungwirth, S., Lenzen, M., Lewis, K., Loh, J., Marchettini, N., Messinger, H., Milne, K., Moles, R., Monfreda, C., Moran, D., Nakano, K., Pyhälä, A., Rees, W., Simmons, C., Wackernagel, M., Wada, Y., Walsh, C., & Wiedmann, T. (2009). A research agenda for improving national ecological footprint accounts. *Ecological Economics,* 68(7), 1991–2007.

Living Planet Report (2012). Retrieved from http://wwf.panda.org/about_our_earth/all_publications/living_planet_report, accessed 11 August 2015.

One Planet Communities (2013). Retrieved from http://www.oneplanetcommunities.org/wp-content/uploads/2013/12/SG_OP_Public-Document_Final_18112013.pdf, accessed 11 August 2015.

Ranganathan, J., Corbier, L., Bhatia, P., Schmitz, S., Peter Gage, P., & Oren, K. (2004). *The Greenhouse Gas Protocol: A Corporate Accounting and Reporting Standard.* Washington, DC: World Resource Institute

Rockström, J., Steffen, W., Noone, K., Persson, Å., Chapin, F.S., III, Laxmbin, E., Lenton, T.M., Scheffer, M., Folke, C., Schellnhuber, H., Nykvist, B., De Wit, C.A., Hughes, T., van der Leeuw, S., Rodhe, H., Sörlin, S., Snyder, P.K., Costanza. R., Svedin, U., Falkenmark, M., Karlberg, L., Corell, R.W., Fabry, V.J., Hansen, J., Walker, B., Liverman, D., Richardson, K., Crutzen, P., & Foley, J. (2009). Planetary boundaries: Exploring the safe operating space for humanity. *Ecology and Society,* 14(2), 32.

12

Business and sustainable tourism

Sextantio—a case study

Salvatore Moccia
Catholic University of Valencia, Spain

The current literature provides abundant information about the growing importance of sustainability in business. Companies in almost every industry, from the food industry to construction, and including petroleum, carmakers, hotels, etc., have jumped on the sustainability bandwagon. However, even if executives and shareholders recognize the importance of sustainability, the challenge lies in how to integrate and implement it successfully in for-profit organizations. In this chapter, we will present the case of Sextantio, a for-profit company dedicated to hospitality—with two hotels running and several other projects in development—which is a pioneer in the field of sustainability applied to hospitality. The company focuses on the reclamation of abandoned areas to create hotels that, apart from being profitable, are also a way to recover marginal areas, and, in general terms, to push the local economy. This chapter is a case study. Considering the emphasis placed on sustainability and business, this case can have some practical implications in the field of sustainable hospitality.

Introduction and purpose

> Happiness lies not in the mere possession of money; it lies in the joy of achievement, in the thrill of creative effort. The joy and moral stimulation of work must no longer be forgotten in the mad chase of evanescent profits ... (Roosevelt, 1933).

The current literature provides abundant information about the growing importance of sustainability in business among businessmen, executives, academics and public. A recent McKinsey (2014) survey among 3,344 executives representing the full range of regions. Industries, company sizes, functional specialties and tenures, found that company leaders believe that sustainability is becoming a more strategic and integral part of their businesses. Regarding the interest of the public, whereas a Google search on the term in February 2009 turned up 28,100,000 entries (Crews, 2010), today, July 2014, the Google search turns up 42,200,000. In fact, scholars agree that sustainability has become a common business buzzword, akin to "going green", "saving the planet", "reducing our carbon footprint", "the three Ps" (people, planet and profit), "TBL", and "environmentally friendly" products and services (Jeffers *et al.*, 2014; Bateh *et al.*, 2013). Companies in almost every industry, from the food industry to construction, and including petroleum, carmakers, hotels, etc., have jumped on the sustainability bandwagon. Crews (2010) notes: "Business leaders must be wondering [if sustainability is] just the latest management fad or a concept that will fundamentally change how businesses are managed and measured". In addition to that, the scholar underlines that sustainability is more than a fad, creating a permanent shift in the very nature of business. However, even if executives and shareholders recognize the importance of sustainability, the challenge today lies in how to integrate and implement it successfully in for-profit organizations. According to Epstein *et al.* (2010):

> How to manage the paradox of improving social, environmental and financial goals simultaneously is one of a company's biggest challenges. Integrating corporate social, environmental and financial impacts into operational and capital investment decisions come with a lot of tension. While social and financial initiatives may benefit one another in the long term, they're often conflicting in their need for resources and agendas in the short run.

Regarding the definition of sustainability, it is a challenge. In fact, several scholars note there is still a certain disagreement on the definition and notion of sustainability (Bateh, *et al.*, 2013). For the purpose of this chapter, we would use the definition of sustainability articulated in 1987 by the United Nations: "development that meets the needs of the present without compromising the ability of future generations to meet their own needs" (United Nations, 1987).

As already noted before, sustainability has also become a white-hot issue in the hospitality industry. People are beginning to look at sustainable solutions in a whole new way. In fact, Wang & Wang (2009) underline that "as a sign of its sweeping popularity" one of the best-attended sessions at the recent Lodging Conference in Phoenix was "Going green: Environmentally profitable hotels". In this chapter, we will present the case of Sextantio, a for-profit company dedicated to hospitality—with two hotels running and several other projects in development—which is a pioneer in the field of sustainability applied to hospitality. The company focuses on the reclamation of abandoned areas to create hotels which, apart from being profitable, are also a way to recover marginal areas, and, in general terms, to push the local economy. Daniele Kihlgren, founder and President of Sextantio, has been the driving force behind the company's effort to transform abandoned areas into luxury hotels. According to him:

> Ancient settlements are an important part of Italian patrimony but they have been systematically violated. We have the moral obligation to deliver them to new generations. In addition to that, they can represent an important economic value. From this perspective, I got the idea to restructure ancient settlements with the aim of creating a touristic destination, for a highly qualified tourist, loving history, civilization and culture.

This chapter is a case study. It has been developed thanks to the help of Mr Kihlgren, founder and president of Sextantio, who has been interviewed by the authors in different occasions. Considering the emphasis placed on sustainability and business, the case can have some practical implications in the field of sustainable hospitality.

Sextantio in Abruzzo: The beginning

The company started its pioneer project in 1999, in Abruzzo, Italy, buying an old settlement in Santo Stefano di Sessanio. The most accredited hypothesis is that the name Sessanio derives from a corruption of Sextantio (which gives the name to the company), a small Roman settlement near the present-day town, probably six miles away from an important Roman *pagus* (village). It is located high in the mountains, at 1,251 metres above sea level. This picturesque village rose in the 11th century and for a long time belonged to the Barons of Piccolomini from Siena until 1569, when the whole territory was bought by Francesco de Medici, Grand Duke of Tuscany. The Medici family owned these lands until 1743. Their presence was very helpful for the economy of the village, because of their strong relationships with Florence, especially in wool trade. At the end of the 18th century Santo Stefano came under the rule of the King of Naples. The age-old practice of transhumance marked the economy of this village, and has exerted an enormous historical and cultural influence on the character, lifestyle and traditions of the local people. The decline of the village started together with the transhumance crisis, and at the end of the 19th century most of the local people moved, both in other parts of Italy and America. Agriculture was the main occupation of the people who decided to stay here. At the beginning of the 20th century there were about 1,500 inhabitants, which became about 900 after the Second World War. The decrease continued in the following decades. In 2004 the local population amounted to just 112 inhabitants.

The village of Santo Stefano di Sessanio is perhaps the most fascinating of all of man's achievements in the entire Parco Nazionale del Gran Sasso e dei Monti della Laga. It is built entirely out of white limestone, which has become dulled with time. All the houses are covered with clay tiles, providing a harmonious overall view to those gazing down on it from the top of the Medici tower. The village is considered one of the most beautiful in Abruzzo, for its pure environmental values, architectural dignity and stylistic homogeneity. Although there are no real fortified walls, the village is entirely surrounded by an unbroken line of buildings, which served as both houses and defence walls, as is further evidenced by their very few and small windows.

Sextantio: The project

According to Daniele Kihlgren, he discovered the village of S. Stefano just by chance. He was driving around the area, and then he lost the road. Finally he found a paved road that led to the village. When he saw the village for the first time he got the impression that time had stopped there. Everything was still as it had been in the past. Then, he went back the city and he visited a consulting company. They suggested he develop a business analysis to see—from a financial point of view— whether it was possible to create a touristic activity in the area. Not following the advice of the consultants, Mr Kihlgren instead started dreaming about the revitalization of the area, firmly convinced of the merit of the model. Subsequently he further developed the concept of "Albergo Diffuso", which implies that urban planning and architecture, for certain specific and historical sites, should not bend to their final destination but is the history and the respect for it which impose the final destination. For example, at the Sextantio Albergo Diffuso in S. Stefano di Sessanio, reception is inside a cave used to rear pigs, and at the Sextantio Albergo Diffuso Le Grotte della Civita in Matera a rock church is the common room for guests. The company decided to purchase nine of the few preserved historical villages, some of them built in the Middle Ages, located on top of the Apennine mountains, others more rural but in a seductive fusion with the surrounding area.

The mission of the company is to save all forms of the territorial identity: from the landscape, to the history and the architecture and local materials cultures, to the craft tradition and the cuisine of the areas.

The Sextantio strategy is based on the following pillars:

- Development of the local economy
- Increase in the buildings' value

- Restoration of old professions

- Development of agriculture

- Economic sustainability

The general idea of Mr Kihlgren was not to offer tourists an old area refurbished as a new one, but an old area alive with old traditions, and the old spirits. In accordance with that, when he started to analyse the local area in more depth, he asked old people about the old traditions, including old dishes, old furniture, old materials, old colours, old stories and old rituals. All these elements were, then, supported by academic research.

Mr Kihlgren undertook all the analysis and already drawing a sort of business plan, even if he does not like to call it a business plan but rather "intuition and enthusiasm", he signed an agreement with the local municipality and with the regional authority responsible for the environmental protection of the area, with the aim of rediscovering the old flavour of the village, and maintaining the traditions. Based on this agreement, Mr Kihlgren bought abandoned areas of the village and started the restoration.

Figure 12.1 **The Sextantio Project in Matera. The area as it was before**

2006/06/10

Figure 12.2 The Sextantio Project in Matera. The area as it is now

Figure 12.3 The Sextantio Project in S. Stefano di Sessanio. The interior as it was before

Figure 12.4 The Sextantio Project in S. Stefano di Sessanio. The interior as it is now

Figure 12.5 The Sextantio Project in S. Stefano di Sessanio. The interior as it is now

Figure 12.6 The Sextantio Project in S. Stefano di Sessanio. The interior as it was before

Figure 12.7 The Sextantio Project in S. Stefano di Sessanio. The interior as it is now

Figure 12.8 The Sextantio Project in S. Stefano di Sessanio. A typical dish of S. Stefano

Figure 12.9 The Sextantio Project in S. Stefano di Sessanio. A picture of a loom in the area of S. Stefano de Sessanio

The restoration was undertaken taking into account the following:

- Maintaining the design of the building as it originally was

- Regarding the interiors, maintaining, as much as possible, the same elements as in the past, including small details, like cutlery, chairs, blankets, etc.

- When it was no longer possible to find some elements for the restoration process, he decided to produce them, using the same age-old techniques

As for traditions, Mr Kihlgren was also worried about recovering the old novels and stories, so the restored area was used also to tell stories and tales. And as for gastronomy, also in this case, the idea was to retain the old traditions as much as possible. In accordance with that, the menus have been developed taking into account the old recipes, and the old ways of preparing and serving food.

The results

Development of the local economy

When Mr Kihlgren started the analysis of the area of S. Stefano, the population was declining fast. The decline is even worse compared with other Italian touristic locations.

Figure 12.10 **Demographic trends between 1861 and 1981 in two famous touristic locations in The Alps (Courmayer and Selva di Val Gardena), in two touristic winter locations in Abruzzo (Roccaraso and Pescocostanzo) and one in the Abruzzo mountains where touristic presence is not significant (S. Stefano di Sessanio)**

Source: Sextantio

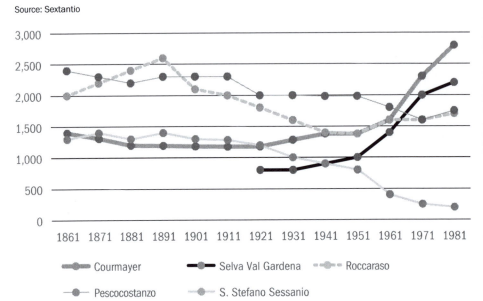

In 2001 the touristic presence in the area of S. Stefano di Sessanio was limited to 285 per year. The availability of beds in the village was limited to 79.

In 2008, following the establishment of Sextantio in S. Stefano di Sessanio, the touristic presence in the area has been growing to up to 7,300 people per year, underlying the exponential growth caused by the hotel.

In addition to that, it was possible also to see a real explosion of other touristic capabilities, like bed and breakfasts, restaurants, coffee shops and wineries.

Increase in the buildings' value

Regarding the prices of buildings in the municipality of S. Stefano de Sessanio, the analysis of the Regional Agency for the territory has given the following results:

Table 12.1 **Population, hotels, number of beds available and yearly number of tourists in S. Stefano di Sessanio**

Source: Sextantio

Population	No. hotels	No. beds	No. tourists
112	3	79	285

Figure 12.11 Touristic presence in the area of S. Stefano di Sessanio between 2005 and 2008

Source: Sextantio

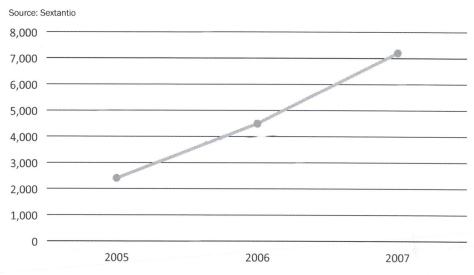

It is possible to see that every year, since the beginning of the project, the values of buildings in the specific area has been rising quickly. In addition to that, if we compare this rise with the prices in similar areas of the same region, we can easily understand that this growth has been significant (Source: Regional Agency for the territory).

If we analyse the difference between the first geographical area (S. Stefano di Sessanio) and the second one, there is a difference of €637.50. If we multiply this difference for the square metres available in the area (50,187.55 m²), the final result is €31,994.690.63. This number represents the increase in the buildings' value on account of the presence of the Hotel Sextantio in the area.

Restoration of old professions

The economic development of the area has also allowed the resurgence of age-old professions like blacksmithing, weaving, woodworking, crocheting and restoring.

Development of agriculture

The impact on agriculture has been double. From one side, there has been a positive change due to increasing demand from tourists for local products and, from another side, due to the recovery of old seeds and old cultivation techniques in producing the dishes prepared in the hotel restaurant.

Table 12.2 Number of touristic infrastructures in the area of S. Stefano di Sessanio, year 2010

Source: Sextantio

Type	No.	Beds/chairs
Agritourism	4	42
Bed and breakfast	15	329
Camping	1	
Restaurants	8	430
Small shops	17	
Coffee shops	7	

Table 12.3 Market value euro/square metre in the village of S. Stefano di Sessanio, year 2006–2008

Source: Regional Agency for the Territory

Typology	Market value (€/mq) 2 semester 2006	Market value (€/mq) 1 semester 2007	Market value (€/mq) 2 semester 2007	Market value (€/mq) 1 semester 2008	Market value (€/mq) 2 semester 2008
House—historic centre	Min. 370 Max. 540	Min. 405 Max. 590	Min. 485 Max. 710	Min. 580 Max. 850	Min. 700 Max. 1,020
House—economic	Min. 300 Max. 440	Min. 330 Max. 485	Min. 395 Max. 580	Min. 470 Max. 700	Min. 560 Max. 840
Garage	Min. 290 Max. 430	Min. 320 Max. 475	Min. 385 Max. 570	Min. 460 Max. 680	Min. 550 Max. 820
Penthouse	Min. 390 Max. 550	Min. 430 Max. 610	Min. 520 Max. 730	Min. 620 Max. 880	Min. 740 Max. 1,060

Table 12.4 Average market value euro/square metre in the village of S. Stefano di Sessanio compared to neighbouring villages, year 2010

Source: Regional Agency for the Territory

Municipality	Average market value (€/mq)—House historic center, 2010
Barisciano	€657.50
Calascio	€875.00
Carapelle Calvisio	€431.25
Castel del Monte	€925.00
Castelvecchio Calvisio	€428.75
S. Stefano di Sessanio	€1,562.50
Villa S. Lucia	€428.75

Economic sustainability

The economic data, in general terms, reveal sound business development. It is clear enough that since 2010 they have been changing the pricing policy, and it is giving them good results. In fact, even if the Average Room Rate[1] has been declining, on the other side there has been a rise in the percentage of rooms occupied and, consequently, an increase in the revenue (source: Sextantio).

Figure 12.12: Room occupancy between 2010 and 2012 in the two projects

Source: Sextantio

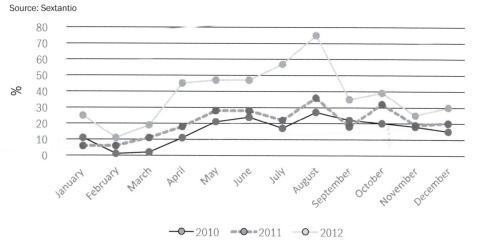

Sextantio in Basilicata: The second intervention

The second intervention of Sextantio was in Matera, in the south of Italy, a place declared a UNESCO world heritage site. According to the UNESCO web page: "Matera is the most outstanding, intact example of a troglodyte settlement in the Mediterranean region, perfectly adapted to its terrain and ecosystem". The first inhabited zone dates from the Palaeolithic era, while later settlements illustrate a number of significant stages in human history. These ancient settlement are internationally well known as the "Sassi di Matera"[2] (stones of Matera). The Sassi are houses dug into the rock itself, representing a collection of caverns that have been used during the last 7,000 years as houses.

---

1 The Average Room Rate is the hotel revenue divided by the number of rooms sold. Therefore, if a hotel made €100,00 and sold 400 rooms, the Average Room Rate would be 100,000/400 = €250.

2 http://whc.unesco.org/en/list/670, accessed 8 May 2013

Table 12.5 Comparison, by year and months, of room occupancy in the two projects

Source: Sextantio

Room occupancy			
	2010	**2011**	**2012**
January	11%	6%	25%
February	1%	6%	11%
March	2%	11%	19%
April	11%	18%	45%
May	21%	28%	47%
June	24%	28%	47%
July	17%	22%	57%
August	27%	36%	75%
September	22%	18%	35%
October	20%	32%	39%
November	18%	19%	25%
December	15%	20%	30%

Table 12.6 Comparison, by year and months, of the Average Room Rate in the two projects

Source: Sextantio

Average Room Rate			
	2010	**2011**	**2012**
January	€232	€252	€121
February	€309	€171	€105
March	€166	€104	€103
April	€184	€171	€154
May	€176	€174	€140
June	€215	€171	€145
July	€215	€277	€139
August	€213	€183	€144
September	€208	€162	€145
October	€278	€190	€145
November	€130	€105	€115
December	€227	€187	€145

Figure 12.13 The Sextantio Project in Matera. The hotel

Figure 12.14 The Sextantio Project in Matera. The interior of a room

Figure 12.15 The Sextantio Project in Matera. The interior of another room

Table 12.7 Turnover of Sextantio in 2008–2012 and average room occupancy in percentage

Source: Sextantio

Year	Average room occupancy (%)	Turnover
2012	38%	€520,000.00
2011	20%	€360,000.00
2010	16%	€280,000.00
2009	13%	€255,000.00
2008	20%	€330,000.00

Sextantio Albergo Diffuso Le Cave della Civita is divided into 18 rooms, some of exceptional size, a common sight in a cave church, and a reception. The whole complex is located in caves in the cliff on the river, against the dramatic scenery of the Parco della Murgia and rocky churches, and located in the oldest part of the poor and degraded Civita. For the restoration project in the Sassi of Matera, the company maintained the proportion of the rooms, used original and recycled architectural materials, hid as far as possible the modern technology used for heating and plumbing, and used minimalist contemporary design solutions. The unique architectural setting of the Sassi cave habitations of Matera posed particular questions for their conservation philosophy. Traditionally the Sassi of Matera have used more impoverished internal furnishings than the hill towns of Santo Stefano. The farmers in the Sassi were labourers, and not small landholders like their hill-town counterparts. The Sassi cave homes were subsistence living. The Sassi had less of a domestic function than hill-town homes. Life in the Sassi was more focused on the community, so attention was paid to the external appearance of the houses, the communal wells. The furnishings and household objects in the Sassi, though similar to those in the mountain communities, were less refined. Taking all of these differences into consideration, the conservation project was much more minimalist than in Santo Stefano di Sessanio—fittings and fixtures were simpler and fewer. Much of the furniture was built-in, in order to maintain a continuity of form and function with the original structure. With such irregular buildings, free-standing furniture was out of context. Where it was necessary to furnish with desks, chairs and wardrobes, they used reclaimed wood and architectural materials. These designs were simple, and were completely sympathetic with the existing structure, the context of the Sassi caves and the lives of the people who once lived and worked there. The project shows how it is possible to successfully restore the identity of vernacular buildings. Through a researched understanding and an honesty with the buildings' origins—combined with a touch of poetic licence—it was possible to recreate the soul of a building, even when the life lived there was one of poverty—as in the case of the Sassi caves.

Figure 12.16 The Sextantio Project in Matera. The dining room as it is now

Conclusions

> ... a great deal of economic life depends for its viability on a certain limited degree of ethical commitment. Purely selfish behaviour of the individual is really incompatible with any kind of settled economic life (Kenneth Arrow, Nobel Laureate in economics in 1972).

In the business world, it is quite common to talk about profits. What is really not common is to link profits to sustainability. It seems that the two elements are irreconcilable enemies.

This chapter, presenting the case of Sextantio, a company created with the aim of earning profits and recovering old villages and old traditions, is an example of how profits and sustainability can work together. The example of Sextantio, with the protection of this heritage, pursues not only ethical and cultural values, but also a great economic return—not only for the investor but also the whole territory—as the first experience in Santo Stefano di Sessanio has taught.

In short, it can be said that the Sextantio strategy is based on the following:

- Development of local economy: in 2008, following the establishment of Sextantio in S. Stefano di Sessanio, the touristic presence in the area has been growing to up to 7,300 people per year, underlying the exponential growth caused by the hotel. In addition to that, it was possible also to see a real explosion of other touristic capabilities, like bed and breakfast, restaurants, coffee shops and wineries

- Increase of the buildings' value: every year, since the beginning of the project, the value of buildings in the area has been rising enormously. In addition to that, if we compare this rise with the prices in similar areas of the same region, we can easily understand that the growth has been important

- Restoration of old professions: the economic development of the area has been used also to reinstate some old professions like blacksmithing, weaving, woodworking, crocheting and restoring

- Development of agriculture: the impact on agriculture has been double. From one side, there has been a positive impact due to the increasing demand from tourists for local products and, from another side, due to the recovery of old seeds and old cultivation technique for producing the dishes served in the hotel restaurant

- Economic sustainability: the economic data, in general terms, reveal sound business development

The chapter has been developed thanks to the collaborative effort of Sextantio, in the person of its founder and President, and it represents an attempt to argue that profits and sustainability are not enemies. It contains some limitations, the most important being the difficulty to replicate the model everywhere. It is clear enough that the business model is strictly connected to a special form of territory, the sort of territory with enough history, tradition and architecture. Another limitation derives from the fact that it could be very difficult to evaluate the results of the intervention in larger areas. In fact, it is almost impossible to calculate the impact of the second intervention of Sextantio in Matera, as Matera is a declared UNESCO world heritage site, and already receiving tourists from that designation.

References

Bateh, J., *et al.* (2013). Defining sustainability in the business setting. *American Journal of Business Education*, 6(3), 397–400.

Crews, D.E. (2010). Strategies for implementing sustainability: Five leadership challenges. *SAM Advanced Management Journal*, 75(2), 15–21.

Epstein, M.J., Yuthas, K., Buhovac, A.R. (2010). Implementing sustainability: The role of leadership and organizational culture. *Strategic Finance*, April, 41–7.

Jeffers, A.E. *et al.* (2014). Is it time for companies to capitalize on sustainability? *CPA Journal,* March, 6–10.

McKinsey (2014). Sustainability's strategic worth. Retrieved from http://www.mckinsey. com/insights/sustainability/sustainabilitys_strategic_worth_mckinsey_global_survey_ results, accessed 11 August 2015.

Roosevelt, F. (1933). First inaugural address. Retrieved from http://historymatters.gmu. edu/d/5057, accessed 12 October 2015.

Sextantio, http://www.sextantio.it/santo-stefano/?lang=en, accessed 11 August 2015.

UNESCO (1993). The Sassi and the park of the Rupestrian churches of Matera. Retrieved from http://whc.unesco.org/en/list/670, accessed 11 August 2015.

United Nations (1987). Report of the World Commission on Environment and Development: Our common future. Retrieved from http://www.un-documents.net/wced-ocf.htm, accessed 11 August 2015.

Wang, J.-Z. & Wang, J. (2009), Issues, challenges and trends facing hospitality industry. *Management Science and Engineering*, 3(4), 53–8.

13

Compliance or the deviant response?

Implementation patterns of the TTTIC quality practice in Trinidad & Tobago

Marlon Delano Nangle

John Molson School of Business, Concordia University, Canada

While pursuing business objectives, organizations face the challenge of balancing competitive and institutional demands. However, for some firms, conformance to institutional pressures to adopt and fully implement a practice does not imply that the most effective and efficient choice is made. By drawing on theoretical insight from institutional theory, organizational agency, competitive strategy and issue interpretation I argue that a firm's competitive strategy influences the extent of implementation a practice receives. To conduct this study I examined the implementation patterns of a quality practice introduced to the tourist accommodation industry in the Republic of Trinidad & Tobago. The competitive factors that lead managers to interpret the practice as an opportunity for gain versus a threat for loss were examined to understand better the motivations towards an adopted practice in a competitive environment. Results suggest that the competitive environment does indeed influence how an adopted practice is interpreted. Further results demonstrate a strong association between issue interpretation and the extent of practice implementation, which is arguably decided by top management beliefs regarding the value of the practice. Limitations of the study and potential avenues for future research are discussed, followed by practical implications rendered applicable to business and society.

Introduction

Quality assurance is at the very essence of tourism as it impacts each of the sub-sectors of the industry. To promote sustainability, a nation may choose to incorporate a certification system that targets its tourist operators to comply with a set of standards. This chapter investigates what occurs with a quality certification practice that has been newly introduced to the tourist accommodation sector—strictly speaking, the level of implementation that the practice receives. With attention on motivation and cognition surrounding the implementation decision, the central focus becomes how the practice is actually interpreted by adopting decision-makers. While the decision to conform to institutional pressures to adopt a practice may appear to be in a firm's best interest for legitimating reasons, it does not imply that the most effective or efficient choice is made. Addressing the call for more research to understand what factors might predict issue interpretation (Jackson & Dutton, 1988), the competitive factors that lead decision-makers to interpret a practice as an opportunity versus a threat towards business objectives are examined. Further, results illustrate that the value a decision-maker places on a practice does, indeed, influence the level of implementation the practice receives from the adopting firm.

In an effort to diversify the economy and make it strong enough to withstand economic shocks, the government of the Republic of T&T (Trinidad & Tobago) has been making a concerted effort to promote sustainable economic growth and development. Now one of the nation's goals is to transform the country into a premiere tourist destination. Yet a key issue that has always plagued T&T's tourism sector is a reputation for second-rate quality in its product and service offerings. In 2006, the TTTIC (Trinidad & Tobago Tourism Industry Certification) programme was reintroduced as a process by which an independent body gives written assurance that accommodation providers conform to a set of specified requirements contained in the national standard. However, as of 2012, if one were to research tourist destination reviews, there exists an inconsistency in customer evaluations of quality service among T&T's tourist accommodation providers. One would see reviews ranging from the extreme positive to the extreme negative among tourist accommodation providers who have the TTTIC certification.

Unreliable results in the level of quality achieved among tourist accommodation providers suggest a need to explore the factors that cause this variability in order to provide solutions that will make for better success with this sustainable government initiative. Furthermore, a dominant paradigm in business policy literature is that firms employ generic business-level strategies in pursuit of their economic and competitive goals (Porter, 1980, 1985). That said, since the chosen business strategy denotes a way for a tourist accommodation provider to view and respond to changes in its environment, this variation would probably be seen among tourist accommodation providers responding to institutionalized pressure to adopt a practice as well, such as the TTTIC initiative.

With the central focus of this inquiry being institutional pressures to adopt, the extent of implementation an adopted practice receives and the resultant dissimilarity among industry participants, the two related research questions become:

- Does a tourist accommodation provider's business strategy influence how the quality practice is interpreted?

- Does the interpretation of the quality practice influence the level of implementation that the quality practice receives by adopting organizations?

It is rare to see a study examining how organizations experience isomorphic pressures, interpret them and learn to manage them (Boxenbaum & Jonsson, 2008), making the objective of this study to examine how organizations in the tourist accommodation sector of T&T interpret, experience and manage the TTTIC practice. Using an organization's business strategy as a predictor variable in issue interpretation, this study includes the role of adoption motivation to help understand how adopters interpret issues they face and what are the likely outcomes of these interpretations.

The role of institutional context in the tourism industry

Institutional theorists emphasize that, in order to gain and maintain support, an organization is expected to follow the laws dictated by governing bodies, meet the standards set by accreditation agencies, perform the duties as members of various associations and promote the products and services desired by end consumers. Isomorphism takes place since organizations in the same field are exposed to the same isomorphic pressures described above and thus a certain degree of conformity seems inevitable since all organizations have legitimacy concerns. Oliver (1991), however, reaffirmed the possibility for agency within the institutional context by envisioning alternative strategic responses to institutional pressures other than just conformity. A central remaining debate in institutional theory is whether organizational behaviour derives from and is guided by the larger social forces that be, or by the agency-type behaviour that exercises the right to evaluate and make choice. While proponents of agency agree that all organizations succumb to institutional pressures, each at the very least can exercise varying discretion in its response (DiMaggio, 1988; Oliver, 1991).

With a newly introduced practice to the tourist accommodation sector, one could assume that, to avoid social sanctioning, all tourist accommodations wishing to maintain legitimate standing will undertake some form of implementation. Internalization, however, is described as the state upon which the recipients view the practice as valuable and therefore become committed to it (Kostova & Roth, 2002). It is argued that internalization is of key importance since the positive perceptions of a practice are reflected in "action-generating" properties that go beyond initial adoption to create persistence and stability of the practice over time (Tolbert & Zucker 1996, p. 177). However, an adopted practice not perceived as valuable by recipients is argued to lead to ceremonial adoption (Kostova & Roth, 2002). Many argue this outcome to be likely when there is high uncertainty surrounding a practice or the belief that it is not valuable, matched with strong pressures for its adoption from the legitimating environment (Meyer & Rowan, 1977; Tolbert & Zucker, 1983).

Issue interpretation

One way to examine interpretations by decision-makers is to assign constructs to categorize environmental events (George *et al.*, 2006). Opportunity and threat constructs have been found to be useful in executive decision-making (Dutton & Jackson, 1987; Jackson & Dutton, 1988) as they each imply a sense of urgency and difficulty, which probably leads to organizational action (George *et al.*, 2006). Introduced by Staw *et al.* (1981), the threat-rigidity hypothesis posits that, when faced with a threat, individuals and organizations have a tendency towards rigidly pursuing routine activities, which results in restricted information processing and constriction of control (Staw *et al.*, 1981). The reasoning is that by strictly adhering to well-established—thus predictable—behaviours and routines, individuals and organizations can regain control over what seems uncontrollable after being perceived as a threat. Staw *et al.* (1981) imply that, when an organization chooses to pursue an opportunity, it will go beyond usual routines, thus risking action that is perceived to result in benefit and gain. Therefore, framing an issue, whether positive or negative, affects organizational change by influencing the cognition and subsequent motivation of the organization's decision-maker (Dutton *et al.*, 1983).

Competitive strategy

Through executing an effective competitive strategy, a company discovers its industry focus and learns about the customers it serves (Porter, 1980). Porter's theory consists of two essential key elements to a competitive strategy. The first element is a schematic one used to describe a firm's competitive strategy according to its market scope, which is either broad or niche focused. The second element refers to the firm's chosen source of competitive advantage, which can be through cost or differentiation (Campbell-Hunt, 2000).

Low cost

This generic strategy focuses on cost reduction wherever possible. A low-cost strategy addresses costs associated with operations, facilities, overheads and the savings attainable from experience. The intended purpose of pursuing such efforts is to position the business to gain competitive advantage by having the lowest cost in the industry (Porter, 1979, 1987, 1996) for its products and services. For this strategy to be effective, price should be an important factor among rivals and the product or service being offered should be standardized since the features are acceptable and recognizable to many customers.

Differentiation

This strategy is aimed at establishing fundamental differences in its product and service offerings so that buyers are able to perceive definable attributes of the product and service in contrast to those of the firm's competitors (Porter, 1979, 1987, 1996; Hlavacka *et al.*, 2001). Hence, this strategy focuses on creating uniqueness that is in demand so much as to justify incurring additional costs since the firm is rewarded by commanding premium prices of its customers. Although there are many ways to differentiate a product to provide value to customers with diverse needs, the firm must make sure to differentiate on the right things. This means firms using this strategy must differentiate on features that buyers perceive as providing value and guard against over-differentiating to make product features exceed buyers' needs.

Trinidad & Tobago tourism industry certification

To date, there are a number of factors that affect the potential of T&T's tourism industry to play a more significant role in the nation's economy. Of these factors, the major issues central to this study include: quality of tourist accommodation establishments, adherence to international standards and customer service (Ministry of Tourism, Trinidad & Tobago, 2010). Due to T&T's historical heritage and assortment of social factors, there still exists a strong underlying perception among the population that service means servitude (Newsday, 2010). As such, this attitude results in many cases of slow or indifferent service delivery, which contributes to reducing the tourism industry's competitiveness.

The purpose of the TTTIC practice is to increase the quality level of the nation's accommodation providers by having them meet minimal international standards through annual audits and continual monitoring. An inherent flaw of this mandate is the fact that, although quality is a term used frequently among policymakers and managers alike, it is also quite ambiguous. For one, quality could be simply a job well done and, although this could be seen as common sense, it still proves difficult to effectively define the term broadly as such (Sheehan & Presenza, 2011). Quality for another could be assuring the compliance of products and services with a given set of standards and procedures identified through a form of certification (Sheehan & Presenza, 2011). Although the second proposed definition seems to align itself with the mandate of the TTTIC, it also stands to complicate the definition further as it relates to the tourist accommodation sector since manufacturing-based definitions have proven inapplicable to service quality, requiring that new conceptualizations be made. In the tourist accommodation sector, the definition of quality becomes extremely elusive because outputs from the sector can be standardized and customized as well as tangible and intangible (Sheehan & Presenza, 2011). Therefore, it seems impossible to adequately represent what quality is in the tourist accommodation sector by conformance to and/or exceeding a set of broad standards.

The TTTIC has a set of standards for bed & breakfast/self-catering properties and a set for hotels/guesthouses. To encourage practice adoption, the TTTIC offers benefits such as promotion on the TDC (Tourism Development Company) website, operator credibility enhanced by a recognized logo, promotion in a TTTIC certified operator brochure listing as well as receiving special badges, decals and other marketing material to identify a certified operator (Romain, 2009). In addition, operators also have access to free and subsidized training through STEP (Small Tourism Enterprise Project), which provides training, capacity building and institutional strengthening for tourism operators.

TTTIC competitive strategy and issue interpretation

Although the TTTIC practice gives prospective adopters a broad definition of what quality is, those using a differentiation strategy already have their own well-articulated definition to go by. As such, the decision-makers of these firms should positively frame the TTTIC practice since for them there is no ambiguity surrounding what quality is to their customer base; thus, they have perceived control as to what the practice will mean to them. With this perception of control, the decision-maker's cognition should motivate them to see the practice as an opportunity for economic and social gain since adoption of the practice could help the firm distinguish itself from other organizations (e.g. Abrahamson, 1991), and even help them be regarded as one of the market leaders in their respective segment.

By contrast, firms pursuing a low-cost strategy in T&T are typically small bed & breakfast establishments as well as "no frills" self-catered apartments—the majority being converted private residences that are owner-occupied and operated. Past research demonstrates that a low-cost strategy is ideally suited to a stable and predictable environment (Hambrick, 1983; Miller, 1988; Kim & Lim, 1988) as it allows firms to better control costs and improves efficiency (Miller, 1988). As stated earlier, with the TTTIC practice still relatively new to T&T's tourism industry, this creates a new learning curve that low-cost firms must navigate in order to see what economies can be realized as well as diseconomies to be avoided. Since the TTTIC

Figure 13.1 **TTTIC certification process for tourist accommodation providers**

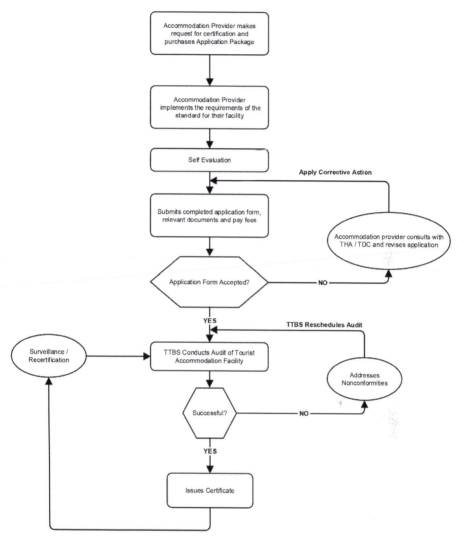

practice's minimal requirements are broad in nature and rendered applicable to all accommodation types, ambiguity is likely to exist surrounding what denotes quality. Given that the majority of low-cost providers in this industry have limited economic resources, this presents obstacles that can cause the perception of having less control in the environment. This loss of control should cause decision-makers to frame the TTTIC practice negatively in the sense that it will do nothing towards improving efficiency, thus causing low-cost firms to revert to familiar routines in order to regain control in their environment (Staw *et al.*, 1981). The introduction of the TTTIC as a mainstay in the tourist sector will also create normative pressures and legitimacy considerations to adopt the practice. As such, it becomes socially unfavourable for the low-cost firm to be seen to be out of step with what has become legitimate and standard, thus they will adopt the practice to stay in tune with industry developments. Thus, even though the low-cost firm perceives no economic or social benefit in the TTTIC practice, it will not risk incurring any economic or social loss from failure in adopting it.

TTTIC issue interpretation and practice implementation

Based on the stance by agency scholars, organizations at the very least experience differing levels of discretion in responding to institutional pressures (Heugens & Lander, 2009). That said, when faced with institutional pressures, it will be key decision-makers who will interpret and choose the best response that suits the organization. The relationship between a newly adopted practice and the organization does not cease at the moment of adoption. Rather the decision-maker's reasons for taking up the practice should affect how far they go in implementation.

Opportunity perception

Examining the relationship between motivation and implementation prior research suggests that, when the decision-maker interprets an issue as an opportunity, it will facilitate the organization's potential for action (Kostova & Roth, 2002). With the issue being the adoption of the TTTIC practice, it is argued that decision-makers who believe they can achieve gains associated with practice adoption will work harder to implement it. Members in the same organizational field are typically insouciant to certain amounts of differentiation, which allows each a range of leeway (Deephouse, 1999) around the institutionalized template. This means that organizations are free to customize a prescribed template such as the TTTIC practice to enhance its contribution to quality and efficiency (Westphal *et al.*, 1997; Zbaracki, 1998) for the firm.

Threat perception

Similarly, the threat-rigidity hypothesis suggests that, when an organization is faced with an issue that is perceived as a threat, it will respond by reverting to familiar routines and becoming "rigid" (Staw *et al.*, 1981). As such, it is expected that this perception will lead the organization to restrict information and conserve its resources (Staw *et al.*, 1981). In similar vein, it is argued that, as opposed to achieving gains, no belief in such benefits will lead a firm to work less hard to implement the TTTIC practice. In a similar fashion, Kostova & Roth (2002) studied the adoption of organizational practices by MNC subsidiaries and found that ceremonial adoption was typical of subsidiaries that did not agree with the practice but were, nonetheless, forced to adopt it. As such, firms perceiving the TTTIC practice as a threat to their economic and social standing are expected to put forth less effort towards implementation, but still do just enough to save face and maintain their legitimacy.

Methods and analysis

Previous empirical studies of strategy have focused both temporally and geographically on environmental control (DeSarbo *et al.*, 2005), whereas study of managerial cognition has concentrated on specific industries in order to better understand the comparisons between firms (Kennedy & Fiss, 2009). With the research context being the tourist accommodation sector of Trinidad & Tobago, the first objective was to identify all tourist accommodation providers who were audited and TTTIC approved as well as those pending certification. A survey coupled with an open-ended interview was chosen for this study. Suitable informants were those who were knowledgeable about their company's involvement with the TTTIC practice, including regulatory bodies such as the TTBS (Trinidad & Tobago Bureau of Standards) and the audit process towards achieving certification. Informants needed to answer various questions regarding perceptions surrounding the TTTIC practice as well as various questions regarding implementation outcomes. Survey participants were restricted to shift supervisors, managers and owners who were knowledgeable of or directly involved with their company's adoption of the TTTIC practice. The complete survey can be reviewed in Appendix A.

A total of 32 (16 in Trinidad, 16 in Tobago) from a list of 105 accommodation providers responded to the survey, resulting in a response rate of 30.5%. Additionally, this list contained tourist accommodation providers representing hotels, guesthouses, bed & breakfast and self-catering facilities that were spread throughout the entire country. These variations in types and locations suggest that the target firms are representative of the general characteristics of tourism accommodations of the population.

Measures used in study

All of the multi-item measures in this study were those that have already been validated from extant literature and used a seven-point Likert scale, which was the same as for the original scales. Additionally, all multi-item measures were modified in order to make them applicable to the research context and participant sample of this study.

Competitive strategy

In order to decipher what type of strategy each accommodation provider was pursuing, it was decided to refer to pre-existing data. Given T&T's many market niches, the majority of tourist accommodation providers have a narrow-focused strategy based on a specific type of customer or geographic region. The majority of bed & breakfast establishments in T&T are owner-operated and geared towards budget travellers. As a result, this type of accommodation and its pricing were used as a benchmark to categorize low-cost providers versus differentiators. The average daily rate of a bed & breakfast was calculated, as well as the maximum and minimum price. As a result, any accommodation provider that advertised a daily

Table 13.1 **Differences in the tourism products of Trinidad & Tobago**

	Trinidad	**Tobago**
Unique selling proposition	• Culinary diversity • Religious and ethnic mix	• Semi-rustic, idyllic island-environment • Close proximity to Trinidad
Main types of visitors	• Business travellers • Returning residents • Independent travellers (not on pre-paid packaged holiday)	• European travellers • Trinidadians on short trips, weekend visits and holidays
Main source markets	• USA • Caribbean region	• Europe • Trinidad
Accommodation types	• Large branded hotels • Boutique hotels • Bed & breakfast • Apartments	• Small non-branded hotels • Apartments and villas • Bed & breakfast
Market niches targets	• Business • Events and cultural attractions • Ecotourism • Diving • Yachting • Shopping and nightlife • Historical sites • Health • Sports	• Ecotourism • Diving and water sports • Events and cultural attractions • Weddings and honeymoons • Historical sites • Health

rate below $100 (US dollars) was considered a low-cost provider. Any accommodation provider higher than this price was considered a differentiator. To further validate the accuracy of this method, the websites and any available advertisements of the targeted accommodation providers were reviewed to verify their scope and whether they articulated the type of customer targeted. Additionally, as a final confirmation of competitive strategy and scope, the first question asked during the interview was, "Does your business target a specific type of customer or do you cater to many types of tourists?"

Issue interpretation
Testing the role of issue interpretation required a set of variables reflecting the motivations for firms that have adopted the TTTIC practice. A modified measurement instrument used by Kennedy & Fiss (2009) was based on a series of survey items asking informants, "On a scale of 1 to 7, how important were the following reasons for your business's decision to implement the TTTIC?" The measure then

listed eight items that relate to economic and social gains and losses as reasons for TTTIC adoption.

Implementation extent

The extent to which the TTTIC practice was implemented was defined as the accommodation provider's overall commitment to the TTTIC practice and was measured with a scale modified from Mowday et al.'s (1979) organizational commitment questionnaire.The measurement instrument was based on a series of survey items asking informants, "On a scale of 1 to 7 relating to your experience with the TTTIC, how much do you agree with the following statements?" The measure then listed seven items that reflected informant's attitudes towards the quality practice.

Organizational size and age

Organizational size and age were controlled due to their potential influence on the directionality of organizational actions towards the TTTIC practice. Organizational size was accounted for by counting the number of rooms at each establishment. This measure of size was chosen since it is a commonly recognized practice in the literature of hospitality establishments to use the number of beds or the equivalent number of rooms as indicative of size (Baum & Mezias, 1992; Chung & Kalnins, 2001; Fernàndez & Marìn, 1998). The age of each establishment was simply accounted for by asking participants to indicate the year that their establishment commenced operations.

Top management belief

The beliefs held by top management are expected to have a significant influence on the relationships being tested in this model and, therefore, needing to be controlled. Top management belief was measured using a modified three-item scale borrowed from Liang et al. (2007). The measurement instrument was based on three survey items asking informants, "On a scale of 1 to 7, indicate how much you agree with the following statements. The head(s) of this tourist accommodation believes that…" The measure then listed the three items relating to top management belief towards the TTTIC practice

Open-ended interview questions

In an attempt to further qualify quantitative responses and add explanatory value to the arguments put forth in this study, four open-ended interview questions were included and asked of each participant. The interview questions allowed informants the opportunity to further reflect on their environmental perceptions of the adopted practice and how it relates to their business. Similarly, the interview also gave the researcher a further in-depth look at the underpinnings of the institutional context of this study. A summary of primary responses to the interview questions can be reviewed in Appendix B.

Results and discussion

The objective of this study was to investigate the implementation of the TTTIC practice among tourist accommodation providers that belong to and are influenced by the same institutional context. The questions asked were: whether a tourist accommodation provider's business strategy influences how the quality practice is interpreted; and whether the interpretation of the quality practice influences the level of implementation that the practice receives by adopting organizations. The analysis and reporting of the results in this section were structured to answer these broad questions.

Competitive strategy and issue interpretation

Regarding competitive strategy's predictive ability of issue interpretation, it is important to note that strategies were determined using existing and subjective data. That said, results may have differed if a different methodology or measure was used to assess the strategy dyad. However, given the salient characteristics of most tourism industries like budget versus luxury accommodations, or bed & breakfast establishments versus hotels, it is believed that the existing data used in addition to the accompanying qualitative question relating to strategy sufficed in providing an accurate depiction of the competitive strategy used by participants in this sample. It is also important to note that the majority of informants indicated that they believed that having quality standards was important to the industry, regardless of the competitive strategy they identified with. However, variation between the strategy types was evident from responses relating to the perceived utility of the TTTIC practice. The majority of differentiation strategists saw more utility of the TTTIC practice for their business compared to low-cost strategists who had a more sceptical outlook of TTTIC's utility for their business.

Issue interpretation and implementation extent

It was postulated that opportunity and threat perceptions are significantly associated with the extent of implementation that the TTTIC practice has received. It is important to reiterate that the correlation between variables does not imply that one causes the other. That is to say, from results it can only be concluded that tourist accommodation providers who have extensively implemented the TTTIC practice can be expected to have an opportunistic view about the practice. Conversely, those who have implemented the practice less extensively can be expected to have a contrary and less positive view towards the merits of the practice.

Interestingly enough, regarding the control variables, the models relating to implementation extent and issue interpretation all demonstrated that a firm's top management belief towards the TTTIC practice had a significant effect in predicting implementation extent. Based on results, it is highly likely that top management belief towards an adopted practice antecedes how the practice is interpreted. This lends support to the argument that, in responding to stimuli from the environment, top management develops "belief structures" to use as a basis for making inferences (Walsh, 1988), which can arguably lead to a positive or negative interpretation.

Open-ended responses

Many firms mentioned the criteria used to assess some properties were based on standards representative of chain hotels and inapplicable to every situation. To illustrate, an informant from a boutique hotel refused to comply with a request to replace various light fixtures, as lighting was rendered too dim in main corridors:

> They [TTTIC auditors] said I have to change all the lights because they were not bright enough for guests ... I explained that guests come to my hotel for the ambience and prefer dim lighting ... And I will not comply with rules that are clearly made for big-name hotels at the expense of my customers' experience.

Another major sentiment shared by the majority of respondents was that the TTTIC practice could be greatly improved by assessing proposed requirements to ensure that they are applicable and relevant to T&T's unique context. Many informants complained that some of the standards were clearly copied from North American guidelines and refused to comply, based on merited grounds. The quote below is one of a few informants complaining about the ridiculous request to use stainless steel garbage cans on premises in Tobago:

> The one rule that takes the cake ... Can you believe that they [TTTIC auditors] said that I need to replace all my plastic garbage bins with stainless steel ... Hello! This is Tobago, and common sense must tell you that if we are in a tropical climate close to the sea, all the [garbage] bins will rust in no time! Why would that rule apply in the tropics? ... Now where is the quality in that?

Study limitations

In addition to a small sample size, this research investigation refers only to a specific geographical area with its own unique institutional context. Secondly, in interpreting the results from data collection it would be impossible to rule out the possibility of common method bias. The bias is likely to have a potential impact on results due to the way questions were constructed, the way in which they were asked and potentially due to the audience to which the questions were asked to.

Conclusion

A key finding from this study is that top management belief towards an adopted practice is influential towards predicting the level of implementation the practice receives. Hence, future studies could start by testing whether top management beliefs and even top management demographics could better predict issue interpretation. This study has attempted to rethink the role of issue interpretation during the implementation of an adopted practice in an organizational field. Specifically, it has been argued that a firm's chosen competitive strategy is a significant factor towards predicting issue interpretation. Indeed, it is evident that, due to the accompanying internal processes and environmental perceptions held by firms pursuing a specific competitive strategy, the compatibility of a new practice with a chosen strategy will go far towards determining the value that the practice receives by adoptees. Despite the fact that organizations and decision-makers are constrained and subject to varying institutional pressures, it is naïve to believe that adoption and implementation decisions are as mindless as once thought (Kennedy & Fiss, 2009). Indeed, this study further strengthens the agency debate in institutional theory by pointing out that strong organizational field-level isomorphic forces can result in acts of resistance and deviance by decision-makers (Heugens & Lander, 2009), regardless of whether they interpret an institutionalized template in a positive or negative light.

Finally, policymakers must be able to detect where, when, why and how adapted versions of a practice take place in order to improve on subsequent versions of the practice. Referring to the TTTIC practice, policymakers promoting the practice would be wise to pay close attention to the opinions and implementation patterns of adopters in order to alter and improve the practice as needed, before disseminating new versions. On the other hand, policymakers may also be interested in assuring conformance to and faithful implementation of the practice (Ansari *et al.*, 2010). In this case, policymakers should bear in mind that, when designing quality practices such as the TTTIC, competitive implications for affected businesses must be considered with the same seriousness as institutional purposes if any real sustainability is to be achieved.

References

Abrahamson, E. (1991). Managerial fads and fashions: The diffusion and rejection of innovations. *Academy of Management Review*, 16, 586–612.

Ansari, Shazad M., Fiss, Peer C., & Zajac, Edward J. (2010). Made to fit: How practices vary as they diffuse. *Academy of Management Review*, 35, 67–92.

Baum, J.A.C. & Mezias, J.S. (1992). Localized competition and organizational failure in the Manhattan hotel industry. *Administrative Science Quarterly*, 37, 564–80.

Boxenbaum, E. & Jonsson, S. (2008). Isomorphism, diffusion and decoupling. In R. Greenwood, C. Oliver, K. Sahlin, & R. Suddaby (eds). *Handbook of Organizational Institutionalism*, pp. 78–98. New York: Sage.

Campbell-Hunt, C. (2000). What have we learned about generic competitive strategy? A meta-analysis. *Strategic Management Journal*, 21(2), 127–54.

Chung, W. & Kalnins, A. (2001). Agglomeration effects and performance: A test of the Texas lodging industry. *Strategic Management Journal*, 22, 969–88.

Deephouse, D.L. (1999). To be different, or to be the same? It's a question (and theory) of strategic balance. *Strategic Management Journal*, 20, 147–66.

DeSarbo, W.S., Di Benedetto, C.A., Song, M., & Sinha, I. (2005). Revisiting the Miles and Snow strategic framework: Uncovering interrelationships between strategic types, capabilities, environmental uncertainty, and firm performance. *Strategic Management Journal*, 26, 47–74.

DiMaggio, P.J. (1988). Interest and agency in institutional theory. In L.G. Zucker (ed.). *Institutional Patterns and Organizations: Culture and Environment*. Cambridge, MA: Ballinger.

Dutton, J. & Jackson, S. (1987). Categorizing strategic issues: Links to organizational action. *Academy of Management Review*, 12, 76–90.

Dutton, J.E., Fahey, L., & Narayanan, V.K. (1983). Toward understanding strategic issue diagnosis. *Strategic Management Journal*, 4, 307–23.

Fernàndez, N. & Marìn, P.L. (1998). Market power and multimarket contact: Some evidence from the Spanish hotel industry. *Journal of Industrial Economics*, 46(3), 301–15.

George, E., Chattopadhyay, P., Sitkin, S.B., & Barden, J. (2006). Cognitive underpinnings of institutional persistence and change: A framing perspective. *Academy of Management Review*, 31, 347–65.

Hambrick, D.C. (1983). An empirical typology of mature industrial product environments. *Academy of Management Journal*, 26(2), 213–30.

Heugens, P.P.M.A.R. & Lander, M.W. (2009). Structure! Agency! (and other quarrels): Meta-analysing institutional theories of organization. *Academy of Management Journal*, 52, 61–86.

Hlavacka, S., Bacharova, L., Ruskanova, V., & Wagner, R. (2001). Performance implications of Porter's generic strategies in Slovak hospitals. *Journal of Management in Medicine*, 15(1), 44–66.

Jackson, S. & Dutton, J. (1988). Discerning threats and opportunities. *Administrative Science Quarterly*, 33, 370–87.

Kennedy, M.T. & Fiss, P.C. (2009). Institutionalization, framing, and the logic of TQM adoption and implementation decisions among US hospitals. *Academy of Management Journal*, 52, 897–918.

Kim, L. & Lim, Y. (1988). Environment, generic strategies, and performance in a rapidly developing country: A taxonomic approach. *Academy of Management Journal*, 31(4), 802–27.

Kostova, T. & Roth, K. (2002). Adoption of an organizational practice by subsidiaries of multinational corporations: Institutional and relational effects. *Academy of Management Journal*, 45(1), 215–33.

Liang, H., Saraf, N., Hu, Q., & Xue, Y. (2007). Assimilation of enterprise systems: The effect of institutional pressures and the mediating role of top management. *MIS Quarterly*, 31(1), 59–87.

Meyer, J.W. & Rowan, B. (1977). Institutionalized organizations: Formal structure as myth and ceremony. *American Journal of Sociology*, 83, 340–63.

Miller, D. (1988). Relating Porter's business strategies to environment and structure. *Academy of Management Journal*, 31, 280–308.

Ministry of Tourism Trinidad & Tobago (2010, October). National tourism policy of Trinidad and Tobago.

Mowday, R., Steers, R., & Porter, L. (1979). The measurement of organizational commitment. *Journal of Vocational Behavior*, 14, 224–47.

Newsday (2010, November 1). Ministry launches STAR programme to address poor quality service, http://www.newsday.co.tt/features/print,0,130126.html, accessed 11 August 2015.

Oliver, C. (1991). Strategic responses to institutional processes. *Academy of Management Review*, 16, 145–79.

Porter, M. (1979). How competitive forces shape strategy. *Harvard Business Review*, March–April, 137–45.

Porter, M. (1980). *Competitive Strategy*. New York, NY: Free Press.

Porter, M. (1985). *Competitive Advantage Creating and Sustaining Superior Performance*. New York, NY: Free Press.

Porter, M. (1987). From competitive advantage to corporate strategy. *Harvard Business Review*, May–June, 43–59.

Porter, M. (1996). What is strategy? *Harvard Business Review*, November–December, 61–78.

Romain, Kenrick (2009). Trinidad and Tobago boosts tourism quality through standards. *ISO Management Systems*, May–June, www.iso.org/ims, accessed 11 August 2015.

Sheehan, L. & Presenza, A. (2011). The organizational impacts of quality management in tourism firms: An empirical investigation of the Molise Region, Italy. *Tourism*, 59(4), 427–46.

Staw, B., Sandelands, L., & Dutton, J. (1981). Threat-rigidity effects in organizational behavior: A multi-level analysis. *Administrative Science Quarterly*, 26, 501–24.

Tolbert, P.S. & Zucker, L.G. (1983). Institutional sources of change in the formal structure of organizations: The diffusion of civil service reform, 1880–1935. *Administrative Science Quarterly*, 28, 22–39.

Tolbert, P. & Zucker, L. (1996). The institutionalization of institutional theory. In S. Clegg, C. Hardy, & W. Nord (eds). *Handbook of Organization Studies*. Thousand Oaks, CA: Sage, 175–90.

Walsh, J.P. (1988). Selectivity and selective perception: An investigation of managers' belief structures and information processing. *Academy of Management Journal*, 31(4), 873–96.

Westphal, J.D., Gulati, R., & Shortell, S.M. (1997). Customization or conformity? An institutional and network perspective on the content and consequences of TQM adoption. *Administrative Science Quarterly*, 42, 366–94.

Zbaracki, M.J. (1998). The rhetoric and reality of total quality management. *Administrative Science Quarterly*, 43, 602–36.

Appendix A: Questionnaire items

1) In what year did your business implement the TTTIC?

On a scale of 1 to 7, how important were each of the following reasons for your business's decision to implement the TTTIC?

(2) I was concerned with *LOSING some of my market share*
1☐ 2☐ 3☐ 4☐ 5☐ 6☐ 7☐
Not important   *Extremely important*

(3) I was concerned with *COMPETITION from my competitors*
1☐ 2☐ 3☐ 4☐ 5☐ 6☐ 7☐
Not important   *Extremely important*

(4) I wanted to *IMPROVE quality standards for customers staying at my accommodation*
1☐ 2☐ 3☐ 4☐ 5☐ 6☐ 7☐
Not important   *Extremely important*

(5) I wanted to *IMPROVE operational efficiency*
1☐ 2☐ 3☐ 4☐ 5☐ 6☐ 7☐
Not important   *Extremely important*

(6) I wanted OTHERS to see me as *a market leader*
1☐ 2☐ 3☐ 4☐ 5☐ 6☐ 7☐
Not important   *Extremely important*

(7) I wanted to *IMPROVE service quality*
1☐ 2☐ 3☐ 4☐ 5☐ 6☐ 7☐
Not important   *Extremely important*

(8) I wanted to *IMPROVE customer satisfaction*
1☐ 2☐ 3☐ 4☐ 5☐ 6☐ 7☐
Not important   *Extremely important*

(9) I was concerned with *INFLUENCE or PRESSURE from ANY of the following bodies: Trinidad & Tobago Bureau of Standards; Tourism Development Company; Tobago House of Assembly; Trinidad Hotels, Restaurants & Tourism Association; Tobago Hotel & Tourism Association*
1☐ 2☐ 3☐ 4☐ 5☐ 6☐ 7☐
Not important   *Extremely important*

On a scale of 1 to 7 relating to your experience with the TTTIC, how much do you agree with the following statements?

(10) I have put a great deal of effort towards implementing the TTTIC
1□ 2□ 3□ 4□ 5□ 6□ 7□
Strongly disagree　　　　　*Strongly agree*

(11) I speak about the TTTIC to my friends as a great way to improve business
1□ 2□ 3□ 4□ 5□ 6□ 7□
Strongly disagree　　　　　*Strongly agree*

(12) I find that my values and the values promoted by the TTTIC are very similar
1□ 2□ 3□ 4□ 5□ 6□ 7□
Strongly disagree　　　　　*Strongly agree*

(13) The TTTIC programme really inspires the very best in me in the way of involvement at my work
1□ 2□ 3□ 4□ 5□ 6□ 7□
Strongly disagree　　　　　*Strongly agree*

(14) I am extremely glad that I am involved in the TTTIC programme
1□ 2□ 3□ 4□ 5□ 6□ 7□
Strongly disagree　　　　　*Strongly agree*

(15) I really care about the TTTIC programme and its future
1□ 2□ 3□ 4□ 5□ 6□ 7□
Strongly disagree　　　　　*Strongly agree*

(16) Often I find it difficult to agree with what the TTTIC programme suggests
1□ 2□ 3□ 4□ 5□ 6□ 7□
Strongly disagree　　　　　*Strongly agree*

On a scale of 1 to 7, indicate how much you agree with the following statements. The head(s) of this tourist accommodation believes that …

17) The TTTIC has the potential to provide significant business benefits to the firm
1□ 2□ 3□ 4□ 5□ 6□ 7□
Strongly disagree　　　　　*Strongly agree*

18) The TTTIC will create a significant competitive environment for the tourist industry in this country
1□ 2□ 3□ 4□ 5□ 6□ 7□
Strongly disagree　　　　　*Strongly agree*

19) It is NOT necessary to use the TTTIC to conduct business activities
1☐ 2☐ 3☐ 4☐ 5☐ 6☐ 7☐
Strongly disagree   *Strongly agree*

20) What is your gender?
Male   *Female*

21) What is your age group?
Under 26   *26 to 35*
36 to 45   *46 to 55*
56 to 65   *66 or older*

22) What is your highest level of education?
Did not complete high school   *High school diploma*
Associates/2-year degree   *Bachelor's degree*
Master's degree   *Doctorate degree/professional degree*

23) Which of the following terms best describes your position with your company?
Shift supervisor   *Manager*   *Owner*

24) In approximately what year did you start working in the tourist accommodation industry?

25) In approximately what year did your company open for business?

Appendix B: Open-ended interview summary

"What were the major reasons why your company adopted the TTIC practice and how did you react to this decision?"	"Has the TTIC practice helped you to better understand what 'quality' means for your business?"	"Are there ways that the TTIC programme can be improved to better help your business and Trinidad & Tobago's Tourism Industry as a whole?"
• The majority of respondents indicated that a major reason for adopting the TTIC practice was that they believed quality standards were necessary and overdue for T&T's tourism industry • Others indicated that, prior to the launch of TTIC, the government had initiated a similar predeceasing programme associated with the TDC. Those who were already part of that programme indicated that they automatically transferred over to the TTIC once it came into effect • Many of the low-cost strategists indicated that a major reason for adopting the TTIC was based on the promise of government incentives	• The majority of differentiator strategists indicated that they already had predefined standards of quality for their business. They indicated that the TTIC opened their eyes to quality practices for which they may have previously been unaware or that they found inapplicable to their business • The majority of low-cost strategists indicated that the TTIC programme opened their eyes to specific aspects of quality that they did not previously consider • With the exception of a few larger hotels, the majority of informants indicated that the definitions and criteria used to explain quality had to be redefined and made applicable to many different accommodation types. There was a contextual factor that was subject to varying interpretations	• An overwhelming number of informants attested that they believe legislation to make the TTIC practice mandatory was needed. Additionally, most believed that the standards need to be constantly re-examined to ensure that they remain applicable to T&T's tourism context. Some elaborated further on this by stating that T&T should refrain from merely copying North American and European standards of quality and should define it to be applicable to the Caribbean context • Some informants mentioned that they had not yet been audited for the calendar year despite the fact that the associated fees were paid. They went on to state that actions such as this gave them less confidence in the programme and that a central issue for any T&T initiatives was the general lack of follow-through • Many of the low-cost strategists indicated that the incentives to align with the TTIC practice were disproportionate to those given to larger hotels. They indicated that governing bodies needed to provide more incentives and smarter configuration of quality standards made applicable to low-cost establishments. Interestingly enough, many informants pursuing a differentiation strategy also mentioned that standards for smaller owner-operated establishments (low-cost) were unfair and needed revision

Human trafficking
Why it's time for the hotel industry to act

Fran Hughes
International Tourism Partnership

The focus of this chapter is in providing facts, figures and practical information to help a hotel or hotel company understand the issue of human trafficking and how it is relevant to their business. Presented in the form of practical guidance directly aimed at the hotelier, the chapter defines human trafficking, gives key statistics on the nature and prevalence of trafficking, explains what the risks are to a hotel and gives guidance on measures a hotel or hotel company can take to reduce the risk of trafficking affecting their business. It also includes a selection of case studies highlighting best practice from the hotel sector.

Introduction

Human trafficking is the acquisition of people by improper means such as force, fraud or deception, with the aim of exploiting them. It is a complex problem brought about by interrelated economic, social, cultural, political and personal factors. Those trafficked are exploited into prostitution, forced labour, for the removal of their organs and other emerging forms of trafficking including organized begging, benefit fraud, domestic servitude and forced marriage. In short, it is modern-day slavery:

> The UN Palermo Protocol definition is globally accepted: "Trafficking in persons" shall mean the recruitment, transportation, transfer, harbouring or receipt of persons, by means of the threat or use of force or other forms of coercion, of abduction, of fraud, of deception, of the abuse of power or of a position of vulnerability or of the giving or receiving of payments or benefits to achieve the consent of a person having control over another person, for the purpose of exploitation. Exploitation shall include, at a minimum, the exploitation of the prostitution of others or other forms of sexual exploitation, forced labour or services, slavery or practices similar to slavery, servitude or the removal of organs (UNODC/United Nations Office on Drugs and Crime).

Human trafficking is, by nature, a "hidden" crime. Available statistics (detailed below) are only an estimate of the size of the problem and can vary from different organizations. Figures on the impact on the hotel industry specifically are hard to come by. However, government and law enforcement agencies pinpoint the hospitality industry as being high risk, and the increasing number of national initiatives in many countries highlights the growing focus on this issue as one which is particularly relevant for hotels. Whether statistics are available or not, there should be no threshold of interest and engagement with this issue—no level of human trafficking is acceptable.

- The ILO claims there were almost 21 million victims of forced labour. Of those exploited by individuals or enterprises, 4.5 million are victims of forced sexual exploitation.[1] According to the ILO, human trafficking is the third-largest illicit moneymaking venture in the world, after drug dealing and the arms trade

- According to the UN (United Nations), human trafficking is a global criminal business that impacts on every country in the world and is estimated to have a global worth of $32 billion and it is recognized as a high-profit, low-risk crime. There are even reports that some trafficking groups are switching their cargo from drugs to human beings, in a search of high profits at lower risk (UNODC)

- The UNODC (2012) *Global Report on Trafficking in Persons*[2] states that:
  - Women account for 55–60% of all trafficking victims detected globally; women and girls together account for about 75%
  - Twenty-seven per cent of all victims detected globally are children. Of every three child victims, two are girls and one is a boy
  - Trafficking for sexual exploitation is more common in Europe, Central Asia and the Americas. Trafficking for forced labour is more frequently

---

1   http://www.ilo.org/global/topics/forced-labour/lang--en/index.htm, accessed 9 November 2015.
2   https://www.unodc.org/documents/data-and-analysis/glotip/Trafficking_in_Persons_2012_web.pdf, accessed 9 November 2015.

detected in Africa and the Middle East, as well as in South and East Asia and the Pacific

- Trafficking for the purpose of sexual exploitation accounts for 58% of all trafficking cases detected globally, while trafficking for forced labour accounts for 36%. The share of detected cases of trafficking for forced labour has doubled over the past four years
- Victims of 136 different nationalities were detected in 118 countries worldwide between 2007 and 2010
- Between 2007 and 2010, almost half of victims detected worldwide were trafficked across borders within their region of origin. Some 24% were trafficked inter-regionally (i.e. to a different region)
- The number of convictions for trafficking in persons is, in general, very low. Notably, of the 132 countries covered, 16% did not record a single conviction between 2007 and 2010

Implications for the hotel industry

Human trafficking can impact on a hotel in a variety of ways:

- Use of a hotel for the sexual exploitation of adults and children

- Staff, and in particular those recruited or subcontracted via unscrupulous agencies, being victims of forced or bonded labour

- Products and services supplied to the hotel being produced by forced or bonded labour, labour exploitation and unethical labour practices

Child exploitation is probably the most disturbing aspect of human trafficking. Hotels and tourism are not causing child exploitation, but hotels can be used by criminals to carry out their crimes. This is a compelling argument to raise awareness with staff and reduce the risk of this happening on your property.

There is no evidence to suggest that large chains or smaller independents are more at risk. The risk is higher in properties where there is subcontracted staff, hiring of migrant workers, but lack of policy and enforcement and lack of awareness in staff put any hotel at risk. The business case for action is a strong one. Naturally, there is a moral obligation to ensure their business is not open to the exploitation of children and adults for sexual purposes and forced labour, and in most countries there is a legal obligation to protect against forced labour and sexual exploitation. Ignorance of the law and failure to carry out the right checks are no defence in a court of law. There is a growing move to legislation requiring companies to disclose their anti-trafficking policies and activities, such as the California Transparency in the Supply Chain Act of 2010 in the USA. The UK Modern Slavery Act 2015 requires businesses with a turnover of more than £36 million and which operate in the UK, wherever they are headquartered, to report what they are doing to tackle trafficking risk. Similar legislation has been proposed in the US. So while legal requirements for companies to disclose may be limited, it is clear that companies should be in a state of preparedness to report.

Investor groups are increasingly asking questions of a company's anti-trafficking policies and activities. Julie Tanner, Assistant Director of Socially Responsible Investing at CBIS (Christian Brothers Investment Services Inc) explains:

> Faith-based and socially responsible shareholders have worked for more than twenty years with leading companies across many sectors on good practice around supply chain transparency and accountability, and they are stronger and more resilient as a result. As a natural outgrowth of this work, investors have engaged the hospitality sector, recognizing that lack of attention to human rights issues poses real risk to companies, including reputational, legislative and regulatory risk. Awareness of these risks and knowledge of the ways that traffickers may use a company's premises, products and services in connection with their trafficking activities can help companies avoid negative publicity, business interruptions, potential lawsuits, public protests and a loss of consumer trust, all of which can impact shareholder value.
>
> Beyond the obvious moral reasons, there is a need for companies to develop a holistic and long-term human rights due-diligence process, including human trafficking, based on an analysis of company activities and relationships and how these affect people and their rights. Comprehensive assessments of potential exposure to human rights violations are an essential measure of sound governance, help to build trust and value in the brand. In addition to helping shareholders and consumers make investment and purchasing decisions, many corporations find that their efforts to strengthen global labour standards and to eradicate slavery and human trafficking not only uncover human rights issues that have the potential to impact their position in the marketplace, but also reveal opportunities for improvement.
>
> We call on hospitality companies to not only create and implement comprehensive, transparent, and verifiable human rights policies and systems for their direct operations and supply chains but also to disclose information to stakeholders, including shareholders, about their implementation measures, management processes, goals and evaluation techniques. As socially responsible shareholders, we view a commitment to transparency and disclosure as evidence of proactive and attentive management and an important aspect of corporate social responsibility that is a critical tool for building trust with investors and the public. It also provides a basis for analysis and allows shareholders to evaluate a company's progress over time and compare company performance to that of its peers. Leadership in transparency and disclosure may enhance a company's public profile with investors, current and future customers, and result in a competitive advantage within the sector.

A plan for action

With such a complex and difficult topic, it is important to make a plan. The following suggested approach will help a hotel or hotel company build robust policies and activities to reduce risk of exposure to trafficking and forced labour. Remember: human trafficking is not just about child or sexual exploitation but also includes forced labour. When developing policies and procedures for human resources relating to human trafficking, the SEE Formula[3] from the Staff Wanted initiative is a great place to start. Developed by the Institute for Human Rights & Business and Anti-Slavery International, SEE provides clear and simple guidance on the steps needed to combat the exploitation of vulnerable workers, trafficking and forced labour.

When planning, bear in mind the following:

- What information do you need?
- What do you need to do?
- Who needs to be involved?
- What timescales are realistic for implementing activities?
- How will you know if your plan has been carried out successfully?
- How can you measure your impacts?
- What will you report on—to whom and how?

Inform yourself

There are many resources available on human trafficking. Speak to organizations working in this area to understand the issues. Don't be scared—they are likely to be delighted you are engaging with them! Know the law and what is required of you in terms of hiring policy, reporting and your liabilities. For current information on applicable legal instruments and standards, see the ILO.[4] As the policy landscape is always changing, it is your duty to keep up to date with local laws.

Identify any key risk areas

Do you use agency staff? Are any staff migrant workers? Are you operating in a region known for sex tourism? Are there large events in your area where there may be an increased risk of trafficking? Studies indicate that mega sporting events such as the Olympics, World Cup and Superbowl could lead to an increase in trafficking because of the need for short-term labour and increased demand for sexual

---

3   http://www.staff-wanted.org/see-formula, accessed 10 August 2015.
4   http://www.ilo.org/global/topics/forced-labour, accessed 10 August 2015.

services. The 2012 report from CBIS on the London Olympics, *Corporate Strategies to Address Human Trafficking*[5] gives an excellent insight into the issues and suggested approach.

Develop and include in policy and governance procedures

Corporate governance should include a human rights policy, which is an essential part of any CSR matrix. This will ensure that there is responsible reporting and management of the risks as part of the corporate governance structure. Ensure your human rights policy, hiring policy, supplier code of conduct etc. state your zero-tolerance stance on human trafficking. Best practice is to include the definition of trafficking as laid out in the Palermo Protocol (above) in your policy statement and to reference support of the Guiding Principles outlined in the UN's "Protect, Respect and Remedy" framework for Business and Human Rights.[6] Ensure that policies and codes governing relations with suppliers of staff, goods and services also define the same stance on human trafficking.

It is important to check out recruitment agencies before contracting them to provide staff. What checks do they have in place to ensure workers are not being exploited? Check for yourself. Are contracts fair and transparent? For more detail, Verité[7]—a US-based NGO—hosts a wealth of resources, including sections on auditing the labour supply chain, indicators of human trafficking in the labour supply, strengthening vendor codes of conduct, taking remedial action and multi-stakeholder approaches.

Make a statement

This should reinforce your commitment to human rights and to reduce the risk of trafficking in your business. The ITP (International Tourism Partnership) developed a human trafficking position statement[8] specifically for hotels, which is a good reference and which may be adapted to the individual business.

There are several codes of conduct developed by organizations working in this area. These can be helpful tools for business to help shape policy and activities going forward and to publicly demonstrate a commitment to addressing trafficking. But remember—addressing trafficking is about more than making a statement or signing a code. It needs to be an active programme engaging staff and be integrated into core business.

---

5 http://cbisonline.com/us/wp-content/uploads/sites/2/2012/09/FINAL_OlympicsReport_9_28.pdf, accessed 10 November 2015.

6 http://www.business-humanrights.org/SpecialRepPortal/Home/Protect-Respect-Remedy-Framework/ GuidingPrinciples, accessed 10 August 2015.

7 http://www.verite.org, accessed 10 August 2015.

8 http://tourismpartnership.org/human-trafficking, accessed 10 August 2015.

Engage staff

Awareness raising through good training needs to be a key part of your strategy. Given the sensitive nature of the issue of human trafficking and the misconceptions there may be around it, it is recommended to seek advice and expert input before training staff and to ensure the trainer is confident with the subject. Different staff will need different information. For example, security staff will be dealing with different situations to housekeepers, human resources and senior management. Several online training resources on human trafficking are available. Ensure training covers both sexual exploitation and forced labour.

Once awareness is raised, staff are likely to be concerned and will want to know what to do with this knowledge. It is essential that you work out strategies for handling suspected cases of trafficking and that your training covers this. Note that many situations may not be as they seem—how do you know that the child is not a relative of the guest? Challenging a guest directly or calling the police could have very serious consequences. The best approach is usually to cascade issues up to senior management where a decision may be made.

Join local and global networks

In some countries, there are groups that share knowledge, information and best practice on trafficking, as well as forming solid networks to work actively against trafficking. These may have trafficking as their main focus (such as the Global Business Coalition Against Human Trafficking),[9] be national awareness campaigns (such as the Blue Campaign in the US),[10] or address trafficking as part of a broader scheme of work (such as the Institute of Hotel Security Management[11] in the UK, specifically for security staff). As many include government, civil society, law enforcement and business, they can be excellent forums for keeping up to date with the issues.

Report on your activities

While this may take time, it may be worth it in the long run as it provides the information stakeholders, such as investor groups and interest groups, need without them having to come and ask for it. It can be useful to track progress and, furthermore, reporting can help build profile and brand by demonstrating publicly your commitment to act on human trafficking. According to CBIS, companies should report on:

- How human trafficking risks have been assessed

---

9   http://www.gbcat.org, accessed 10 August 2015.
10   http://www.dhs.gov/blue-campaign, accessed 10 November 2015.
11   www.hotelsecuritymanagement.org, accessed 10 August 2015.

- Training: it is insufficient to say "we have trained our staff"; investors want to know what staff, where, how many, what kind of training?

- Supply chain management: what policies and codes are in place and what checks are in place to ensure suppliers, including recruitment agencies, comply?

What industry is doing: Best practice and case studies

There are many examples of businesses—collectively and individually—taking action to tackle trafficking. Here are just a few of them.

International Tourism Partnership

The ITP has a working group dedicated to human trafficking. Through the group, members have been able to discuss the issues and share resources, such as training materials and policy statements, and best practice. ITP has a secure shared platform where members can access key documents and resources. Together, the group developed a position statement, which has helped direct and underpin members' human trafficking work. ITP's strong network of contacts in the field ensures members are kept up to date with news and developments relating to trafficking and forced labour.

Marriott International

This group first established its working group on human rights back in 2006. Having been approached by various external organizations on the subject of human trafficking, Marriott drew in internal and external experts to inform them on the issues. It soon became clear to them that, though the global hotel and tourism industry was not the cause of exploitation, it could be used by criminals to exploit people. As such, it was incumbent on the business to take action. Since then, Marriott has incorporated clauses on human trafficking rights into its Principles of Responsible Business, which encompass supply chain, environment, employment and human rights issues. A key factor in this was having buy-in and support at the executive level to put human rights at the heart of the business.

Marriott leadership realizes that it is not just about policies. As Barbara Powell, Senior Director, International Social Responsibility for Marriott, states, "Setting policy is the easy part; the difficult part is making it work." Despite the real challenge of raising awareness on a global scale, Marriott has delivered tailored training to its associates and security officers globally. In addition, this training was shared with, and now forms the basis of the AH&LA human rights training. The company has also spoken about human rights at a variety of events and is an active member of ITP's human trafficking working group.

Central to Marriott's strategic approach to human trafficking is the support of the YCI (Youth Career Initiative) programme—a 24-week education and training programme for vulnerable young people in 12 countries. According to Powell:

> YCI helps us address the root cause of human trafficking and give young and potentially vulnerable people legitimate employment opportunities. We can provide a very tangible solution and get young people into employment, which is directly relevant to our business. This has real traction in helping reduce trafficking, and provides opportunities to rehabilitated victims of trafficking.

Marriott International supports YCI by providing hands-on training as well as in-kind support to students in the programme. Marriott properties in nine countries currently participate in the programme. Additionally, the J. Willard & Alice S. Marriott Foundation, a private family foundation, has committed $1 million in grant funding (over ten years) to support YCI's general operating expenses as well as its strategic vision to grow in countries where it currently operates and to expand into new countries. Marriott's comprehensive policy documents[12] make excellent reference points.

Carlson

Carlson is a founder member of gBCAT (Global Business Coalition Against Human Trafficking),[13] which is a global coalition of corporations committed to eradicating trafficking in supply chains, including forced labour and all sex trafficking, notably child prostitution. gBCAT is a thought leaders' forum to develop and share best practices for addressing the vulnerability of businesses to human trafficking in their operations. Sharing knowledge and support across industries is hugely important in the fight to eradicate trafficking in supply chains, and it is great to see the hotel industry taking the lead.

Youth Career Initiative

The YCI[14] is leading a pioneering project to integrate the victims of trafficking into its six-month education programme for vulnerable young people. Since 2010, and thanks to the support of the US Department of State's Office to Monitor and Combat Trafficking in Persons, YCI started incorporating rehabilitated survivors of human trafficking as part of the target group in selected locations. In Mexico City

---

12 http://www.marriott.com/corporate-social-responsibility/corporate-values.mi, accessed 10 August 2015.
13 http://www.gbcat.org, accessed 10 August 2015.
14 http://www.youthcareerinitiative.org, accessed 10 August 2015.

and Hanoi, 18 young people who came from shelters caring for rescued survivors of trafficking, successfully completed the programme and have started developing careers in hospitality, as well as other business sectors such as retail. This amounts to 20% of the total number of graduates in those markets. By 2015, YCI hopes to expand the work with trafficking survivors to cover four new locations. *See also* Marriott International, above.

Institute of Hotels Security Management

The Institute of Hotels Security Management[15] in the UK is a professional association for security staff. It meets regularly to discuss issues related to hotel security, including trafficking, and has a secure alert system for members.

Sabre

The global travel technology company Sabre launched its Passport to Freedom initiative in 2012, in order to raise awareness in the global travel industry about human trafficking, to advocate for legislation change and to provide opportunities for leaders to collaborate.[16] Sabre is training its employees and encouraging them to share the message and create awareness among their customers and suppliers, such as travel agencies, hoteliers, airlines and cruise lines. Sabre hopes to widen the scope of its activities over the coming years.

15 www.hotelsecuritymanagement.org, accessed 10 August 2015.
16 http://www.sabre.com/index.php/about/corporate-responsibility/passport-to-free-dom, accessed 10 August 2015.

About the contributors

Co-editors

Miguel Angel Gardetti, PhD, has been the head of the Center for Study of Corporate Sustainability (IESC) since its foundation in 2002; he also holds the same position at the Center for Study of Sustainable Luxury. He is head professor in MBA and masters' programmes both in Argentina and abroad. He has provided training within frameworks of executive education and in house programmes to CEOs and corporate managers both from domestic and multinational companies in Argentina and Latin America. In the field of Luxury and Sustainability, he was the founder and director of the IE Award for Sustainability in the Premium & Luxury Sectors. He developed several publications such as a special issue on "Sustainable Luxury" for the *Journal of Corporate Citizenship*; a book, *Sustainable Luxury: Managing Social and Environmental Performance In Iconic Brands* (Greenleaf Publishing, 2014); and the two volumes of the *Handbook of Sustainable Luxury Textiles and Fashion* (Springer 2015). For his contribution to this field, he was granted the "Sustainable Leadership Award" by the Indian World CSR Congress, February 2014, in Bombay, India.

Ana Laura Torres holds a Bachelor's degree in Ecology from La Plata National University (Argentina), specializing in corporate sustainability at the Center for Study of Corporate Sustainability. She played a significant role in the creation and development of the Centre for Study of Sustainable Hotels. She has worked as an environmental consultant for the German Institute of Investment and Development (DEG) in Cologne.

Contributors

Theresa Bauer iis professor of international management and marketing at SRH FernHochschule Riedlingen, Germany. She has work experience as a lecturer at Raffles University Iskandar, Malaysia, and as a public relations manager in Germany. She received her PhD from Humboldt-University Berlin, Germany, and holds degrees in History and Multimedia from Karlsruhe University, Germany, and degrees in Economics and Business Administration from Hagen University, Germany. Her current research focuses on CSR, Responsible Lobbying and CSR Communication.

Arthur Braunschweig is a management consultant, specializing in the integration of sustainability issues into management of companies and other organizations. He works as managing partner of E2 Management Consulting AG (Zürich, Switzerland). Arthur has worked with numerous companies from various industries such as food and beverage, finance, tourism and energy, as well as NGOs. In addition, Arthur has developed various methods and standards of environmental management, such as the Swiss ibex label for sustainable hotels, the GRI's first sector supplement, and the "Ecopoints" weighting method for LCA (life cycle assessment) and company ecobalance. Arthur has been teaching at various universities and at the Eidgenössische Technische Hochschule Zürich for many years.

Beverly K. Burden is the sustainability coordinator at Singita Serengeti, responsible for overseeing the delivery of the project's sustainability strategy (One Planet Action Plan). This includes managing infrastructure upgrades (LED light bulbs, PV, composting equipment), staff training, guest engagement and community programmes. Beverly has been working in conservation and tourism in Africa for five years.

Eun Kyong (Cindy) Choi is an Assistant Professor at the Kemmons Wilson School of Hospitality & Resort Management at the University of Memphis. She holds a PhD in Hospitality Administration from Texas Tech University and an MS in Hospitality Management from Florida International University. Her expertise lies in social media marketing, green hotels and service quality management. Dr Choi has published several papers in scholarly journals including the *Journal of Foodservice Business Research, Journal of Quality Assurance in Hospitality and Tourism* and the *Journal of Teaching in Travel & Tourism*. In addition, Dr Choi has given more than 15 proceedings and presentations at international conferences.

Alison L. Dempsey, JD, LLM, PhD is an internationally experienced lawyer and business professional with nearly 20 years' experience of focusing on corporate governance, ethics and responsible business. She holds a doctorate in law (UBC Law, 2012) and is the author of *Evolutions in Corporate Governance—Towards an Ethical Framework for Business Conduct* (Greenleaf Publishing, 2013). Her particular interest is in the role of mandatory and voluntary regulatory frameworks—in combination—enabling business and institutions in economically, environmentally and socially responsible practices, sustainable success and the mitigation of adverse impacts on society and the environment.

Benjamin H. Gill, MA (Cantab), MSc, C.Env, is the Technical Manager of the One Planet Programme, setting the headline standards and guidance and ensuring all endorsed projects are on track to meet the Common International Targets. He also supports the delivery of the sustainability strategies for a number of partners including Villages Nature, an eco-resort under construction in Paris for 900,000 visitors a year in phase one, and Singita Serengeti, a world leading conservation-led tourism project.

Z. Gulen Hashmi is a research consultant and DBA candidate at Business School Lausanne, specializing in hotel sustainability and action research. She is also a hotel manager of a three-star hotel in Bucharest, Romania. Her experience as a hospitality professional spans over 20 years, having worked in various hotel operations both in chain hotels and individual mid-sized hotels, as well as consultancy work related to water management in hotels. She holds a Bachelor's degree in European Hospitality Management in the Netherlands, an EMBA from Turkey and a second Master's in Environmental Governance from the University of Essex, UK. She has published one journal article on corporate sustainability, and two hotel case studies that have been accepted for publication in December 2015. Her articles are on systemic collaborative challenges of our time, such as collaboration for sustainability, well-being and employee engagement in the hotel industry.

John Hirst is Lecturer in Management at Durham University Business School and Senior Fellow of the Higher Education Academy. His career has spanned senior management posts in UK commerical, charitable and educational sectors. His particular interest in sustainable development draws on his experience as a geographer and a manager: he is a Fellow of both the Royal Geographical Society and the Chartered Management Institute. John was instrumental in founding the multidisciplinary Centre for Environmental Change at Oxford University where he was also a Governor of Manchester (now Harris-Manchester) College. At Durham University, he co-founded the multidisciplinary Centre for Applied Ethics & Relational Studies, the forerunner of the Institute for Advanced Studies (IAS). In addition to teaching and supervision, John is developing Durham University Business School's relationship with the Academy of Business in Society (ABIS) and the UN-supported Principles of Responsible Management Education (PRME) UK & Ireland regional chapter, to both of which the Business School is currently affiliated.

Fran Hughes is Head of Programmes at the International Tourism Partnership, which brings together the world's leading international hotel companies to provide a voice for environmental and social responsibility in the industry. ITP works to demonstrate in a very practical way that environmental and social responsibility make good business sense by highlighting best practice, offering a range of practical products and programmes and tackling emerging sustainability issues through its collaborative working groups. Fran has over 20 years' experience in the tourism industry, having worked as an adventure tour leader, in sales and marketing, tour operations and a variety of consultancy work. She holds a Masters in Environmental Strategy and is an Associate of the IEMA (Institute of Environmental Management and Assessment).

Kevin D. Lynch is the Leadership Executive-in-Residence at the Center for Values-Driven Leadership at Benedictine University in Lisle. Dr Lynch also serves as an associate faculty member of the College of Business. As a practitioner, academic and consultant, Dr Lynch specializes in assisting organizations that are experiencing rapid change, particularly with regard to strategic growth decisions, and the implementation of appropriate organizational infrastructure. His research interests include scholar-practitioner interactions, social, environmental and financial sustainability, and values-driven business. Dr Lynch earned his PhD from Benedictine University. He holds an MBA specializing in finance and systems from the University of Illinois and a BBA in accounting from Baylor University.

Ruth Mattimoe completed a PhD entitled "An institutional study of room rate pricing in the Irish hotel industry" with Professor Bob Scapens, Emeritus Professor of Management Accounting at the Manchester School of Accounting & Finance (now Manchester Business School). Since then, her sole research has earned a Fáilte Ireland (Irish Tourist Board) Applied Industry Fellowship for research into the financial management aspects of small and micro Irish tourism businesses, while her joint research on UK hotels and restaurants (with Professor Will Seal of The Business School, Loughborough University) gained a CIMA grant. At two Irish Academy of Management conferences, her papers were awarded the Fáilte Ireland prize for the best paper in the Tourism Track. Real-life issues in hotels and other tourism entities and professional service firms provide a sustaining platform for her research.

Salvatore Moccia is Faculty MBA and Director of External and International Development at the Catholic University of Valencia. He is also Visiting Professor at Ramkhamhaeng University, Bangkok, Thailand. He has worked as an officer with international experiences at NATO, United Nations and EUROFOR. Dr Moccia holds a PhD from the University of Navarra (Spain) in Management and Cultures of Organizations and an MBA—International Finance—from St John's University, USA.

Katrin Muff serves as Dean of Business School Lausanne since 2008. Her international business experience includes nearly a decade with Alcoa in various countries and then with P&G. She has also co-founded a European incubator for early-seed start-ups. Katrin has co-founded the World Business School Council for Sustainable Business and is actively engaged in GRLI's (Global Responsible Leadership Initiative) project 50+20, a vision of management education for the world.

Marlon Delano Nangle is a 2013 graduate of the Master of Science in Administration Program at Concordia University in Montreal, Canada. His research interests include managerial cognitions, institutional agency and organizational culture. Currently working as a training & development specialist, Marlon aspires to pursue his doctorate and become an industrial-organizational psychologist.

Zabihollah Rezaee is the Thompson-Hill Chair of Excellence and Professor of Accountancy at the University of Memphis and has served a two-year term on the SAG (Standing Advisory Group) of the PCAOB (Public Company Accounting Oversight Board). He received his BS degree from the Iranian Institute of Advanced Accounting, his MBA from Tarleton State University in Texas and his PhD from the University of Mississippi. Professor Rezaee has published over 200 articles in accounting and business journals and made more than 210 presentations. He has also published seven books: *Financial Institutions, Valuations, Mergers, and Acquisitions: The Fair Value Approach*; *Financial Statement Fraud: Prevention and Detection*; *US Master Auditing Guide* 3rd edition; *Audit Committee Oversight Effectiveness Post-Sarbanes-Oxley Act*; *Corporate Governance Post-Sarbanes-Oxley: Regulations, Requirements, and Integrated Processes*; *Corporate Governance and Business Ethics*; and *Financial Services*

Firms: Governance, Regulations, Valuations, Mergers and Acquisitions; and has contributed to several other volumes.

Domenico Saladino is an environmental and sustainability oriented consultant to hotels and other organizations in Switzerland and abroad. Before that, Domenico worked as a hotelier for many years. In addition to his consulting work, he has helped build up "La Capriola", a foundation offering touristic vocational training for handicapped. He is the lead auditor for the ibex fairstay certification scheme and auditor for the EU Eco-Label for tourist accommodation in Switzerland. He also teaches "ecology management in the hotel industry" at Swiss Schools of Tourism and Hospitality.

Susan Tinnish is the Dean of Kendall College's School of Hospitality Management located in Chicago. There, she is responsible for overseeing and managing all aspects of the school including faculty and curriculum selection, assessment and programme direction. She also serves as a member of Kendall's academic leadership team. Dr Tinnish has also been involved in establishing sustainable practices for business meetings, events and trade shows. She chaired the ASTM (American Society for Testing and Materials) committee, which established the Convention Industry Council's APEX/ASTM International Standards for environmentally sustainable meetings and events and served as the US Chair for the ISO (International Standards Organization) effort to develop a worldwide sustainable events management system. Dr Tinnish earned her PhD from Benedictine University. She holds an MBA specializing in finance and marketing from University of Chicago's Booth School and a BS in communication studies from Northwestern University.

Duane Windsor (PhD, Harvard University) is the Lynette S. Autrey Professor of Management in the Jesse H. Jones Graduate School of Business at Rice University, Houston, Texas. His research focuses on corporate social responsibility and stakeholder management theory. Dr Windsor's work has appeared in a number of journals.